PLANET
OF THE APES

PLANET OF THE APES

The Complete History

Sean Egan

APPLAUSE
THEATRE & CINEMA BOOKS

GUILFORD, CONNECTICUT

APPLAUSE
THEATRE & CINEMA BOOKS

An imprint of Globe Pequot, the trade division of
The Rowman & Littlefield Publishing Group, Inc.
4501 Forbes Blvd., Ste. 200
Lanham, MD 20706
www.rowman.com

Distributed by NATIONAL BOOK NETWORK

Library of Congress Cataloging-in-Publication Data available

Names: Egan, Sean, author.
Title: Planet of the apes : the complete history / Sean Egan.
Description: Guilford, Connecticut : Applause Theatre & Cinema Books, an imprint of the Rowman & Littlefield Publishing Group, Inc., [2021] | Includes bibliographical references and index. | Summary: "Planet of the Apes examines the entire history of the Planet of the Apes phenomenon, from books to films to comic books to television shows to video games to merchandise. With the help of new and exclusive interviews, it examines the contributions of producers, directors, writers, actors, and makeup artists in an attempt to gain an understanding of how this media property has changed the world"— Provided by publisher.
Identifiers: LCCN 2021022425 (print) | LCCN 2021022426 (ebook) | ISBN 9781493057252 (paperback) | ISBN 9781493057269 (epub)
Subjects: LCSH: Boulle, Pierre, 1912-1994. Planète des singes—Adaptations. | Planet of the apes (Television program) | Planet of the Apes films.
Classification: LCC PQ2603.O754 Z65 2021 (print) | LCC PQ2603.O754 (ebook) | DDC 791.43/75—dcedtf
LC record available at https://lccn.loc.gov/2021022425
LC ebook record available at https://lccn.loc.gov/2021022426

∞™ The paper used in this publication meets the minimum requirements of American National Standard for Information Sciences—Permanence of Paper for Printed Library Materials, ANSI/NISO Z39.48-1992

Contents

Introduction

Planet of the Apes started life in 1963 as a work by French literary novelist Pierre Boulle. His quirky but thoughtful conceit of a world where savage humans are ruled over by talking, thinking apes went on to become one of the biggest multimedia sensations in history.

The 1968 motion picture adaptation of Boulle's book was a game-changingly classy science fiction film that helped confer respectability on a genre previously dismissed as pulp. It also boasted one of the most iconic endings in cinematic history. That quality went hand in hand with box office success and an attendant public appetite for more. By 1973, said picture had spawned four sequels. The franchise then spun off a live-action television series, which in turn generated an animated TV show. What with this, comic books, novelizations, and a tsunami of merchandising, the late 1960s and first half of the 1970s had a distinctly simian flavor.

The property then began a long sleep. With filmed Apes action no longer being produced and merchandisers and fan clubs ceasing operations, it seemed that what had been dubbed "Apemania" was definitively over. However, in 2001, a new generation was introduced to the concept when cinemas hosted director Tim Burton's updating of the concept. Although derided by critics, it was a box office success. A decade later came yet another lease on life with a reboot series, starting with *Rise of the Planet of the Apes*. Its acclaimed and successful opening trilogy is to be followed by more films set in the same universe.

Planet of the Apes has always been marked by both gravitas and groundbreaking. It has explored serious themes alien to most franchises, let alone SF ones. Boulle's original novel was a Swiftian satire. Within Planet of the Apes movies can be found discussion—oblique and overt—of such crucial issues as race, religion, authoritarianism, vivisection, and war.

Another thing Planet of the Apes pioneered was continuousness: the original quintet of films was the first in any genre to directly carry on the story lines from previous installments. This series-orientation is now the bedrock of the film industry.

It was because of Planet of the Apes that motion picture makeup gained a new credibility. The extraordinary ape prosthetics created by John Chambers for the original Apes movie won an Oscar when there was no specific regular award for the craft. In the twenty-first century, realistic, talking apes were taken to the next level: the new Planet of the Apes film trilogy employed modern computer-generated imagery to breathtaking effect.

Another Apes innovation is not so intellectually or artistically vital but is nonetheless important to the issue of sustaining a film industry. Planet of the Apes led the way in merchandising. In the mid-1970s, it seemed like every other commercially available artifact in the world was emblazoned with an ape face or the Planet of the Apes logo. It was this craze, not *Star Wars*, that proved to movie studios that ancillary product could be a substantial and integral part of a film's profit plan.

Planet of the Apes: The Complete History examines the entire Apes phenomenon, from books, films, and television series to comic books and merchandise. With the help of new and exclusive interviews with writers, directors, actors, makeup artists, and others, it attempts to gain an understanding of why a media property changed the world.

1

THE UNLIKELY ORIGINATOR

Frenchman Pierre Boulle was the most improbable progenitor of a mass-media science fiction franchise. For a start, Boulle even disputed the SF categorization of his novel *La planète des singes*, published in France in 1963 by Éditions Julliard. "It is a story, and science fiction is only the pretext," he told Jean Claude Morlot of *Cinefantastique* magazine. A World War II hero and intellectual, Boulle would have probably even detested the word *franchise*. He was delighted with the 1968 motion picture adaptation of his novel, but the resultant relentless commercial exploitation of his original idea by media and merchandise manufacturers was a world removed from his stern-browed hinterland.

Boulle was born in Avignon, France, in 1912. He graduated from college in 1932 with a degree in engineering, but, as with so many people in that era, his professional plans were disrupted by Herr Hitler. His army stint was followed by a post-invasion sign-up to the Free French, for whom he worked as a spy, helping to repel Japanese invasion forces in China, Burma, and Indochina.

Boulle began writing at the dawn of the 1950s. His first novel was spy tale *William Conrad*, which gained enough attention to be adapted for an episode of *Playhouse 90* on American TV network CBS. He came to true prominence in 1952 with his third book, *Le pont de la rivière Kwaï*, a powerful and harrowing novel set during World War II in a Japanese prisoner-of-war camp. It was translated into English two years later as *The Bridge over the River Kwai*. The book sold six million copies in the United States, but English was one of only twenty-two languages in which it was ultimately issued.

In 1957, director David Lean turned the book into a classic piece of cinema under the slightly different title *The Bridge on the River Kwai*. The film depicts the rollercoaster mental ride of British Lieutenant Colonel Nicholson (Alec Guinness) as he first attempts to sabotage the bridge built by POW Allied manpower on the Burma-Siam railway, then begins to take pride in his work, before finally being jolted back to reality as he realizes he is aiding the enemy. It picked up seven Oscars, including Best Picture.

La planète des singes was Boulle's eleventh book. He later explained to *Cinefantastique* that its origins lay in a visit to a zoo. "I watched the gorillas. I was impressed by their human-like expressions. It led me to dwell upon and imagine relationships between humans and apes."

For its English-language publication, *La planète des singes* was tackled by Pierre Boulle's usual translator, Briton Xan Fielding. The latter's adaptation is generally smooth, although occasionally stilted ("They are now accustomed to this unusual manifestation on my part"). In fact, the biggest problem with it stems from nomenclature. In French, the only way of distinguishing between *monkey* (a small simian with a tail) and *ape* (a large simian *sans* tail) is by placing the word *grand* in front of the word *singe*. There are no monkeys in the narrative, but Fielding chooses to use *monkey* throughout, with just ten uses of *ape* or one of its variants in the entire text. (One of them, in fact, occurs when the protagonist tells a simian that on Earth the verb "to ape" means "to imitate.") The British edition even extended this linguistic and zoological error to the cover: whereas the 1963 American publication of the book from Vanguard Press was wisely titled *Planet of the Apes*, in 1964 Britain's Secker & Warburg gave the book the name *Monkey Planet*, which, in addition to being wrong, lacks flow.

Boulle's novel uses a framing device, the narrative bookended by the third-person portrayal of Jinn and Phyllis, a wealthy couple who are spending a blissful holiday in the vacuum of space, far away from inhabited stars. Pseudo-science gives way to an unexpectedly—and probably consciously—antediluvian note when the pair discovers floating in the cosmos a classic message in a bottle. Its contents transpire to be a large number of very thin sheets covered in tiny handwriting "in the language of Earth," with which Jinn is familiar after having been partly educated on that planet. (This notion of a universal Terran language will be contradicted several times in the text.) When the two begin to read the manuscript, the narrative switches to the first-person account of Ulysse Mérou, the French author of the discovered manuscript.

Mérou—a journalist by profession—explains that in the year 2500 he set off with two companions for Betelgeuse on a spacecraft funded and built by cynical elderly scientist Professor Antelle, a journey that would take them two years but would equate to more than three hundred on Earth. The third crew member is young physician Arthur Levain.

When they reach said star, the trio discovers revolving around it an Earth-like planet. They set off in a launch to investigate. It soon becomes clear that the planet is inhabited by advanced lifeforms: they find themselves flying over a town with streets and moving vehicles. There is also plenty of greenery, which reminds Mérou of the meadows of Normandy. They christen this Earth-twin Soror—French for "sister."

Taking a dip in a lake, they are startled to find watching them a beautiful and stark-naked woman. Mérou instinctively dubs her Nova, thinking only the name of that brilliant star suitable for such a transcendent sight. However, something is amiss. Nova is strangely blank eyed and, when she engages in horseplay, unable to make any sounds other than mewing and whining. Other members of Nova's species, male and female, show themselves. Like her, they are beautiful but mute. They are also clearly unnerved by the crew's volubility, clothes, and weapons. They destroy the crew's launch, before marching the three now naked Earthmen off to their encampment where they are held prisoner, if not particularly maltreated.

The next morning, the encampment erupts into panic at the sound of strange noises in the surrounding forest, which include drums, metallic bangs, and gun shots. It occurs to Mérou that the noises are reminiscent of those made by beaters in a hunt. His notion turns out to be correct, but—astonishingly—it is the humans who are the prey. One-fifth of the way in, the book's central conceit is revealed as the spacemen are confronted by the sight of a gorilla on horseback wearing a jacket that resembles the product of the best Paris tailor. He also sports a check shirt and breeches, but instead of boots his stirruped lower extremities are encased in gloves. What might seem a comical apparition is no laughing matter: the gorilla shoots a fleeing human in the back. The gun of one of his hairy companions lays Levain to waste. Mérou tries to escape but is enmeshed in a net.

The human game is transported to an urban area. Mérou and Nova are part of a group separated from the others and taken to what Mérou later learns is the research and experimentation department of the Institute for Advanced Biological Study. They are placed in individual cages with straw bedding. The next morning brings the appearance of a female chimpanzee named Zira, the head of the department. When Mérou apologizes to her for his state of undress, she can't understand his words but is clearly intrigued by the very fact of a human possessing language skills.

The party remains in its cages. (Boulle delicately draws a veil over what must be an absence of toilet facilities.) A few days later, Zira brings an orangutan who, despite his comically long arms, is plainly of high status. Significantly, he and Zira make for Mérou's cage. Mérou addresses him by what is clearly his name, Zaius. The latter is left flustered by this and is immediately hostile to the idea that this human is something special. Certainly, Mérou is not held in sufficiently high regard as to be spared participation in a study in mating practices. His shame and humiliation are at least lessened by his designated partner being Nova.

Mérou puts up with this situation for another month before the thought of what his admired Professor Antelle would make of his bestial circumstances prompts him to snatch the notebook from Zira's hand and draw her the theorem of Pythagoras. Zira is exhilarated by this development. Via further drawings, Mérou manages to convey to Zira precisely how he came to be on this planet.

Careful to keep these revelations from Zaius, Zira begins educating Mérou. There follows the quick mastering of a communication gap that, through necessity, is common in literature but never quite plausible ("In less than two months we were capable of holding a conversation on a variety of subjects"). Mérou also teaches Zira French.

Zira explains ape society to Mérou. Chimpanzees are the innovators; gorillas gravitate to organizing, directing, and hunting; and orangutans are the scholars, if rather hidebound ones. She also explains Soror's theory of evolution, one which orangutans continue to resist, asserting that species are immutable. While that theory states that man and ape have a common source, it is believed that man has stagnated in his animal state because of the advantage that apes enjoy in the shape of four hands and long, nimble fingers. (How apes are able to construct cities, cars, jet planes, and weapons without the benefit of fully opposable thumbs is something Boulle doesn't address, possibly deliberately.)

Through reading the books Zira supplies him, Mérou discovers that intellectual differences are the only disputes in a world that has no nations. He is shocked to be told of the scientific experiments apes conduct on humans. These experiments explain the jungle drives, which are conducted to renew supplies. Zira is in turn shocked to be told that things are pretty much the opposite on Earth.

Zira starts working on a plan to enable Mérou to recover his liberty. To this end, she takes him to meet her fiancé, a chimpanzee named Dr. Cornelius, who works at the influential Scientific Academy. On the journey, Zira explains that the remains of Mérou's launch have been discovered and have aroused the curiosity of ape scientists, not least because Soror has only just developed satellites (crewed, of course, by humans as oblivious of their place in scientific history as was Laika the dog back on Earth). On a later outing to a zoo, Mérou is horrified to find Antelle in a cage, reduced to a savage state with no intelligence lighting his eyes.

Zira decides to circumnavigate orangutan obstinacy by presenting Mérou at an important biological conference. On being addressed by this talking and plainly intelligent human, the place erupts—a far more deafening proposition than on Earth as apes can clap with four hands. Mérou promptly moves from the role of guinea pig to scientific collaborator.

Cornelius informs Mérou that archaeologists have discovered some curious ruins and asks him to accompany him on a visit. The buried city existed over ten thousand years previously, an era science knows nothing about. Digging there for a month, they discover motor cars and airplanes. They also discover a china doll. Like many dolls, it talks, enunciating *papa* (a word that is handily the same in Sororian and French), but oddly it is a human doll.

Cornelius and Mérou agree that man had once been Soror's dominant species and that their society had been overtaken and perpetuated by apes through the latter's pronounced capacity for imitation. Mérou decides to be the savior of this regressive human race. This plan is assisted by the news Zira relates to him that Nova is pregnant by him.

Cornelius introduces Mérou to Helius, a chimpanzee who experiments on human brains. Helius has made a remarkable discovery. Not only has he induced humans to talk, but with one particular subject he has succeeded in awakening what he terms "the memory of her species." Under the influence of electrical impulses, the subject repeats snatches of speech of different people, which cumulatively provide an explanation for how apes took over the world. "They are becoming arrogant," says one forgotten ancestor through the woman. "We have been wrong to . . . use them as servants. . . . One day I was jostled in the street by a chimpanzee. . . . One of them has succeeded in talking. . . . The first use they make of speech is to protest when they are given an order."

Another voice continues the narration of the decline of humanity: "I walk on all fours; I turn somersaults. . . . I'm not unhappy. I have no more worries or responsibilities."

The authorities are alarmed when some of these discoveries leak out and are picked up by the press. When Nova gives birth to a boy who shortly begins to speak, both Mérou and child come to be regarded as a danger to the ape race. Cornelius informs Mérou, "The orangutans hate you because you are the living proof of their scientific aberrations, and the gorillas consider you too dangerous to be left in liberty much longer. They are frightened you might found a new race. . . . You must leave this planet." An astronomer friend of Cornelius has determined the location of Mérou's spaceship. Mérou, Nova, and their son can reach it by taking the place of humans scheduled to be placed on an upcoming satellite launch. The departing Mérou has an instinct to share a farewell kiss with Zira, even though he thinks her face "grotesque." She seems to share the inclination ("We are about to kiss like lovers"), but then Zira suddenly bursts into tears and protests, "You really are too unattractive."

Mérou, Nova, and the boy Mérou has named Sirius make the long journey back to Earth. As they are arriving seven hundred years after they have left, Mérou is not expecting to see much that is familiar, but not even he could have imagined the sight that greets them at Orly airport when a senior army officer arrives to meet his party. Nova lets out a scream as she registers that the officer is a gorilla.

Cut to Phyllis and Jinn coming to the end of the manuscript whose opening ("Lord have pity on us! . . . I have set off again with my family in the spaceship") now makes sense to the book's reader. Not to Phyllis and Jinn, though. When Jinn had first opened the mysterious object, it was reported that Phyllis pawed the ground in impatience—the first of several clues about something that is now made explicit. Dismissing the tale they have just read as a practical joke, Jinn begins to manipulate the spaceship's driving levers with his four nimble hands while Phyllis gets out her compact to touch up her muzzle.

Boulle's novel put critics in mind of both the concern with individual rights of Enlightenment scribe Voltaire and the section of Jonathan Swift's *Gulliver's Travels* concerning the talking-horse race the Houyhnhnms. There is the additional possible influence of Aldous Huxley's *Ape and Essence* (1948), which depicts a post-nuclear-holocaust society wherein man is dominated by baboons. However, Boulle brings his own innovations to the party. His detailed description of ape society is ingenious. Those who saw the movie first (i.e., the vast majority of people who have experience of both book and film) take it for granted, but the demarcations among chimpanzees, gorillas, and orangutans had to be painstakingly thought through.

On the debit side, Boulle's idea of apes rising through imitation is not wholly convincing, nor does he entirely persuade us that large elements of ape society would feel threatened by Mérou. It is curiously on human psychology that the author mainly falls down. The idea he propounds via the regression of both Antelle and the planet's once-dominant humans—that within a lifetime intelligence can just melt away—is simply nonsense. The species-memory idea is also baloney, a painfully transparent means of engineering expository dialogue. Writing in 1976 in Marvel Comics' *Planet of the Apes* magazine, Jim Whitmore had reservations based on particular knowledge. "The book is a *French* science fiction satire," he noted. "This is important. It partially explains the opening sequence and the simplistic reversals that run throughout the book; this kind of thing is a hallmark of French

SF, always more concerned with style and trappings than with content. . . . Unlike its philosophical predecessor *Gulliver's Travels*, it lacks the detailed conceptions necessary to put the point across."

For all this, it cannot be denied that *La planète des singes* is a remarkable and intriguing work, an outlandish fantasy with a serious undertow and a satisfying narrative arc, replete with not one, but two twist endings.

"I don't consider it one of my best novels," Boulle told *Cinefantastique*. "For me, it was just a pleasant fantasy. . . . I hadn't achieved what I had started out to do." Perhaps the fact that Boulle's name was now considered gold dust by Hollywood explains why *Planet of the Apes* was immediately optioned by Tinseltown in defiance of his own conviction that it was unfilmable. He told the same publication that he had never thought his vision could be successfully translated to the screen because "it seemed to me too difficult, and there was the chance that it would appear ridiculous." His fee from Hollywood of around $100,000 may have alleviated his qualms.

Although classy in its own way, the film version coarsened the material, dispensing with much of its philosophical subtext and putting the emphasis on action and spectacle. Boulle himself conceded that, although he found some of the many changes to his vision "disconcerting," contrary to his fears "nothing was ridiculous because it had been very well made." However, Boulle's vision also rapidly slipped beyond his proprietorship. It being the case that movies are, by both direct exposure and osmosis, far more wide-reaching than literature, the Hollywood interpretation of Boulle's ideas came to define them in the public mind.

Boulle's vision might have come back into his intellectual orbit had producer Arthur P. Jacobs accepted *Planet of the Men*, the screenplay

Boulle wrote for a putative *Planet of the Apes* sequel. Although small elements of it found its way into follow-up movie *Beneath the Planet of the Apes*, the script was rejected. Instead Boulle had to sit back and watch as, over the following years, his original vision was reworked, reshaped, and extended in ways he cannot ever have imagined or, in some cases, wanted. Meanwhile, the vast bulk of the kids who attended the films, watched the TV shows, or devoured the merchandise had no idea who Pierre Boulle was.

Boulle returned to his extremely successful writing career, his oeuvre ultimately consisting of more than thirty works encompassing novels, short stories, and nonfiction. Of the style of that body of work, Hugh Schofield of BBC News noted, "Boulle writes in simple French, and his books are made easier to read by a strong narrative flow (generally not a strength among modern French writers)." Much of his work was adapted for French-language films, plus one further Hollywood production. All of it was marked by deep thought. Or as Boulle put it, "A novel is built around an abstract idea, on the logic of the absurd. Only after having got the thing precisely plotted do I add my own memories and experiences and research documents. One cannot write a good novel if it is not given the support of one master idea." Boulle died in 1994, aged eighty-one.

Pierre Boulle was ambivalent about the most iconic moment of the first Planet of the Apes movie, wherein devastated astronaut Taylor realizes that he is actually on Earth a long time after man was the dominant force. There is an irony in this traducing of his ideas, at a reach a subliminal mark of respect. The device used to bring about Taylor's insight was the remnants of the Statue of Liberty. It is, of course, a symbol as all-American as you could get, but it was made in France.

2

THE TWILIGHT ZONE MEETS THE FORBIDDEN ZONE

Hollywood is littered with discarded script drafts and rejected screenplays. The Planet of the Apes franchise is no exception, and multiple intriguing Apes-related projects never quite made it to the screen. The first, and most famous, carries the exclusive credit of science fiction legend Rod Serling.

Born in 1924 in Syracuse, New York, Serling started as a radio scriptwriter. This, in turn, led to work in the newer dramatic medium of television. As was common with up-and-coming writers of that era, the likes of *Kraft Theatre*, *Playhouse 90*, and *The Hallmark Hall of Fame* dotted his résumé. Not so usual was his multiple Emmy awards, in his case for *Patterns* (1955), *Requiem for a Heavyweight* (1956), and *The Comedian* (1957). In 1959, Serling devised his most celebrated creation, *The Twilight Zone*. Both the name and theme music of this shock-ending SF/supernatural television series entered the language as synonyms for eerie occurrence. Serling contributed ninety-two episodes to the CBS show across its five seasons, picking up another clutch of Emmys in the process. A non–*Twilight Zone*–related drama called *It's Mental Work*, based on a John O'Hara story, saw him garner yet another. When Boulle's *Planet of the Apes* was optioned by filmmakers, *The Twilight Zone* was still on the air. With the show having done more than anything else to provide SF and fantasy a place in the mass media, Serling was a natural fit for the adaptation job.

The chronology of the making of the first Planet of the Apes film has been confused by the fact that some parties have suggested that Arthur P. Jacobs was the first to option Boulle's book, among which parties numbered Jacobs himself. Although the latter producer would go down in history as the man who finally brought the project to the screen, Serling's recollection would mean that his own involvement with a putative Planet of the Apes movie predated that of APJAC, Jacobs's production company. In late 1963, Serling was working on a *Planet of the Apes* adaptation under the aegis of the King Brothers, a trio of sibling producers who specialized in speed and cheapness. "The King Brothers had a notion about doing the Pierre Boulle book as a nickel-and-dime picture," Serling told Marvel's *Planet of the Apes* magazine in 1974. "I did a whole treatment for them, a scene-by-scene breakdown of how we would lick the problem. They ultimately discarded it because of the ape population." Elsewhere, Serling said that he baulked when he learned that the budget was a paltry $200,000 and that the special effects would consist of the actors wearing masks.

It would seem to be that in reality it was only after the Kings' abortive efforts that Jacobs got involved. Arthur P. Jacobs was born in Los Angeles in 1922. He majored in cinema at the University of Southern California at a time when motion pictures were not widely deemed worthy of serious study. At MGM Studios, he worked his way up from messenger to publicist, passing through Warner Bros. before, in 1956, opening his own public relations company, APJAC, a title formed by his first two initials and the first three letters of his surname (although nobody seemed to know what that *P* stood for). However, he clearly had creative juices bursting for release, and in 1963, that acronym was transferred to a production company.

Securing financing for his first picture was a fairly easy matter because his Hollywood PR work meant he knew many stars, among them Marilyn Monroe. Tragically, the Blonde Bombshell died just as she was about to take the lead role in that first Jacobs production, *What a Way to Go!* This 1964 black comedy was nonetheless a box office and critical success, inaugurating a fruitful partnership with the 20th Century-Fox studio.

Similar success seemed preordained for Jacobs's second movie, *Doctor Dolittle* (1967, but the Rex Harrison musical about a man who could talk to the animals wasn't as charming as it clearly imagined it was, and it flopped at the box office. It had taken Jacobs six years to make *Dolittle*. Much of its preparation period overlapped with that of *Planet of the Apes*. In fact, the post-*Dolittle* period must have been a frightening time for Jacobs: if *Planet of the Apes* had tanked, that would have made two flops in a row. Luckily for him, the two films were not cross-collateralized so the losses incurred by *Dolittle* were not offset against the profits of *Planet of the Apes*.

Around the turn of 1964, Jacobs was arranging meetings with literary agents in order to find material to adapt to the big screen. He later claimed—caveats are necessary when relating Jacobs anecdotes because he had a reputation for being an unreliable narrator when it came to his career—that he had in his head a vague idea to alight upon something like *King Kong*, although he wasn't envisaging a remake as such. This inchoate yearning led a Parisian agent, after failing to interest Jacobs in a Françoise Sagan work, to mention Pierre Boulle's book. When Jacobs immediately expressed interest in purchasing the rights, the agent is said to have responded, "I think you're crazy, but okay." If true, this would not be the last time that Jacobs's enthusiasm for the project was met by amused disbelief.

Jacobs was originally in partnership on *Planet of the Apes* with director J. Lee Thompson. When the project was met with scorn by movie studios, Thompson sold his share back to Jacobs and moved on. However, Jacobs—as he would with all Apes-related setbacks—persevered. He obtained a commitment from Blake Edwards to direct the picture and an expression of interest from Warner Bros. in financing and distributing it. That Rod Serling would be the common factor in the separate King Brothers and Jacobs putative Apes projects was something facilitated by Mort Abrahams, who would be the film's associate producer. Speaking in 2007 to Apes fanzine *Simian Scrolls*, Abrahams recalled that another, unnamed writer had prepared a "quite bad" script for Jacobs. "I said, 'Well, I've been working with Rod Serling for some years in other television projects. He's a very good writer, with a very good system of ideas. Let me call and speak with him.'" It was by no means the last time that Abrahams fulfilled for Jacobs a Planet of the Apes function that merited at the very least a coproducer credit. Some have even suggested that Abrahams was the first Apes film's de facto producer and Jacobs more like its executive producer.

Serling said that, in contrast to the King Brothers, Edwards told him money was no object. Certainly, Serling's own fee supported that: $125,000 equates to more than $1 million today. Unfortunately, Serling went too far. "I think the estimate of the production people was that if they had shot that script it would've cost no less than a hundred million dollars," he told Marvel. Serling said he worked on his Jacobs-aegis Planet of the Apes adaptation for well over a year, turning out thirty to forty drafts. Although none of them were filmed, one version would seem to have come very close, judging by third-party markings indicating which scenes had been designated second-unit shoots.

In Serling's vision, four astronauts go on a space voyage in a deep sleep induced to make the two-year journey seem to pass quickly. One of them doesn't make it, and the fact that said crew member is now a space-suited skeleton suggests a passage of time has occurred that is far greater than two years. Serling introduces the device of main astronaut character John Thomas sustaining a bullet through the throat. This prevents him initially communicating his intelligence to his simian captors following the literal manhunt he finds himself in. Serling also presents strange scarecrows on X-shaped mounts, something that would be a permanent motif in Apes films, reoccurring with different rationales in every new franchise iteration.

It is on an operating table directly before a lobotomy ordered by Zaius that Thomas finds his voice, screaming to the amazement of the assembled white-coated apes, "No! Get away! Let me alone!" Following his presentation to the conference (here called a congress), Thomas is quickly made a free—and tailored—man, holding court to clamoring reporters. It turns out that his ship landed in an area that has been quarantined for centuries because of historical radioactive contamination. As the simian history books claim that there was no civilization prior to the present one, the source of that contamination is a mystery.

Zaius broods about what Thomas has told ape society about the wars on his planet. The orangutan's point about man's capacity for conflict and destruction is well taken by Thomas—up to the moment he finds his colleague Dodge stuffed and mounted in a museum. Thomas gets increasingly lonely and belligerent at his privileged freakshow status, something Zira tries to alleviate by bringing Nova to his apartment. When within five weeks, Thomas teaches Nova not only to speak but also to reason, Zaius is even more unnerved, and this is before he and Thomas attend an archaeological dig overseen by Cornelius that finds evidence of ancient but developed human culture, including a talking doll. "You laid bare a question," says Thomas. "Which came first—the chicken or the egg? The ape . . . or the man?" A glum Cornelius tells Zaius that they haven't so much found something as lost it: "A birthright. . . . While we swung from trees, they had a language." More diggings reveal that man was wiped out by a nuclear war. In the aftermath, Thomas postulates, simians became the dominant species by mimicry, thus explaining the apes' lack of a technological time line. Zaius says, "Way down deep, Mr. Thomas . . . I've known that man has been a menace." It's obvious what these words presage. As the excavation site is filled in, Thomas steals a helicopter in order to evade his death sentence.

In Serling's undated first draft, Thomas escapes into space. By the time of his March 1965 version, he had opted for a far more pessimistic ending. Zira and Cornelius track down Thomas to his spaceship. They find him despondent: he has realized from the ship's tapes that he and his colleagues were asleep for two thousand years. Meanwhile, the spaceship is out of fuel, has a smashed guidance system, and can't be operated by one man. The two apes transport Thomas to the edge of the jungle so that at least he can rejoin his own kind. Saying their farewells, Thomas asks Zira if she minds if he kisses her. "Not at all," she replies. "Except—you're so damned ugly!"

Approaching airplane sounds indicate danger, but Thomas is suddenly oblivious. As Dr. Zaius emerges from the plane, Cornelius pleads with the frozen Thomas to run. "I'm afraid there's no place to run to," the human responds. He has just realized the significance of a curious metal object jutting from the ground nearby.

"What did he mean—no place to go?" asks Cornelius after Thomas has been shot dead by the new ape arrivals, trussed up, and placed on a pole. Dr. Zaius shruggingly indicates he doesn't know to the backdrop of the ruins of the Statue of Liberty.

Serling's grounding in the low culture of TV is apparent in corny exchanges on the level of "I don't like it—it's too quiet," as well as a nonsensical suggestion from Zira that Taylor's erudition could be some sort of hoax. The reverse-role conceit is occasionally rendered clunkily (an ape guard says, "Damned animals! Why don't they keep 'em in a zoo where they belong!"). Taylor quickly teaching Nova both to speak and think coherently is preposterous. The twentieth-century modernity also feels slightly ridiculous, although in fairness that is probably because the '68 film's blend of eras, though illogical, now subconsciously feels to us correct.

Yet fans of the film will recognize much of its narrative structure and several of its iconic scenes. There are also components that, had they been included in the film, would have improved it. One is the pathos deriving from the surviving astronaut's melancholy about his situation. Another is Thomas's observation to Zira about the resemblances of Earth to this planet, "The language is the least understandable of the similarities. Even as a coincidence. That's the native tongue of my country. And perhaps two or three other countries on Earth."

The apes' treatment of humans is less sensationally sadistic than the film's, essentially a way of keeping them at bay so that they don't steal ape food. Meanwhile, man destroying his own civilization with a nuclear war provides a more legitimate reason for simians to fear him than to be found in either Boulle's book or the eventual film (which doesn't explicitly discuss it).

The most important change Serling makes from the Boulle template, of course, is to move the events from an alien planet to Earth. The sight of Lady Liberty devastatingly reveals to Taylor that he is not on an alien world as he had assumed but a future version of his own. It serves to give the narrative a far greater power, making the horror immediate instead of abstract. It also engenders a twist in the tale to end them all. Most impressive of all, Serling takes an only moderately cinematic story and gives it a traditional Hollywood arc, one furthermore sprinkled with a goodly number of "bumps." (For those unaware of what that is, the Statue of Liberty moment is an uber-bump.)

Serling never worked with Michael Wilson, the man to whom the finished film's screenplay was co-attributed. Wilson made significant alterations and improvements to Serling's screenplay. However, there's no disputing that Wilson was standing on the shoulders of a giant.

JACOBS'S LADDER TO DESTINY

After the King Brothers had failed in their objective of bringing *Planet of the Apes* to the screen, it initially seemed it was Jacobs's turn to do the same. He later estimated that he spent three and a half years vainly seeking financing from Hollywood studios. The design sketches he commissioned to demonstrate the concept didn't stem the point-blank refusals any more than the screenplay he obtained from a master like Serling. A frustrated Jacobs said he even took the step of looking for capital beyond his home country's industry, approaching Britain's J. Arthur Rank and Samuel Bronston, the latter an American who made epics from a Spanish base. Along the way, Blake Edwards followed J. Lee Thompson out of the exit door for similar disillusionment-based reasons.

With rejections once again ringing in his ears, Jacobs hit upon the idea of attaching a star to the project. Studios would theoretically find less cause to turn down the idea if they knew it was to feature an actor who put backsides on seats. After refusals from the likes of Marlon Brando and Paul Newman, he ended up with Charlton Heston. Jacobs reported that Heston said yes to *Planet of the Apes* within an hour of him starting to pitch it to him. Heston's published journals *The Actor's Life* date this pitch as happening in the first week of June 1965.

Heston was born John Charles Carter in Illinois in 1923. He had the Damascene conversion to the profession common in actors' backstories, in his case getting the thespian bug after auditioning on impulse for a high school play. From there, he obtained a university acting scholarship. Also, as with many thespians, serendipity played as much a part in his success as talent. Heston could undoubtedly act, but the fact that he was tall and chiseled secured him more plum parts than equally talented but plainer types. Also, as with many actors, he changed his identity. "Charlton Heston" was a combination of his mother's maiden name and his stepfather's surname.

He made large strides appropriate to his six foot, three-inch frame. Legendary director Cecil B. DeMille cast him as the circus manager in the Oscar-winning *The Greatest Show on Earth* (1952). In 1956, Heston took on the role of Moses in DeMille's *The Ten Commandments*. Historical parts would from here on abound on his résumé. Following 1959's *Ben-Hur*, Heston had his pick of leads, his performance in the title role having garnered him a Best Actor Academy Award.

Although an impressive career, it was not one that made him an obvious candidate for the role of the lead human in *Planet of the Apes*. "You wouldn't think Heston would play that part because he's always played bigger-than-life religious parts," observes Linda Harrison, who would ultimately play Heston's silent leading lady in *Planet of the Apes*. "But . . . Heston, who knew scripts, thought this was an incredible picture to be in." Heston had spurned the occasional offers to appear in SF, even the more thoughtful productions like *Destination Moon* and *War of the Worlds*, but recognized *Planet of the Apes* as offering very different possibilities. In 1980, he mused to Don Shay of *Fantastic Films*, "The irony of a man so misanthropic that he almost welcomes the chance to escape *entirely* from the world finding himself then cast in a situation where he is spokesman for his whole species and forced to defend their qualities and abilities—it was a very appealing thing to act."

When Heston signed up for *Planet of the Apes*, it marked the first time a star of such stature had agreed to appear in a science fiction vehicle. A corollary of the stardust and gravitas Heston lent the production was personal power in the form of influence on the script. He made an intelligent suggestion in saying that, when awaking from suspended animation, the astronauts should have beards—a no-brainer but one that wouldn't have necessarily occurred to filmmakers in an age where real-life astronauts were clean-cut and clean shaven and beards were synonymous with hippies and radicals. He also said that it was his idea for Taylor to be stripped naked during the section where he is put on trial by orangutan elders. He usually refused disrobing scenes, considering them a distraction from the story. "In this case I saw no way you could more clearly and effectively make the point . . . that to the apes Taylor is an animal," he reasoned to Shay. Harrison suspects Heston may have had an additional motive. "He said, 'I was thin and so I developed my body,'" she recalls. "He liked to show it off."

The actor's engagement led to a fine director coming aboard in the shape of Franklin Schaffner, who was award-bedecked, if mostly in television. Yet again, though, the answer from the studios was in the negative. Heston's faith in the picture began to waver, and he found Jacobs's dauntless optimism about it "laughably unrealistic." The reason for Jacobs's endless knock-backs was the fact that talking apes in a dramatic, as opposed to comedic, production was something that had never been done before. A way needed to be found for movie executives to get their heads around it.

In March 1966, four actors assembled on 20th Century-Fox's lot in order to participate in a very unusual screen test. Fox was the studio Jacobs was currently trying to convince of the viability of *Planet of the Apes*. He was indefatigable in that quest to convince. At one point, Richard D. Zanuck, Fox's head of production, had threatened to have Jacobs thrown off the lot if he ever brought up the project again. Now, though, Zanuck relented and agreed to fund a screen test in which Heston would have a philosophical debate with an actor wearing ape makeup.

Born in 1934, Zanuck was Hollywood royalty. "It was William Fox and Darryl Zanuck [who] started the studio 20th Century-Fox," points out Richard D. Zanuck's future wife Linda Harrison. The 1935 merger of the Fox Film Corporation and Twentieth Century Pictures created one of the behemoths of the motion picture industry. The new studio's logo of wandering spotlights soundtracked by a syncopated, martial-drum fanfare became famous around the world. "The genes were very aware," Harrison says of Zanuck Jr. "You have to remember, it's not power, but what they know. . . . He grew up watching all the films." Not that "Dick" didn't have to work his way up in his father's company. "He did every job imaginable you can do." After that, though, the younger Zanuck's rise was meteoric. "His father put him in as head of the studio at twenty-seven years old, and he just knew what he was doing," says Harrison. "He was like the mother of all the hens. He made these movies and [hired] producers and directors and writers and actors. . . . Dick was tremendously ambitious. . . . I remember Darryl saying, 'Dick has so much more ambition than I had.'"

"It was a project I had always liked a lot, but when he [Jacobs] first proposed it, it seemed to be just too expensive of an idea," Zanuck told Samuel James Maronie in Marvel's *Planet of the Apes* magazine. "Plus, there was some concern that I had about whether or not the apes themselves would appear comical." To address that concern, Jacobs had got Serling to provide a mini-script for a screen test in which John Thomas and Dr. Zaius engaged in philosophical jousting while Zira and Cornelius looked on. Schaffner was directing. Two of the thespians performing it were young Fox contract players, Harrison and James Brolin. As the romantic partner of Fox's head of production, Harrison was privy to how crucial this day was. "[I] remember Dick at the restaurant saying, 'It's all gonna depend on the test, whether we can get the makeup right,'" she says. "I played Dr. Zira." Brolin took the part of Cornelius. The other half of the cast was rather better known. Heston was present to play Thomas, while portraying Zaius was a screen legend of an older vintage, Edward G. Robinson.

Harrison was more than a little distracted by the appliance plastered across the lower part of her face. "I didn't like it at all," she says. "You felt like you're smothering to death. You had to be so still so they get your right features in, then they put pieces on there." It should be said that the makeup she and her colleagues had to put up with that day was nothing compared to what actors endured in the actual *Planet of the Apes* movie. The segments of the screen test that have subsequently been released show that its prosthetics are rather basic stuff, with Harrison's muzzle as much human deformity as ape mouth and Robinson's hirsuteness mainly represented by what resemble overgrown sideburns.

Adding to the perfunctory aura is prosaic clothing that doesn't have the feeling of anything related to science fiction: Brolin wears a garish button-front shirt that could conceivably be seen on any contemporaneous young man on Sunset Boulevard, while Harrison sports a conservative blouse-and-skirt outfit that might be worn by that young man's mother.

"It went well," Harrison nonetheless says. "Because of that test they said, 'We can do it.' . . . It didn't seem like it would be a determination but that's what I was told." "The footage convinced us that we could do it for a reasonable cost," Zanuck told Marvel. "The question of whether the apes would look comical was also satisfied because they looked very real and it all looked very good on screen."

From the recollections of Tom Burman, who would work in the film's makeup department, Zanuck and Harrison may be compressing events a little. "The studio's executive board didn't think it had a chance of making any money," Burman says. "Following that test, the board was even more sure than ever that they didn't want this project to go any further. But Richard Zanuck held his ground." It's also widely claimed that the 1966 box office success of SF picture *Fantastic Voyage* (plot: a submarine and its crew are shrunk in order to be injected into the body of an important scientist so as to neutralize a blood clot in his brain that is threatening his life) was another factor in convincing Zanuck that the public had an appetite for the way-out. "He wasn't ever skeptical," Harrison insists of Zanuck. "He was talking about this incredible film, the book, Pierre Boulle. And he said, 'If it gets made'—he had such power—'you can play Nova.'"

Although *Planet of the Apes* did get made, it wasn't with Serling's screenplay. Abrahams told *Simian Scrolls*, "Rod called me and said, 'I don't think I can do any more with it, I'm written out.'" As Jacobs and

Abrahams looked around for a replacement writer, they decided that in any new script they wanted more naturalistic dialogue, more developed main characters, and greater suspense. There was another consideration. "We had to bring it in under six million, which means we didn't have to go to the board to get consent," says Harrison. "In the book, [the apes] were very high end, very advanced with airplanes and everything else. We made them more primitive because it was a lot cheaper. They did a lot of imaginative things to get this picture made."

Rewriting duties were initially handed to a young unknown named Charles Eastman, but his submitted work was deemed too comedic. The producers instead turned to Michael Wilson. Wilson was born in 1914. His résumé was for many years shrouded in mystery. From 1951, there is little dispute about what he wrote, and it was that year that saw the release of *A Place in the Sun*, for which he and Harry Brown took the Academy Award for Best Screenplay. However, '51 was also the year that Wilson—an ex-communist—refused to name names to the House Un-American Activities Committee. His hostile-witness status had an effect standard in the days of the Red Scare: unofficial blacklisting by the motion picture industry. The self-same industry also effected its usual solution: continuing to use his talents but under a pseudonym or uncredited. This eventually led to a dilemma. When the script written by Wilson and Carl Foreman for *The Bridge on the River Kwai* won a deserved Oscar, it had to be awarded to the man whose name had been placed for the sake of convenience and camouflage in the screen credits: Pierre Boulle. Similarly, Wilson could not be credited for his contributions to another Lean classic, *Lawrence of Arabia* (1962), as well as a slew of other movies. By the second half of the 1960s, though,

McCarthyism was over, and the likes of Wilson were free to openly ply their trade again.

"Mike Wilson . . . took away almost all of my dialogue and used his own," Serling told Marvel. Serling admitted that his dialogue was much more somber. "What I felt it needed was satire," Wilson himself told Marvel. "It was too straight and too serious." Wilson recalled working on the script for around five months, attending story conferences with Jacobs, Abrahams, and Schaffner. Candidly admitted Serling, "I blew it and Wilson did it." It wasn't necessary to go to the Writers Guild of America for arbitration over screen credit. "They offered me collaborative credit almost immediately," said Serling. "But it's really Mike Wilson's screenplay, much more than mine."

It should also be mentioned that John T. Kelley, a writer of nothing like the renown of either Serling or Wilson, made subsequent uncredited contributions whose extent and quality will never be determined. All we know is that he was brought in after Wilson for dialogue adjustments.

~

Only those who have never read Boulle's original novel or never watched the subsequent films thinks Planet of the Apes is nothing more than straight science fiction, a shallow role-reversal premise, or even just straightforward entertainment. The franchise has always been suffused with analogies and messages. Paul Dehn confirmed this way back in 1972 when he enthused to *Cinefantastique* about the job of Apes screenwriter, "One can make so many comments about present-day life."

The 1968 *Planet of the Apes* film touched upon a fear that was ever-present in contemporary society: nuclear annihilation. It's of course shockingly revealed—if implicitly rather than explicitly—in the famous ending. The film's Nova was of the generation familiar with nuclear-attack drills. "In school, we were taught to go underneath our desk," says Harrison. For her, it is stuff like this that gave the picture such a resonance. "It's one movie that just has legs. It's incredible. My psychiatrist saw it and he said, 'It's because we hold that fear that one day we could blow up our country or our world.' There's a lot of interesting parallels."

"Wilson's building it off of something Serling wrote and Serling was very big into commentary," notes Rich Handley, author and editor of several Planet of the Apes books. Rod Serling was indeed well known for the progressive symbolism he would insert into *Twilight Zone* scripts, but Wilson made his own social-critique contributions to the screenplay. He ensured that the tribunal trial of Taylor by three austere orangutans, for instance, was flavored with his own Kafkaesque ordeal at the hands of the House Un-American Activities Committee.

While the above-mentioned men were proud to claim their part in making *Planet of the Apes* synonymous with social criticism, some of their colleagues were ambivalent about it or even oblivious. Richard D. Zanuck told author Brian Pendreigh, "The object of the picture was entertainment. We weren't trying to send any profound messages, most of which have been concocted and interpreted as time has passed." Meanwhile, Jacobs seems to have been actively hostile to the idea judging by an exchange reported in *The Studio*, the book that John Gregory Dunne wrote about 20th Century-Fox after being granted access to its offices and backlots during the time of the '68 movie's production:

> "The dailies look great, Chuck," Jacobs said.
>
> "I think we've got something more than mere entertainment here," Heston said.

"Jesus, as long as it's not a message picture," Jacobs said nervously.

"We've got entertainment *and* a message in the picture, Arthur," Heston said.

While the entertainment-oriented Arthur P. Jacobs may have cared little about the Apes series' social commentary, he surely deserves credit for allowing and enabling it, even if passively.

Meanwhile, the idea of Charlton Heston being ignorant of any subtext in *Planet of the Apes* seems to be tied in to the conservative opinions he held in later life, with it becoming logical (and in some cases ideologically necessary) to dismiss his motives for association with the project as purely those of a glory-seeking movie star. Again judging by the Dunne-reported exchange, this doesn't seem to be a viable viewpoint.

Planet of the Apes movies did not invent social commentary in science fiction: any number of Fifties and Sixties motion pictures used terror of alien invasion as a metaphor for Red Scare hysteria. However, the APJAC Apes films took it to a new level in terms of depth and breadth. After them, science fiction became a major way of sneaking discussion of social issues into fare that many—most importantly, those being criticized—assumed was merely escapist.

Now that a big star had been secured for the lead human role, it would have been tempting for Jacobs to cast unknowns as the simian characters. With actors destined to be indistinguishable beneath fur and muzzle, who would care who they were? However, Jacobs's masterplan to make the public take a bizarre concept seriously involved injection of class. He set out to obtain genuine stars to play apes. Linda Harrison offers an additional reason for this casting policy: "They chose these incredible actors because they had to come through the mask."

For thespians, though, the natural instinct—possibly even fundamental vocational impetus—is to be visible and recognizable. Burman recalls of Jacobs, "He was especially worried that it would be hard to find a leading actress who would allow her face to be covered up." This situation was exacerbated by the reluctance of actors to spend hours in the makeup chair. Julie Harris (*Rebel without a Cause*) expressed interest in playing Zira, but once apprised of the prosthetics process, she backed out. Eventually, Kim Hunter was the performer with sufficient patience and/or lack of ego to take on the role. New York born but sounding strangely English, she had won an Academy Award for her role in *A Streetcar Named Desire* and, just like Wilson, was regaining career momentum after a period of McCarthyism-related disruption. Maurice Evans, who was English, was mostly known for Shakespearian roles. He would give Zaius a dignity even in the midst of his murderous prejudice.

Playing Zira's chimpanzee fiancé Cornelius was Roddy McDowall, an actor familiar to fans of both screen and stage. For a certain generation, McDowall *is* Planet of the Apes. No single actor is as much associated with the Apes live-action franchise, so much so that McDowall had the paradoxical distinction of being its face despite that face being hidden behind prosthetics. He was its ubiquitous chimpanzee good-guy lead, whether as Cornelius (first and third APJAC Apes pictures), Caesar (last two), or Galen (live-action TV series). Meanwhile, his gentle, English-accented voice provided the series a sonic signature.

Roderick Andrew Anthony Jude McDowall was born in 1928 in Herne Hill, southeast London. His Scottish father Thomas was a merchant seaman, and his Irish mother Winifriede can best be described as a professional stage mother. McDowall had an older sister, Virginia, with whom he was always close. McDowall had a stint in modelling when he was five, after which his mum propelled both he and his sister into acting. "My mother was determined that this prodigy of hers would be a miniature superstar," he told George Haddad-Garcia of *Hollywood Studio* in 1982. "I went along with the whole thing eagerly. . . . I don't really think I missed a thing, not having that so-called normal goofing-off childhood."

McDowall made his entrée via *Scruffy* (1938). In 1940, the twelve-year-old McDowall, his mother, and sister crossed the Atlantic with the objective of a berth in Tinseltown. McDowall's US debut was *Manhunt* (1941), but it was his role as Huw in *How Green Was My Valley* (1941), an adaptation of the classic Richard Llewellyn novel about a Welsh mining town, that made his name.

Of his thirteen American childhood films, McDowall was lead in four: *On the Sunny Side*; *My Friend Flicka*; *Lassie Come Home*; and *Thunderhead, Son of Flicka*. With Lassie being a dog and Flicka a horse, for a while McDowall was pigeonholed as a performer almost in the Roy Rogers vein. In the early 1950s, work was scarce for an ex-child actor now grown. McDowall crossed coasts to New York, where he studied acting with Mira Rostova and David Craig to help address that problem. Oddly, though, McDowall never tried to facilitate this process by jettisoning the immature handle "Roddy." Either way, for his friend and fellow actor Don Murray, it was McDowall's appearance in the original 1960 Broadway production of the Arthurian musical *Camelot* that sealed the deal on McDowall's professional maturation. The two had met in 1951 when they were both acting in Tennessee Williams's play *The Rose Tattoo*. "It was [an] interesting time in his life because he was struggling to make the transition from the child superstar," reflects Murray. "I must say that he did it admirably. He played Mordred, the heavy . . . I think that the excellence of that role helped him to make that transition. Without that role, I don't think his acceptance would have happened as thoroughly as it did. . . . He went on from there and did some very interesting work."

McDowall resumed making films in 1960 with *The Subterraneans* but properly announced his movie comeback with *Cleopatra* (1963), being one of the few players to emerge from that troubled production with his reputation enhanced. His role as Octavian/Augustus earned him a Golden Globe nomination for Best Supporting Actor.

Said role saw him reunited on screen with Elizabeth Taylor, with whom he had worked in *Lassie Come Home*. Taylor was another thespian who had fled Britain in World War II, and the two were lifelong friends. Unlike Taylor, however, McDowall never lost his English inflections. It might have been assumed that with McDowall working and living in the States (he was naturalized in 1949), his accent would pose an even greater career difficulty than his status as child actor, yet audiences seemed to unquestioningly accept his anomalous and unexplained tones. "[In] the Ape picture of course there's no reference to an English accent at all," notes Murray. Mort Abrahams told Joe Russo, Larry Landsman, and Edward Gross, authors of *Planet of the Apes Revisited*, "Frank Schaffner and I talked about an ape with an English accent for about thirty seconds and we thought, 'No, he'd be so good and nobody's gonna pay any attention to the accent.' It never really bothered us."

The excellence of the *Planet of the Apes* production wasn't restricted to the acting side. "It had the best people working on every aspect of the crew," notes Harrison, who says Franklin J. Schaffner was "one of the great directors" and Leon Shamroy "the best cinematographer." Jerry Goldsmith (music) had already been nominated for three Academy Awards. It has to be said, however, that Zanuck was undermining that carefully created sophistication with his request to Abrahams to "consider" Harrison for the role of Nova. Harrison admits, "I never really acted before, except in the senior class play."

Linda Harrison was born in 1945 and raised in Berlin, Maryland. An all-American peaches-and-cream brunette, her preternatural attractiveness saw her gravitate to the beauty-contest circuit, which—as she had always vaguely intended—provided a stepping-stone to an acting career. "There was the big beauty contest out in Long Beach on television and I was spotted by Mike Medavoy, who was a little agent and later became a very big producer," she recalls. "He took me to Fox and they signed me up. It's a fairytale story. Then Dick fell head over heels in love with me." Fine, but Zanuck was effectively putting the associate producer in an impossible position. However, Harrison reasons of Zanuck securing her a role in *Planet of the Apes*, "He didn't see it as nepotism . . . I didn't have to talk so he figured, 'She can handle this.'" Harrison's response, when asked whether she ever had to deal on Apes sets with whisperings about favoritism, speaks volumes: "No, because everybody was hired by Dick." Yet, the fact that years later Abrahams, apparently sincerely, spoke warmly of Harrison is testament to the fact that she is considered not just to have acquitted herself well in the Nova role but to have behaved graciously on set.

"I was a very lucky young lady," Harrison says. However, she appends the comment, "I don't want to sound like I'm tooting my horn, but I was a beautiful girl and felt that I would be right for the part." Although she played Zira in the makeup screen test, portraying an ape was never on the cards for the finished film. "Oh no," she says. "They don't take a beautiful girl and put her behind a mask."

As for the man with possibly the film's most difficult and crucial job, Harrison says that head of makeup John Chambers was "a genius." Few would disagree.

For Tom Burman, the rudimentary prosthetics of the March 1966 screen test were due less to an impressionistic approach or to budget than to deficiencies in technique on the part of the man who was head of the relevant studio department. "Ben Nye was hampered by his lack of experience," he says. Dick Smith, Nye's department lab man (the term then in use for makeup effects artist), was also for Burman not up to snuff. "Back then the only one I knew who could handle a job like this was John Chambers."

When *Planet of the Apes* was green-lit in September that year, it was known that a new makeup artist was needed. "Both Ben and Dick had decided to retire if the studio insisted on going any further with this film," Burman says. He notes of Zanuck, "He suggested that they bring in Bud Westmore who was the makeup department head at Universal. He had done a film called *The List of Adrian Messenger*, where he had to create several disguises. What Richard didn't know was that John Chambers was actually the one who had done that work for Bud."

John Chambers was born in Chicago in 1922. He wore his ancestry on his sleeve. "His parents were from Ireland and he didn't like the English because of the Potato Famine," says Burman. This may be the root of Chambers's penchant—also noted by Burman—to fight for the underdog. Chambers graduated with a commercial arts degree. World

War II put an end to his jewelry-designing ambitions. Transferred to Santa Maria, California, he spent three years creating dental plates and prosthetic devices for disfigured soldiers, in the process acquiring an understanding of cosmetics. He would use it as the foundation for a new career, which he began by approaching NBC. After joining said television network in 1953, Chambers worked on, among others, *I Spy*, *Lost in Space*, *Mission Impossible*, *The Munsters*, *The Outer Limits*, *Star Trek*, and *Voyage to the Bottom of the Sea*. By the time of *Planet of the Apes*, he had already devised an iconic prosthetic in the form of Mr. Spock's ears, remarkable for being both otherworldly and natural looking. His extraordinary work on *Adrian Messenger*—several famous actors making cameo appearances were rendered unrecognizable—kicked off his burgeoning movie career.

In putting Zanuck right about who deserved credit for the *Adrian Messenger* makeup, Burman was essentially returning a favor. "It was John who helped me get my apprenticeship at Fox," he notes. One returned favor led to another. Burman says of Chambers, "He came in and picked up the script. That was on a Friday. On Monday, as I was walking out of the makeup department, I see John drive up and get out of his car, waving for me to come to him. He said, 'It's you and me, Tommy.' He held up the script, and I saw the title: *Planet of the Apes*. Then he said, 'I'm going to win the Academy Award.'"

Chambers's can-do-cum-vainglorious attitude is a marked contrast to what Burman recalls as the defeatism of his predecessors. "Dick Smith went ahead and retired while Ben stayed on until he could find the right replacement. Dan Striepeke had been a long-time friend of John Chambers, and John recommended him to take over the department." Chambers ultimately insisted that Nye be mentioned in the film's credits, the type of generosity of which he was just as capable as he was outbursts of cantankerousness.

On *Planet of the Apes*, the Chambers-led team set about a very specific task: creating a design for "evolutionary apes," a creature that wasn't a present-day simian but descended from one. Having, despite his youth, already played a pivotal role in the project, Burman proceeded to influence events further, if more by luck than judgment. Arthur Jacobs was most impressed not by one of the team's main prototypes but by a gorilla design being worked on by Burman in a back room. Although not technically outstanding, it had a quality that would change the entire direction of the designs. "He liked the fact that the sculpture I did was a kind of highbred ape and he thought it had some of the human qualities he was looking for," says Burman.

Not that Burman would ever suggest he was the main driving force in the *Planet of the Apes* makeup work. Chambers's contributions were a revolution. When, in 1968, he spoke of them to *American Cinematographer*, however, Chambers modestly used the collective pronoun. "We had to develop a believable chimpanzee, gorilla, and orangutan makeup that could be worn as long as 14 hours at a time," he said. "So we experimented with a foam rubber so molecularly constructed that, even when worn like a mask, it allows the human skin to breathe naturally under it. Then we came up with a paint—a makeup paint—with which the rubber can be covered without closing the invisible pores. . . . We also produced a new variation of adhesive which allows us to fasten these foam rubber appliances—be they full masks or just cheeks, chins, brows, lips or even ears—to the human skin without irritating it or clogging the pores." By pre-blending the ape makeup and pre-installing parts of the hair, Chambers also cut down dramatically on the time an actor needed to sit in the makeup chair for this elaborate work. Non-cracking paint of Chambers's devising enabled ape actors to wrinkle their facial "skin" and thereby emote. Chambers also made another contribution. "I had to modify the noses on the chimps," he told *Read* in 1972. "The normal chimp has little ugly slits for nostrils. Projected on a big movie screen, those slits could have scared people out of their seats. So I made the masks look more pleasant because we wanted the chimps to be liked."

Burman recalls that the first makeup tests were done on extras. "One was Japanese. He was a male chimp. Another was a Filipino girl testing for a female chimp. Another guy was Chinese testing for the orangutan. We used Asians because they had less prominent features. You can always add to the face, but you can't take away." He also says, "We used a Caucasian for the gorilla. . . . We originally cast a black man for the gorilla, but the studio freaked out." For a time during the casting process this last issue would be a sensitive one, with the studio omitting African Americans because of the fear that giving them ape roles would look like a disparaging act. At a sit-down with the head of the National Association for the Advancement of Colored People, Chambers explained matters, following which, black extras were invited aboard the production.

A new screen test was arranged to try out the developing prosthetics. Recalls Burman of the performers, "Each one was required to exit an ape dwelling which was also being tested, then walk into a close-up in front of camera and slowly turn around. . . . These extras that we tested in full wardrobe would become part of our stock company, so they all had a really profitable run."

With the designs approved and the cameras ready to roll, Chambers now faced the considerable task of recruiting a veritable army of makeup artists. In 1967, the only makeup labs in Hollywood were those of the Fox, MGM, Warner Bros., and Universal studios, while Chambers was just one of two makeup artists who made his living solely through prosthetics. Burman: "So when John had to find a crew to do the application, he decided to use brand new unexperienced people, along with a handful of older friends who had a lot of experience to oversee the new guys." The twelve new recruits were schooled for two weeks. Burman: "Each one would do a full makeup each morning, then take it off and do it again in the afternoon. . . . At the end of the two weeks of schooling, John had a good estimate of how long we would need each morning. Four and a half hours was what we ended up with, and that worked perfectly." In fact, he feels that Chambers was glad of the excuse to recruit rookies. "He didn't want some older guy to put his own signature or interpretation in the makeup and lose conformity." This quest for conformity involved a "paint by numbers" methodology. "Everything was pre-laid out for them: a pre-painted application, three special grease paints, adhesives, mixed crepe wool with real human hair, solvent and so on. John wanted absolute control of how this assembly line was going to operate each day." This mentality becomes understandable when contemplating Chambers's comments to *Questar* in 1980: "Rubber is not like a punch-press operation where you get the identical thing punched out every time. It's an *art*. You mix the rubber, the rubber has a setting time and by the fluctuation of temperature it might set prematurely. . . . Everything is by artistic feel. The men you had doing the work were trained. You'd run the rubber and maybe the whole batch would come out with bubbles in the muzzle or in the nose. Nothing was controlled to that extent."

Burman recalls among the makeup crew "a tremendous amount of enthusiasm and excitement" due to the fact that "we all knew we were doing something that had never been done before; we knew we were making history." However, he also recalls less happy feelings. "There is always a lot of stress when you have that many people all trying to stay on schedule. The most stressful part was that each morning John would stroll through the makeup trailers every thirty minutes checking on everyone to make sure we were doing the makeups as we were instructed to do. He would also call out the time, so you knew where you were at that moment. All of that was okay unless you had some kind of problem and you were running late when for some reason our performer was late or some other reason beyond our control and we had to catch up."

The makeup costs for *Planet of the Apes* have been reported to be fully one-fifth of the picture's (original) overall budget of $5 million. Abrahams later dismissed that as PR, stating that his recollection was a department budget of half a million. With regard to the suggestion that *Planet of the Apes* had the largest number of makeup artists ever assembled—also mentioned in contemporaneous Fox publicity—Burman says, "We had big days when we had over sixty people working, counting hairdressers, body makeup people." However, he offers the caveat that there may have been more makeup and hair people on *The Wizard of Oz* (1939). He seems dubious even about the notion that the makeup department was provided generous resources. "It was only the studio who thought we had a huge budget. They kept pressuring the makeup department to hold it down because they still were not confident that this film would be profitable." This was true "throughout the whole shoot and even in the beginning of postproduction." Even so, the sums concerned were by any standard not small. Chambers told *Read*, "Each time the mask was removed at night, it was ruined, and we had to build a new one." Each set of ape-face appliances cost about $150. Multiplied by the number of actors working and the number of shooting days, this was a tidy sum in 1967.

Chambers had a quite remarkable degree of on-set power. "John had an agreement with Franklin, the director, to be able to stop shooting if he saw anything wrong with the makeups," notes Burman. For Chambers, the circumstances of the shoot made this absolutely vital. He explained to *Questar*, "Most of it was shot outside. . . . The lighting wasn't that subdued in a lot of instances. We had to perfect the makeup enough so we wouldn't destroy the illusion that we were trying to get."

Roddy McDowall wore this sort of makeup more than any other actor. In 1998, he told Danny Savello of *Scarlet Street*, "It was extremely difficult, because trying to register under all that appliance necessitated a tremendous amount of imagination. We had to continually move our faces to show a lot of activity so we didn't look dead." Linda Harrison was thankful to have graduated from ape in the screen test to human in the actual film. "It was a hardship on them," she says of the ape actors. "Getting up at three, and then it would take a lot of vas to get it off." For his part, McDowall didn't so much mind the early starts, time in the makeup chair, or Vaseline-assisted removal, but he told Marvel, "I'm not a true claustrophobe, but after a time, not being able to scratch my nose, eat anything, or drink except through a straw really works on my nerves. After about five hours I really become a basket case!"

As a conscientious actor, McDowall worked hard to complete the effect created by the prosthetics team. This included a convincing walk. Prior to the shooting of the 2001 *Planet of the Apes* film, specialists were employed by the studio to coach the players in ape movement. Back in 1967, actors were on their own. McDowall told *Read* in 1974, "I simply asked myself how an intelligent chimp might walk and stand. Then I invented a semi-animal waddle by crouching as I walk and letting my arms swing loosely."

Despite all this care and craft, there was one thing the makeup crew could not fix. "The prosthetic muzzles caused the actors to speak in a muffled way, so after the film was completed the actors had to do ADR [automated dialogue replacement]," says Burman. "Always a problem with any makeup that covers your mouth and nose."

Chambers's ape makeup would be epoch marking, but was just one part of the film's fantastical visuals. Another was the topography. Art director William Creber later explained to Marvel's *Apes* magazine, "The final concept was to keep any reference to Earth a secret until the tag scene of the picture, the Statue of Liberty shot. This led to the alien look we finally designed." Michael Wilson here claimed another influence on the film. With the production seeking an architectural style for the ape dwellings that looked neither modern-day American nor generically futuristic, he came up with a suggestion. "There's a Spanish architect named Antonio Guadi," he told Marvel. "His architecture suggests a kind of arboreal past; some of the columns of his buildings seem like giant trunks of trees. . . . So the city of the apes in the picture was built in that fashion."

Wilson's suggestion was made manifest by Ivan Martin, head of the studio's construction department. He explained in 1968 to *American*

Cinematographer that the entire Ape-City set was constructed from polyurethane foam. "The material is NKC Coro-Foam, a combination of resin and a catalyst. When these are fired under pressure from a gun, the mix rises like bread dough. Then the heat quickly dissipates, and within ten minutes it is cold—and solid." These upturned dish-like buildings looked substantial, but Creber revealed to Marvel, "Ten men could pick up a whole building!"

Creber, along with costume designer Morton Haack, was also involved in giving each ape species an identity more rapidly apparent than that suggested by their dialogue. "We created a clothes colors standard for each type, somewhat matching their skin coloring, except for chimps which wore green." Clothes were padded to engender an apelike silhouette and stature. Some ingenuity, though, is always more basic: arms were made to look longer by the ruse of shortening sleeves.

~

Shooting of *Planet of the Apes* began in May 1967. Although pleased to be working with an artist like Schaffner, Harrison found that he kept the actors in the dark. "He was extremely private," she says. "In fact, the assistant director who knew Dick, said, 'He never told anyone where the next shot was gonna be.'"

Planet of the Apes opens with a tranquil scene set in the then-near future of 1972. The lead character, Taylor (not, note, John Thomas) of ANSA (not, note, NASA), is seen at the helm of a spaceship—iridescent astral formations visible through the front window—dictating into a microphone the details of his mission while his three colleagues continue their induced slumber. The exposition is better than Serling's opening, which resorted to the device of turbulence causing Thomas's last flight log recording to play to the sleeping ship. "According to Dr.

Hasslein's theory of time, in a vehicle traveling nearly the speed of light the Earth has aged nearly 700 years since we left it, while we've aged hardly at all," Taylor notes. This throwaway reference introduces someone who will be an important component of the series and its mythos.

As well as having a less snigger-worthy name than his Serling antecedent, Taylor is of a markedly different nature. A misanthrope, mildly similar to Professor Antelle in Boulle's book, he caustically signs off, "Does Man, that marvel of the universe, that glorious paradox who has sent me to the stars, still make war against his brother? Keep his neighbor's children starving?" This then highly unusual downbeat rhetoric sets the series' sociopolitical tone.

One of the crew, Stewart, is female. Another of Taylor's colleagues, Dodge, is black. It could be argued that the progressivism is somewhat undermined by both astronauts meeting a grisly fate, first Stewart, who is found to be a skeleton when the ship crash-lands. The ship itself is so stylish that one rather feels it's a shame that we only see it as it's sinking. The submersion in water is the reason the astronauts have to abruptly leave it, a handy device that prevents them looking into their trajectory. (Serling simply has them deciding to do it later, which of course other circumstances then prevent.) However, they are instantly cognizant of the fact from ship readings that they have been asleep for two thousand years in real time.

Heston's long acidic bout of laughter as a colleague plants a tiny American flag sets another tone: almost aggressive pessimism. It also epitomizes the hypocrisy of Taylor's misanthropy: his endless belligerence is the kind of thing that gives rise to the wars he detests. However, this was a day and age just prior to that when feminist theory started to undermine macho assumptions. The bickering astronauts are grimly aware that they are permanently stranded on this unknown world, but Taylor points out to his crewmate Landon that it could arguably be worse. With twenty centuries having passed, "Even if you could get back, they'd think you were something that fell out of a tree."

In a long passage involving the astronauts negotiating inhospitable terrain, Schaffner provides lingering shots of beautiful if barren scenery behind which Jerry Goldsmith proffers portentous, quasi-discordant music. The mysterious scarecrows retained from Serling's script are an eerie note, while the nudity, as the astronauts take a swim upon gratefully encountering water, underlines the fact that this is not by any means a kiddie picture.

The astronauts' clothes are ripped by the feral, mute humans they encounter, although the latter are otherwise peaceable. The same cannot be said, of course, for the simian huntsmen who materialize. As in Serling, Taylor gets a bullet in the throat, which renders him temporarily and conveniently mute. Humans, both dead and alive, are trussed up by the hunters, some of whom pose for photographs with their trophies, the latter something carried over from Boulle's book.

Something else appropriated from Boulle is the ape subspecies hierarchy. Whatever they jettisoned from the author's overall vision or from Serling's solo script, adapters retained this part wholesale, faithfully replicating it in the five films and two TV series of the original Planet of the Apes continuity. The hierarchy might have been ingeniously thought through but was, says Corrina Bechko, "kind of backwards." Bechko has both studied apes and written Apes narratives. Before becoming a comic book writer whose oeuvre includes stories set in the Planet of the Apes universe, she worked in behavioral research for around five years at Los Angeles Zoo. Boulle imagined chimpanzees as the temperate-minded scientists of an ape-dominated world. In fact, chimps would make a mockery of the ninth verse of the twenty-third Sacred Scroll invoked by Zaius in this narrative ("Beware the beast man, for he is the devil's pawn. Alone among God's primates, he kills for sport or lust or greed"). Bechko says, "They are the ones most likely to hold a grudge. They're the ones that actually will war with neighboring chimpanzee troops. . . . I have definitely seen them kill for sport." As for the logic of Boulle's decision to make gorillas the ape-world's warriors, Bechko says, "The gorillas are much more peaceful." It was only in 1979 when the BBC broadcast footage of David Attenborough sitting among a group of wild but peaceable mountain gorillas—a genuinely jaw-dropping sight at the time—that the human race fully came to understand how generations of adventurers and explorers had misled them with their tall tales of gorilla carnivorous savagery. Boulle made the orangutans—red-haired herbivores, native not to the Africa of chimps and gorillas but Indonesia and Malaysia—the ape world's politicians. This makes little sense considering that a gentle temperament hardly chimes with the self-aggrandizement necessary for the Machiavellian mind-set. On another level, though, it has logic. "The orangutans are the real brainiacs," says Bechko. "Orangutans will just stare at a place like a door, maybe for days, and then just go open the door. They figure it out in their heads."

Oddly, Boulle left out completely the other large hairy primate. "Maybe they just didn't know as much about bonobos then," offers Bechko. "They're less well studied." One of the reasons for that lack of research could be that, to the untrained eye, bonobos look the same as chimpanzees. However, they are not just a different species but a contrasting one. "Chimpanzees are more likely to hit and bonobos are more likely to kiss," explains Bechko. "They say bonobos make love not war, and that's actually fairly accurate. They tend to have a lot more intergroup grooming and sex—among all members, not just male-female couplings."

As for the hairless fifth large primate, Bechko observes, "A lot of people would say that we're halfway in between chimpanzees and bonobos. There might be some truth to that."

Not carried over from either Boulle or Serling is the technology, something that, as Harrison points out, was dictated not just by logic but also by budget. These changes result in a confused jumble. How would a society capable of manufacturing cameras and rifles have no electricity, motor vehicles, or telecommunications? Yet the blend of eras surprisingly doesn't jar—not least because rifle-wielding gorillas on horseback just somehow look cool.

A captured Taylor eventually grabs Zira's notepad and pen and, to her astonishment, writes his name. When Zira takes him to see Cornelius, Taylor scribbles out his story for the ape couple. They find it difficult to believe because they have no flight technology. They have also been inculcated with the idea that nobody can survive in the Forbidden Zone, the area where his ship landed, closed to apes for so long that nobody can remember why. Even so, Cornelius has a hypothesis that apes evolved from man, one he keeps quiet because such thoughts are considered heretical.

Meanwhile, Zaius—cognizant of Taylor's intelligence—orders him to be gelded. Taylor understandably makes an escape bid. During the chase, he is horrified to find Dodge stuffed and mounted in a museum. In the act of being recaptured, Taylor finally finds his voice again and says to a gorilla, "Take your stinking paws off me you damn dirty ape!"

It's a descendant of the Serling-written Thomas cry "No! Get away! Let me alone!" but an instantly iconic improvement.

After several more weeks in captivity, Taylor is taken to an "ad hoc Tribunal of the National Academy" constituting three orangutans, including Zaius. This scene may well be Wilson's most important contribution. It is not only possessed of courtroom-drama dynamics but is extraordinarily long for an action-adventure picture, thus adding to the film's aura of class. Zira is accused of having experimented on Taylor to make him speak. Taylor says Landon can prove the veracity of his story, but further horror awaits him when his surviving crewmate turns out to have been lobotomized.

The self-deluding intransigence of the orangutan tribunal is mocked in a visual in-joke wherein they are made to resemble the three wise monkeys. The idea came from Schaffner, perhaps because he was bored by a talky scene. Both he and Heston, however, agreed that it would be out of key for what was otherwise a somber and dramatic passage. The director printed it up in order to provide a laugh in the "dailies." Somehow, it survived from the footage of each day's shooting to the rough cut and from there to the preview. Such was the huge success of the "sneak" that nobody wanted to change anything. "We found ourselves trapped in it," Heston reflected to *Fantastic Films*.

Zaius has a private meeting with Taylor where he informs the human that he has been consigned to brain experimentation, which he happily describes as a "living death." The hostility he has shown Taylor from the beginning begins to make sense as he says, "Your case was preordained. . . . That mythical community you're supposed to come from—Fort Wayne? A fort! Unconsciously, you chose a name that was *belligerent*." This piece of twisted logic is a good touch. However, in Wilson's shooting script, this scene was also used to "hang a lantern" on the statistically impossible fact that the apes on this supposedly alien world converse in English. Zaius demands to know how Taylor could be from another planet when "we speak the same language." It's even better than Serling's tilt at the same issue because it's so fleeting that it doesn't telegraph the surprise that's to come. The fact that it was omitted from the finished film, and the issue is therefore never addressed, weakens the picture. The culprit seems to be Heston, who said in his published diaries, "I had a meeting with Dick Zanuck and Frank on whether or not to make a script point of the fact that the apes speak English. To me, it's patently obvious we should ignore this. English is the lingua franca of film." Although for some people the omission undermines the film's high-grade aura, it has to be said that far more people take the attitude of Tom Burman, who shrugs, "When they are a big success, who cares?"

Cornelius and Zira organize Taylor's escape, enlisting the help of Zira's teenage nephew Lucius. The latter's inclusion creates a surprisingly anti-progressivist strand. Lines like, "What'll probably happen is that some money-mad grown-up'll put him in a circus" cringemakingly betray Lucius as a middle-aged man's scornful idea of a contemporaneous hippie teenager. Matters are compounded when Taylor mockingly instructs the young chimp not to trust anybody over thirty, the famous mantra of 1960s youth.

Taylor insists on bringing with him the beautiful mate Zira had given him upon his first incarceration. Nova (the name given her by Taylor never explained here) is, for a savage, strangely clean of hair, gleaming of tooth, and shaven of leg. However, unlike Serling, Wilson keeps Nova mute throughout, another improvement logic-wise. Taylor decides to head for a fabled area Zaius has told him about, a jungle beyond the Forbidden Zone. Cornelius, Zira, and Lucius are journeying to a location adjacent to that—Cornelius's Forbidden Zone dig, whose contents could disprove the charges of heresy the tribunal has laid on him and his fiancée—so they all travel together. Zira explains that the scarecrows they pass were put up to deter entrance to the Forbidden Zone.

Zaius and armed gorillas gallop in pursuit of the party. When they catch up to it, a rifle-toting Taylor forces Zaius to dispense with his guards. What then occurs is a sort of ideological showdown. In the beachside cave hosting the dig, Taylor points out to the orangutan that among the artifacts Cornelius has discovered there are false teeth, eyeglasses, and heart valves—evidence of ancient human civilization. As if on cue, a human doll with which Nova has been playing startles her by speaking.

As Taylor prepares to make his exit with Nova, he tries to reason one last time with the now-trussed Zaius. The orangutan contemptuously says, "All my life I've awaited your coming and dreaded it. . . . I have always known about man. From the evidence, I believe his wisdom must walk hand in hand with his idiocy. . . . He must be a warlike animal who gives battle to everything around him—even himself. . . . The Forbidden Zone was once a paradise. Your breed made a desert of it ages ago." This soliloquy is one of the few pieces of dialogue remaining from Serling's script, albeit made more emphatic. Another is Zira's protestation to Taylor that he is almost too ugly to kiss, although here given greater resonance by the fact that the human has just rendered himself less ape-like by shaving off his beard.

Part of the ending envisaged by Wilson for the film was one found in the Boulle book. "They had me getting pregnant," recalls Harrison.

"Heston didn't want that because he figured the public would think that they were having sex. He was very proper." Speaking to *Fantastic Films* in 1980, Heston said, "I've forgotten why they changed that." Mort Abrahams told *Simian Scrolls* that he himself had nixed the idea, as the discovery of the Statue of Liberty and a baby being born would effectively constitute two endings.

Although Taylor and Nova escape, in one sense the astronaut's fate is just the same as in the Serling script. For all the changes Wilson made, he was wise enough to retain the ending, even if he enriched it. In this version, the sight of the half-buried Statue of Liberty doesn't merely underline to the astronaut his stranded state but confirms his misanthropic contempt for man and his destructiveness. "There is no parallel with any other film. We have a shocking ending which could stay with the viewers for a long time after they've seen the picture," Rod Serling enigmatically told Herb A. Lightman of *American Cinematographer* in 1968, just weeks before release. When that April readers were able to find out what Serling was hinting at, they discovered he wasn't kidding. The denouement of Pierre Boulle's *La planète des singes* constituted a delightful but whimsical twist in the tale (in fact, a brace of them). What audiences of its screen adaptation saw was also a twist, but one saturated with horror and pathos. Taylor's aghast discovery of the statue that in his time loomed majestically over New York Harbor was shocking, unforgettable, and heartbreaking. It is now arguably the most famous movie ending of all time.

According to Arthur P. Jacobs, the origin of the ending lay in his belief that the astronauts being on another planet as per Boulle's template was "too predictable." At this point, the first screenplay was being worked on, and Blake Edwards was slated to direct it. According to Jacobs, one day he and Edwards were having lunch at the Yugo Kosherama Delicatessen in Burbank, opposite the Warner Bros. headquarters. Jacobs related his misgivings to the director. "Then I said, 'What if he was on the Earth the whole time and doesn't know it, and the audience doesn't know it,'" Jacobs told *Cinefantastique*. "Blake said, 'That's terrific. Let's get ahold of Rod.' As we walked out . . . we looked up, and there's this big Statue of Liberty on the wall of the delicatessen. We both looked at each other and said, 'Rosebud.'" Those who found a verisimilitude in the fact that Jacobs remembered the name of the delicatessen and even the lunch bought (ham sandwiches) will have been confused to note that, in the very same magazine, Serling had a completely different story. "I always believed that was my idea," he said, noting that it attracted him because a fragment of the statue could be shown to the audience without immediately giving away what it was. However, he also admitted that it could have been the case that several people alighted on the idea at the same time. In Marvel's *Planet of the Apes* magazine, meanwhile, Serling said the idea was his "in collaboration with Jacobs." Those who might suspect that this vagueness suggests Serling desperately trying to appropriate credit are directed to both the fact that he publicly conceded the *Planet of the Apes* screenplay to be mainly Michael Wilson's and to Mort Abrahams's unequivocal public statement to author Paul A. Woods, "That was Rod's ending."

"I'm a major fan of *The Twilight Zone* and that is so Rod Serling," says Rich Handley. "I have no trouble believing that Serling is responsible for that." Certainly, the ending bears an uncanny resemblance to a specific *Twilight Zone* climax. In "I Shot an Arrow into the Air," three astronauts land on what they assume to be an asteroid. They wander through the barren landscape. With their water running low, one of them decides that the only way to survive is to kill the others. After carrying out his drastic plan, he is stunned to come upon a road sign stating that Reno, Nevada, is ninety-seven miles away. These plot similarities immediately make it seem like a case-closed scenario. Only—hold on. This is the sole *Twilight Zone* episode whose central idea was provided by an outsider—namely, one Madelon Champion, to whom Serling paid $500 for the right to use the idea when Champion mentioned it in conversation.

Just when everyone thought that there were no new angles to unearth in this convoluted and contradictory saga, Brian Pendreigh offered yet another. Researching his 2001 book *Legend of the Planet of the Apes*, he was told by Blake Edwards that Jacobs had "nothing to do" with the Statue of Liberty ending, but neither did Edwards credit Serling. Instead the director cited somebody whose name had never been mentioned in this context. It had all been, he claimed, a collaboration between himself and Don Peters, a concept artist employed on the project when it was in development at Warner Bros. When Pendreigh tracked him down, Peters refined the story further by asserting, "It was my idea." He showed Pendreigh his concept artwork (reproduced in Pendreigh's book) displaying Lady Liberty and her aloft torch projecting from the ground.

Whoever thought of it, the time-ravaged statue with its torch rising from the sand was a stunning spectacle and remains so even in the age of seamless CGI illusion. The effect was achieved by a combination of an unusually detailed matte painting and a physical construction.

The painting was the work of Emil Kosa Jr. who rendered it on glass so as to facilitate fine detail that the grain of canvas and paper could not. He left transparent areas for live-action insertions. The physical part was the statue's crown, cranium, arm, and torch, constructed of cardboard and papier-mâché by Creber. Harrison: "They had the bare essential of the shape of it, but it wasn't filled out." Although not filled out and only a half-scale model, it required a seventy-foot scaffold. "They had to get a shot of us looking up," recalls Harrison. "The cameraman, the head, couldn't walk up there to shoot because he had bad feet." Luckily Zanuck's roommate from Stanford University was on set. "So finally Dick's friend Bob Dardell went up," says Harrison, adding, "Not too crazy about it."

The horse-mounted Taylor and Nova come into shot through a close-up of metal spikes. The subsequent big reveal that the spikes are part of a famous crown constitutes a shocking moment even despite it not being emphasized with a dramatic blast of music the way such movie scenes usually are. Jerry Goldsmith very wisely opted to let the scene tell its own story, with only Taylor's screams and the lapping waves soundtracking it.

Pierre Boulle, though, was unimpressed. He told Jacobs in a letter that the idea was a "cheap unwarranted effect." Boulle told *Cinefantastique* that one of the reasons he felt unable to share the admiration of the public and critics at the iconic alteration was that "I feel, because I'm a rationalist writer, that things must be explained thoroughly." The public, though, instantaneously understood the nuclear-devastation insinuation, and Boulle's dissenting voice was possibly the only one in the world. Speaking in 2020, Harrison said, "In the Academy Awards this year, they showed the best ending in a movie and [of] course *Planet of the Apes* [was in it], where he's pounding the ocean saying, 'They did it!'"

To be precise, Taylor says, "We finally really did it! You maniacs! You blew it up. Oh, damn you! God damn you all to hell!" The dialogue in Wilson's screenplay is simply "My God!" Heston recalled that he improvised his lines and that this engendered the most friction on a point of script during the entire shoot. "Language was getting more permissive, but still you weren't supposed to say, 'God damn you,'" he told *Fantastic Films*. "I said. 'What do you want me to say? "Shucks! Darn you!"'"

A fault in the film, and one that would run like a seam through Apes movies, is that there is no sense of a wider society. Everything seems to take place in a small area among little more than a cluster of simians. There is some logic to this in the sense that much of the world is out of bounds, but this is not explained or explored properly. Nor does Wilson proffer the information Serling did that ape society has no nations, therefore providing at least some rationale for a concentration of activity and power.

Shooting wrapped on August 10, 1967, fourteen days "overskedge." There were additional expenses other than those caused by being over-schedule, and the film ended up with a spend of $5.8 million as opposed to the anticipated $5 million. Harrison was less concerned by that than the worth of what had been filmed. "I kind of felt, 'Gee, this is a little embarrassing,' she says. 'I'm playing a subhuman. And with these apes . . .' It just seemed farfetched." However, she attaches the qualifier, "I was so young." More seasoned souls on the project were confident. "I think they knew it," says Harrison. "They previewed the movie a couple times. The people write what they feel [on comment cards], and we got good reviews. It was startling for people to see apes."

The picture, of course, was startling for more than that reason. It was a concoction that was both intellectually and viscerally satisfying. Moreover, the first Apes film captured the zeitgeist: the year of its release was one in which the respective values of the long-haired youth and the censorious middle-aged, against the backdrop of the Vietnam draft and the assassinations of Martin Luther King Jr. and Bobby Kennedy, created an unfolding drama that genuinely seemed to auger civil war. And that was just America: there were bellicose uprisings and social movements across the world.

The corollary of this, of course, is that had the original Planet of the Apes films been made in a different era, they might not have been laced with social commentary at all. Rich Handley: "'Specially not in the eighties when *The Cosby Show* was an example of the kind of wisdom being bandied about. The fact that it was made in the sixties is incredibly relevant. That era allowed them to make films like that and get away with saying things that they might not have later on." This might be an opinion informed by hindsight, but something very similar was actually noted at the time in showbiz bible *Variety*. Describing *Planet of the Apes* as "political-sociological allegory, cast in the mold of futuristic science fiction," reviewer "Murf" opined that the screenplay "probably could not have been filmed ten years ago, and the disturbing thought lingers that it might not be possible in another ten years."

Released on February 8, 1968, and running to 112 minutes, *Planet of the Apes* attracted mixed reviews from the professional critics. Esteemed movie writer Roger Ebert said in the *Chicago Sun-Times*, "If you only condescend to see an adventure thriller on rare occasions, condescend this time. You have nothing to lower but your brow." However, as can be seen even sniffy reviews like his noted a serious intent unusual for the genre. (To be fair, it should be noted that *Planet of the Apes* wasn't injecting class into the SF medium single-handedly: '68 was also the year of Stanley Kubrick's phantasmagorical, if slightly boring, *2001: A Space Odyssey*.)

At the 1969 Academy Awards ceremony, Morton Haack was nominated for Best Costume Design and Jerry Goldsmith for Best Original Score. Although right from the get-go John Chambers had talked of winning an Academy Award, some might have assumed him to have been joking, it being the case that regular makeup Oscars didn't then exist. However, Burman says, "Bill Tuttle was given the first special Oscar for his makeup on *7 Faces of Dr. Lao* just a few years earlier. So John was dead serious because he knew the scope of this film and he knew if he could pull this off successfully it would be hard for the Academy to ignore." It was even harder for the Academy to ignore the entreaties of a Fox bigwig. "He got him a special Academy Award," says Harrison of the man who that year became her husband. "Dick did that. He was on the board of the Academy Awards and when Dick believes in somebody, he makes things happen. He had that authority." Zanuck's intervention to secure Chambers an Honorary Award for Outstanding Makeup Achievement raises issues of propriety, not least because the previous year lobbying by Fox had managed to get the studio's badly received flop *Doctor Dolittle* (also, of course, an Arthur Jacobs film) an eyebrow-raising nomination for Best Picture. However, few would dispute Harrison's observation of Chambers and *Planet of the Apes*, "It was groundbreaking and without Johnny it couldn't have been made."

By the time of that '69 Oscars ceremony, *Planet of the Apes* had cleaned up at the box office. Its $15 million in North American rentals made it 20th Century-Fox's biggest earner of the year, it doing twice as much business as the studio's closest contender, *The Boston Strangler*.

"Arthur had taken it to every studio," reflects Harrison. "It's destiny. . . . It was the kind of picture that will either go through the roof or be a flop, and men like Dick need to go by their intuition, and intuition told him it will be a hit."

4

WHAT LIES BENEATH

Whatever the popularity of *Planet of the Apes*, many people would have instantly found the idea of a follow-up to it risible.

Sequels were at that point in cinema history afflicted by an ersatz and exploitative reputation. There had been few, if any, great ones. Moreover, in this specific case any supplement would surely ruin a symmetrical and perfectly tragic story arc. However, Hollywood is in the business of making money, not just art, and the studio whose head of production had once threatened to throw Arthur P. Jacobs off the set if he ever brought up *Planet of the Apes* again felt compelled to ask APJAC for a second Apes film.

Michael Wilson was offered the writing job but turned it down. APJAC turned to Rod Serling. Serling racked up a $200 phone bill discussing what might be done, but the only remnants of his ideas to be found in the finished film are a nuclear-bomb plot device and a section wherein the hero, upon entering a cave, discovers the remains of an old city street from the days when man ruled.

Meanwhile, Pierre Boulle was also expressing interest. Back in April 1965, he had taken it upon himself to proffer a partial screenplay adaptation of his novel. The script spent an inordinate amount of time on the spaceship traveling to the planet, and Boulle's accompanying notes made it clear he disdained the proposed nuclear-holocaust subtext and Statue of Liberty ending. In other words, he wanted it more like his book. Now he offered (unsolicited and unpaid, according to Mort Abrahams) what he called *Planet of the Men* (these days it would probably be given the more politically correct title *Planet of the Humans*). A circulating version carries the handwritten annotation "Copied 7-22-68."

The script is shot through with gaucheries, both linguistic and structural. Not only is it obvious that English is not Boulle's first language, but it's readily apparent that the screenplay is not his preferred writing format. His script is divided into sections denoted by an underline and centered numbers, as though he thinks they are the chapters of a book. More of an issue for the prospective viewer are multiple flashbacks that make for a disjointed narrative. The story line picks up exactly where the first movie left off but then repeatedly lurches forward in time to show us Sirius, son of Taylor and Nova, torn between his father's peaceable intentions and the hatred of apes inherited from his mother. Other faults are convenient coincidences and wodges of expository dialogue.

Boulle takes the opportunity to foist on the public some of the theories and projections from his book. For instance, under attack from Taylor's human army, apes begin to revert to an animal state, dropping onto all fours and climbing into trees—the mirror image of the way in his book the author posited humans rapidly descending into a primordial state as the apes took over, and just as absurd. In other respects, Boulle is essentially making the same point as was made in *Planet of the Apes* (and Wilson made via the ninth verse of the twenty-third Sacred Scroll), something which renders the project a little redundant.

The script is also infused with more than a little snobbery, something startlingly confirmed when it becomes apparent that Boulle hasn't yet bothered to see the *Planet of the Apes* film. He's read the screenplay all right—there are three specific references to the first film's script. However, he portrays Taylor and companions trying to raise the Statue of Liberty back upright when, of course, *Planet of the Apes* never posited it in a toppled state in the first place.

Boulle said he had thrown himself into the project wholeheartedly. "I played the game," he told *Cinefantastique*. "It was an interesting and amusing experience for me, nothing more. It's not the same. When I was writing I was thinking in visual terms, picturing the actors, Charlton Heston, and the others." It was Boulle's belief that his script was not rejected by APJAC as such. "They accepted the treatment that I worked on, but they made so many changes that very few of my ideas were left," he said. Even based as his opinion was on only having read the script for what was ultimately titled *Beneath the Planet of the Apes* (in 1972, he was cheerfully admitting, "I haven't seen the second or the third film"), it's difficult to see how he came to the conclusion that his work was altered rather than dumped. Jacobs later said that the reason Boulle's script was not put into production was that it "wasn't cinematic."

Meanwhile, Serling—who had been shown Boulle's work and suggested ways to improve it—informed APJAC that he would be tied up in other projects for the foreseeable future. Neither APJAC nor Fox were likely to have been heartbroken about this: Serling's own written proposal for a sequel, which he had sent them in April '68, hadn't been ecstatically received.

The task of providing a sequel screenplay was eventually handed to Paul Dehn, who worked off a story cooked up by him and Mort

Abrahams. Born in 1912, Englishman Dehn was from elevated stock, having been educated at Oxford and served as a major in Special Forces during World War II. Writing-wise, he was a bit of a Renaissance man, turning out poetry volumes, song lyrics, sketches for musical shows, and an opera libretti. He was also a film critic for nearly three decades, a period that overlapped with his inauguration into screenwriting. He achieved the remarkable feat of obtaining an Academy Award for his first movie project, *Seven Days to Noon* (1950), for which he and collaborator James Bernard provided the story. When he graduated to actual screenplays, he proved to be highly skilled. He won a British Academy of Film and Television Arts award for his script for wartime intrigue picture *Orders to Kill* (1958). He became a specialist in adapting the printed word to the screen, being responsible for *Goldfinger* (released in 1964 and to this day the greatest-ever James Bond picture), as well as the film of John le Carré's *The Spy Who Came in from the Cold* (1965) and the Richard Burton / Elizabeth Taylor take on *The Taming of the Shrew* (1967).

Although Jacobs was aware of Dehn's talents because they had previously worked together on a project that hadn't reached fruition, it would seem Mort Abrahams was behind the writer's hiring, once again fulfilling a role beyond his pay grade or credit level. The sequel to *Planet of the Apes* was not something one might assume would be in Dehn's wheelhouse—and not just because it would mean devising an original story. However, Abrahams—as much a fan of Dehn's poetry as his screenwriting—felt that someone who excelled at both might provide the property an interesting lateral angle. For his part, Dehn said he leapt at the opportunity, pointing out how he enjoyed darting about from one type of film to another, as demonstrated by him following a fantastical espionage picture like *Goldfinger* with a grittier take on the genre in the form of *The Spy Who Came in from the Cold*, before breaking out of a potential spy-movie typecasting by opting for a Shakespeare adaptation.

The plans for a *Planet of the Apes* sequel hit a snag when Charlton Heston said he wasn't interested. Heston told *Fantastic Films* of his discussions with Zanuck, "'Well, sonofabitch,' he said, 'we really can't do it if you're not in it, you know.' So I said, 'Well, how about if I'm in it at the beginning and you kill me off right away?' . . . After they started working on the script, though, I got another call from Dick Zanuck, and he said, 'Listen, would you mind if we had you disappear in the beginning and then come back at the end and get killed?' Obviously, that was better from their point of view, because if I disappeared everyone would figure that I'd show up again."

To accommodate what might be termed Heston's bookend presence, the narrative was manipulated to provide a lead role for another astronaut. Named Brent, he was played by James Franciscus. Harrison says it was not accidental that this actor was pressed from the same Aryan mold as Heston. "They used him because [of] the facial [resemblance]. But he couldn't replace Heston. . . . He was small. He was self-absorbed. He wasn't really a good actor." Franciscus was fairly well known, but only from television shows like *Naked City*. "For him, this is a real coup to get this part in his career," Harrison says. She does allow, "He was working so hard to get what he thought was the right way of acting." However, Franciscus clearly had issues. Most notably, he seemed afflicted by a mind-set that bespoke a childhood in which his father told him too many times that he was a sissy. The film's director, Ted Post, recalled to Russo, Landsman, and Gross, "Jimmy veers away from being sensitive—he thinks it's not being masculine." Franciscus himself told the same authors that he insisted on changes to the script where his character was effectively saying, "Oh, please help me, I don't know what to do, poor little me," turning it around so that "[h]e was a *man*." Franciscus apparently wasn't able to do what most actors do when they have misgivings about a character they're playing: tell themselves it's only a role and therefore it doesn't diminish them personally. From what Harrison says, Franciscus's problem extended into his private life, with him engaging in bizarre acts of compensation. Before shooting started, she invited Franciscus and his wife to a double date at a high-class restaurant with her and Zanuck. "Dick and him started arm wrestling. The plates went on the floor."

The fact that directing duties went to Ted Post is also something about which Harrison has reservations. "Franklin Schaffner was so much more a greater director than Ted Post," she says. "Ted Post directed *Peyton Place*, . . . Ted Post was a TV director. . . . He was a very easy director. . . . You could get away with a lot of things. . . . Not like Franklin Schaffner—every move you did had to be perfect."

Not that Post was privileged to be working with the quality of material that Schaffner had been. "The script wasn't anything like the first movie," admits Harrison. "I was like twenty-one. As you get older you get much more perceptive and smarter. I didn't really think too much. The part was bigger, which I liked." Nor was the budget the same. Originally, APJAC had been promised $5.5 million, only slightly less than for the first film. They ended up making do with not much more than $3 million. "The studio cut the budget way down on *Beneath* because they had never made a sequel that made money," makeup man Tom Burman says. "We were only able to pull it off because a lot of the work had already been done from the first movie." The reduction meant that ambitious underwater screenplay scenes went unfilmed. Yet, though the combination of inadequate funding and the bad reputation of sequels ostensibly put Paul Dehn in a no-win situation, his craftsmanship ensured that the follow-up was considerably more elevated than the money-grubbing exercise that was widely expected. Consequently, the franchise now became his baby: he had a hand in writing all subsequent films in the quintet (or pentalogy, as some prefer to call the Jacobs series).

Dehn stated that the plot of *Beneath* was suggested to him by the ending of the first movie: if the Statue of Liberty was half buried in the sand, it implied that the rest of New York was under the Forbidden Zone, too. (He may have picked up this idea from Serling's notes, possibly by way of Abrahams.) From there, it was a relatively short jump to facilitate more conflict between apes and humans by populating the now subterranean Big Apple with descendants of the survivors of the nuclear event that had implicitly reduced it to this state so long ago.

Beneath the Planet of the Apes is famously the only live-action Apes project prior to 2001 to not feature the acting services of Roddy McDowall. However, McDowall does technically appear in the film because it takes up directly where the last movie left off, recycling its final iconic scenes from the beach. In fact, McDowall's voice is the first to be heard, as we are treated to a rerun of his Zaius-dictated recitation of the twenty-third scroll's "Beware the beast man" caution. When the Cornelius character crops up later in the narrative, however, it's English actor David Watson who is playing the scientist chimp. Or rather playing McDowall playing Cornelius: he does an uncanny impersonation job.

CHAPTER 4

As in the first film, we are shown a spaceship that would look cool were it not for its unfortunate circumstances. This one is a burnt-out wreck. On the ground beside it are astronauts in spacesuits like those worn by Taylor and his crew. Brent is tending to his unnamed skipper (Tod Andrews). The latter is gravely injured, but before he dies, Brent's dialogue with him establishes that, in following Taylor's trajectory, they have leapt into the year 3955 via a "Hasslein Curve." Brent doesn't know that the fact that his family and friends are centuries dead is the least of his problems: like his ANSA predecessors, he thinks he's on another planet.

Fresh from burying his captain, Brent is startled by the arrival on horseback of Nova. The script is studded with serendipitous occurrences like this, something that sits oddly with the fact that Dehn was responsible for making the plot of *Goldfinger* far more plausible than Ian Fleming's original novel. Nonetheless, Dehn is such a master of narrative that the viewer is less inclined to dwell on the improbability than enjoy the events they set in motion. Although Nova can't communicate anything verbally to Brent, the fact that she is carrying Taylor's dog tags says plenty.

A flashback shows Taylor and Nova being prevented from progressing on their journey by a wall of flame, bolts of lightning, and a fissure opening in the ground. When Taylor steps forward to investigate these phenomena, he disappears. Brent tries to convey to Nova that he wants her to take him to Taylor, but the place she uncertainly points the horse is the City of Apes.

Brent is astonished to see a Citizens Council made up of talking simians. The open-air forum is in heated debate with a general named Ursus currently holding court. It's one of the scattered faint traces of

Boulle's screenplay to be found in the film, the character being similar in name, species, manner, and motivation to a field marshal named Urus in *Planet of the Men.* Another ghost of that script is Ursus stating, "The only good human is a dead human," an inversion of Sirius's motto, "The only good ape is a dead ape." After an opening movie in which gorillas were only bit players, Ursus is the first of what will be several memorable gorilla characters in the franchise. James Gregory superbly communicates the field marshal's glowering belligerence and imperious impatience. The costume department also deserves credit for his distinctive military helmet, high-domed with trailing flaps.

It transpires that there have been strange manifestations in the Forbidden Zone. Eleven ape scouts have disappeared while the twelfth returned with strange stories of huge walls of fire and violent earthquakes. The apes have to venture into the area nonetheless because raids by encroaching humans are threatening famine for Ape City: the reports of life in the Zone imply the presence of food. Deciding that it is his duty as minister of science to find out whether other life forms exist, Zaius decides to join the expedition.

Meanwhile, Nova takes Brent to the home of the now married Cornelius and Zira. When the two chimpanzees see Brent, an unsure Zira exclaims "Taylor?" Only one thing prevents the viewer adjudging this a nice touch: it's not clear whether the line is meant to continue a motif present in both the Boulle book and the first Apes movie that human beings all look alike to the average simian or because a sly acknowledgment is being made that Franciscus is a Hestonalike. Zira tells Brent of the fate of Taylor's crewmates and that Taylor himself was last seen venturing into the Forbidden Zone. She gives Brent some rags that will make him less conspicuous. The upshot of the latter is that for much of the movie two attractive people are wandering around half naked, Franciscus being as ripped as Harrison is curvaceous.

Cornelius and Zira aside, the apes in this movie are even more savage toward humans than they were in the first film. When Brent and Nova are briefly captured, it's stated that their fate is target practice for soldiers. Seeking refuge from the gorillas chasing them, Brent and Nova slip into a cave. Neatly tiled walls, though, indicate that this is not a completely natural formation. Further investigation reveals a pay phone and a sign reading "Queensboro Plaza." "This used to be my home!" Brent gasps. "I lived here. Worked here." Brent is now coming to the same understanding as did Taylor at the end of the previous movie. "Did we finally do it?" he laments. The echoing of Taylor's "They finally really did it!" is not too improbable, as the threat of nuclear catastrophe was a key concern in and around the 1960s. However, it's interesting-cum-amusing how Planet of the Apes is developing into an anti-bomb franchise, something not even in the mind of Pierre Boulle when he penned his book.

There follows a scene in which placard-waving peacenik chimpanzees try to stop the mission marching off to the Forbidden Zone. Ted Post's style is usually merely functional, but he excels here, employing handheld cameras to capture the chaotic, jostling atmosphere of a street demonstration.

With the gorillas prowling outside, Brent and Nova venture further down the subway tracks. Brent blunders into the remains of the old city's cathedral to find a robed man worshipping a gleaming, upright missile, and is then escorted by two similarly weirdly dressed figures to stand before a group of authority figures who telepathically describe themselves as "the only reality in the universe." Jacobs seems to have concluded that if Richard D. Zanuck could apply pressure to get his lover cast in the first Apes movie, there was no reason his own wife, actress Natalie Trundy, shouldn't get part of the action. She plays telepathic mutant Albina. Trundy would henceforth be a fixture of the series. Whatever her abilities, her nepotistic casting as several different characters made a nonsense of continuity.

Other powers the mutants possess include being able to project illusions. When they present to the encroaching ape army an image of simians being tortured by fire, Zaius demands that Ursus order his soldiers to put them out of their misery. Ursus refuses on the grounds that their society's sacred rule is "Ape Shall Not Kill Ape." However, when the mutants show the Lawgiver—the mythical orangutan author of the apes' Sacred Scrolls—weeping blood, Zaius's horror is replaced by skepticism, causing him to gallop toward the illusion and thus shatter the artifice. The telepaths are able to see these events at a remove through methods unknown but which certainly save on exposition. The sight of the failure of their ruse causes the telepaths to decide that they need to set off their "Holy Weapon of Peace," their one mode of defense not based on illusion and mind control.

As the ape army reaches the remains of New York, Brent apprehensively watches the grotesque, gothic act of worship that is the weapon's launch ceremony. Even more grotesquely, the ostensibly diverse telepaths peel off their face masks to reveal that they are uniformly pallid and misshapen apparitions with pulsating veins crisis-crossing their bald pates. It's so striking a visual effect as to almost make the viewer forget that there was no logical reason for them to have covered themselves in the first place.

Brent is escorted to a cell whose resident, to his amazement, is Taylor. "We're a peaceful people," says the guard. "We don't kill our enemies—we get our enemies to kill each other." With their minds psychically manipulated, Brent and Taylor engage in an unwilling fight to the death. Nova, captured with Brent, is being escorted in a nearby corridor. Hearing their voices, she breaks away from her guard. When she sees what's happening, she in her alarm finally manages to enunciate Taylor's name. The distraction enables the astronauts to overcome their captor.

The apes discover the entrance to the subway network and pour in. A gorilla soldier comes across the escaping human trio and guns down Nova. A distraught Taylor doesn't even have time to grieve as he and Brent rush off to stop the launch of the device: Taylor has pointed out that the tail-fin markings that Brent has described identify it as the Doomsday Bomb, a cobalt-plated monstrosity able to destroy the whole planet.

The apes force their way into the bomb chamber, where they shoot dead the mutants' leaders and topple the nuclear weapon. The impact as it hits the floor sets off its launch mechanism. When the two humans try to intervene, Taylor is shot. Brent takes out a few gorillas with a commandeered rifle but is himself riddled with bullets.

Charlton Heston had made it a condition of his return to the role that the script should include his character's death. Dehn went billions better and inserted the demise of every man, woman, child, and ape—not to mention every other living thing—on Earth. That said, the scriptwriter met no resistance: APJAC and Fox could no more see scope for a third film than he. When a dying Taylor begs Zaius for help in stopping the bomb, he is rebuffed ("You ask me to help *you*? Man is evil, capable of nothing but destruction!"). Having after Nova's violent end already bitterly questioned why the planet should be saved, Taylor retorts, "You bloody bastard!" and with his dying breath sets off the weapon. As the screen goes to black, a stentorian voice notes, "In one of the countless billions of galaxies in the universe lies a medium-sized star and one of its satellites—a green and insignificant planet—is now dead." The second Apes movie in a row ends with the credits rolling silently.

Internal production memos show that considerable deliberation went into the story of *Beneath the Planet of the Apes*. However, the plot is still full of holes. Apart from those mentioned above, there are several things never properly explained. Why does Nova lead Brent to Cornelius and Zira, and how does she know the way? How did the telepaths make Taylor disappear in the Forbidden Zone? Why do the telepaths make Brent do violence to Nova before they even meet him? Why do the mutants' mind powers allow them to see what's happening in the Forbidden Zone but not in Ape City? Why don't they merely imprison Brent like they have Taylor instead of forcing the two to fight? The answer to all these questions and more, of course, is that Dehn and his paymasters are more interested in spectacle, shock, and saving on exposition than in logic or plausibility.

Meanwhile, the plot doesn't give Post the opportunity to take advantage of naturally beautiful landscapes the way the first movie's story afforded Schaffner, and the artificial vistas are hampered by substandard special effects: the half-buried New York is a pathetically inadequate matte painting that is particularly risible when remembering the excellence of the Lady Liberty artwork in the previous picture.

Yet the film is an enjoyable romp. Although it's sometimes at the trashier end of the science fiction scale—the self-same end that prevented SF being taken seriously before *Planet of the Apes*—its serious issues also give it a certain amount of gravitas. There are also several fine, nuanced touches: the simmering boredom of gorilla soldiers and orangutan intellectuals alike as they listen to a pompous pre-expedition speech by a minister; the way Brent—tussling with a gorilla guard on top of a prisoner transport vehicle—is saved by luck rather than heroism as his antagonist is felled by a tree branch; the ape soldiers whooping and chattering like conventional perturbed simians when confronted with the illusion of apes being tortured.

Released on May 26, 1970, *Beneath the Planet of the Apes* took $14 million at the box office, a sum that, while lower in absolute terms than the first movie's proceeds, was—when taking into account the reduced budget—actually commensurate with its profits. Aesthetically, it was a reasonably respectable way of bringing the Planet of the Apes movies to an end. And surely it was an end: not even its bottomless appetite for money could enable Hollywood to find a way to continue a series whose entire world had been blown to smithereens.

Could it?

While the Planet of the Apes film franchise was kicked off by a novel, the adaptations stemming from that novel created a veritable library.

The movie series spun off its own books, with each of the *Planet of the Apes*' four sequels having an accompanying novelization. The 1970s live-action Apes television series also generated its own novels. Even the short-lived, little remembered animated TV show *Return to the Planet of the Apes* was transferred into print. This "reverse adaptation" Apes writing has been in recent years augmented by the newer phenomenon of "same universe" writing.

The novelization of *Beneath the Planet of the Apes*, published by Bantam Books, was written by Michael Avallone, whose own tribute to himself—"the fastest typewriter in the East"—indicates where he felt the balance should lie between literary merit and making a buck, as does his claim before his 1999 death to have written more than a thousand books under various names. He claimed to have turned out the *Beneath* novelization in a weekend. Some would testify that it reads like it.

The plus side to Avallone's Apes book pretty much amounts to the fact that he provides at the beginning a symmetrical bookend to the apropos-nothing voiceover at the close of the film, even if it is via the fatuous device of telling us that if the wind could speak this is what it would say. Unfortunately, that plus-point is overwhelmed by downsides. He's pretentious, comparing the tableaux of the assembled mutant priests to a Rembrandt painting, something that juxtaposes oddly with his pulpy writing ("Brent buried his fist on the ape's nose"). He's also lazy, referring to Taylor's crewmates vaguely as "the female astronaut" and "the others." He has a smart-aleck penchant for meaningless postmodernism ("Nova was being similarly manhandled. Gorilla-handled?"). And he's patronizing ("Being female, the woman had not survived the flight," he says of the first film's Stewart).

He also takes liberties with the facts. The habitual novelization reader gets used to discrepancies between a film and its adaptation. So that novelizations can appear in print at the same time as the parent picture, writers work not from movie prints but screenplays. It being the case that rarely has a film made it to cinemas without changes being rendered at the shooting or postproduction stage or both, this regularly results in multiple differences, ranging from subtle alterations of dialogue, to deletion of scenes, and even to significant plot shifts. Movie studios aren't going to go out of their way to keep the adapter apprised of changes: they care little about the contents of a book-of-the-film whose only function from their point of view is to bump up the property's ancillary revenues. However, Avallone introduces additional inconsistencies, the worst one being the gratuitous statement that Cornelius and Zira are at home when the Doomsday Bomb is set off. Not even the filmmakers painted themselves into that corner.

As Pierre Boulle publicly stated in 1972 that he hadn't seen the *Beneath* movie, it's doubtful he would have read the book version. If he did, one wonders what he would have made of the quality of this bastard offspring of his acclaimed work—particularly so in light of Avallone's bizarre dedication: "For Pierre Boulle, for his two very important contributions to the arts of Literature and Film—*The Bridge on the River Kwai* and *Planet of the Apes*."

5

ESCAPE FROM A DEAD END

"I thought, 'That finishes the series. You've blown up the world, and that's the end of it.'" So said Charlton Heston to *Fantastic Films* about the unforgettably absolute finale to *Beneath the Planet of the Apes*. However, the actor added, "But of course, they were cleverer than I was, because they managed to keep on going anyway."

Escape from the Planet of the Apes—the 1971 third entry in the series—was a picture that demonstrated that the intertwined traits of greed and human ingenuity will always find a way. It marked the start of the almost comical process whereby an amused-cum-intrigued public waited to see what desperate-cum-ingenious method APJAC Productions and 20th Century-Fox could next find to prolong the franchise. Few would gainsay, though, that the avarice of both the producers and studio never prevented the series being enjoyable and thoughtful.

From the way Paul Dehn told it, when he had been working on the ending of *Beneath the Planet of the Apes* the strict orders he was under from Fox to not write a script that facilitated a sequel were informed by a moralism: the studio simply did not want the concept milked any further. He was somewhat surprised, then, around four months after the film's release to receive a telegram from Fox reading, "APES EXIST, SEQUEL REQUIRED."

"Zanuck wanted another one," Jacobs recalled to *Cinefantastique*. "That was a tough one, because I spent about three to four weeks with Paul Dehn trying to work it out." Moreover, as was now a pattern, Fox's desire for more Apes product did not go hand in hand with a willingness to provide the sort of financing Jacobs and his associate producer (now Frank Capra Jr.) felt necessary. *Escape* had to be made on just over $2,200,000—less than half the first movie's financing. This limited the room for plot maneuver in what was an already circumscribed situation. "We could not go forward in time without moving to another planet—out of the question on a reduced budget," Dehn told the same magazine. It was only the recollection of the spaceship that Heston's crew had abandoned to the water in the first film that freed producers and writer from their quandary. Dehn concluded that if the ship could go forward in time, there was no reason why it couldn't make the exact same journey in reverse, the sort of logic that scientists would guffaw at but which makes perfect sense in cinema-land. The screenwriter could hardly use the established characters shown to have been killed in *Beneath*, which pretty much left Cornelius and Zira, who—unlike in Michael Avallone's version—disappeared early from the narrative. Dehn proceeded to wrest from these circumstances a story that combined comedy, romance, action, a tragic ending, and a twist in the tale.

The opening scene of *Escape* is quite delightful. On the Earth of 1973, the cool but now worse-for-wear ANSA craft has crashed in the ocean. The army is called out to retrieve from it a trio of astronauts. When they remove their helmets, the astronauts transpire to be chimpanzees. The bump of this revelation was cannily engineered: a prior scene in which the ape trio are seen *sans* helmets inside the spacecraft was left on the cutting-room floor.

The three ape-onauts are Cornelius, Zira, and a friend of theirs named Dr. Milo (Sal Mineo). The latter was responsible for salvaging the spaceship when "war became inevitable." Milo, it turns out, is "a genius well in advance of his time." He'd need to be: we have seen previously in the APJAC films that apes of the future haven't even managed flight, let alone space travel. Moreover, no explanation is offered for how Milo knew that war was going to culminate in a planet-destroying explosion. However, as we saw with *Beneath*, Dehn is adept at keeping the plot moving entertainingly enough to make the viewer not dwell on such logic fissures.

These opening scenes—urgent vistas of scrambled troops and swooping helicopters—see Don Taylor (a prolific TV director since 1956) impressively stamp his mark on the picture. It wasn't, though, the spectacle that Taylor most relished about the project. "Actually, I consider it a love story," he later told *Cinefantastique*. "I didn't try to hammer the sociological overtones." He felt Dehn's script was so close to perfect that it enabled him to concentrate on getting right the many small things that a director doesn't usually have time to address. That didn't stop him, though, tweaking the narrative: "I got Paul Dehn to write in all the stuff about the prizefight and the hotel room . . . and it paid off," he told the same publication.

One plot point Dehn and Taylor seem to have neglected is the chronological detail. The then-futuristic date of 1973 is consistent with the original movie also being set slightly in the future but doesn't quite explain how a culture that is essentially that of 1970 (the year of production) possesses the technological know-how to embark on deep-space missions.

The trio are put into the care of a pair of animal psychiatrists, Dr. Lewis Dixon (Bradford Dillman) and Dr. Stephanie Branton (Mrs. Arthur P. Jacobs). The chimpanzees initially withhold from their hosts the fact of their speech faculties, them concerned that twentieth-century humans would not be best pleased to discover that their fate is to be overtaken by apes. In one of several sections that betray the fact that Dehn has been revisiting Pierre Boulle's novel and consulting with the author, the trio are put through a battery of demeaning tests, just as Mérou was in the book. The humorous shock moment to which Dehn has clearly been building comes when Zira huffily consents to put together a set of interlocking steps and Dixon wonders aloud why she won't take the dangling banana that they put within reach. "Because I loathe bananas," Zira announces to dropped jaws.

The tone at this point is humorous, even slapstick, with scenes so akin to sitcom interplay that at times one is half-expecting *wah-wah-wah* noises. Some of the humor, though, is unintentional. The chimpanzees are temporarily placed in the sick bay of a zoo, where they are dismayed to find that their cage is adjacent to that of a gorilla. The viewer is dismayed to register that the gorilla is a man in an ape suit that is laughably less believable than the chimpanzee makeup. Considering it's a twentieth-century, unevolved gorilla, why not just use the real thing? Meanwhile, when Milo is killed by the gorilla, the scene has no pathos because of the puzzling fact that's it's accompanied by a montage of zoo animals bellowing and screaming, as though the whole of the animal kingdom has psychically gained knowledge of the event and gone into mourning.

The US president decides to present the visitors in a Commission of Inquiry, with the media in attendance. The chimpanzees' speech capabilities are initially dismissed as an elevated form of mimicry, up until—after Zira has done all the talking—someone asks if the other one can speak. "Only when she lets me," cracks Cornelius. Things the simians do not tell their interlocutors are that they saw the world blow up and that they know Taylor, whose whereabouts, of course, are a matter of some concern. Moreover, although they say that they're from the future and admit that apes in their time hunt man for sport, Zira catches herself when about to state that her job involved dissecting humans. The simpatico Dixon and Branton are another matter, and when alone with them, the apes admit the truth about Taylor and the way human beings are treated in their time. They also tell them about the fate of the planet. Perhaps the two zoologists can't find it in themselves to be alarmed because of such things as Zira naively responding in kind to the "Goodnight" of a presenter she is watching on television: it certainly reminds the viewer that human knowledge has progressed much further than that of future ape society.

A lighthearted montage shows Cornelius and Zira checking into the hotel accommodation provided for them and being fitted out with fine clothing, before being presented to the press, again a noticeable echo of a passage in Boulle's novel. The way that they winningly interact with the media is reminiscent, meanwhile, of Serling's script, as is Zira being appalled to see a stuffed member of her species in a museum. At the end of the montage, Zira reveals that a fainting fit is down to her being pregnant. It's a bump created by the crude means of withholding information, Zira for no good reason not having apprised her husband of her condition.

Not exactly overjoyed at the news is the president's science advisor, Dr. Otto Hasslein. The inclusion of a character who is implicitly the man mentioned by Taylor in the first film and Brent in the second is part and parcel of the unprecedented inter-film continuity for which APJAC is striving. The "Curve" man has a convoluted theory about infinite time strands, which he expounds on to a TV interviewer. Something Hasslein (the chillingly excellent Eric Braeden) doesn't vouchsafe to the media is that he considers a future society taken over by apes to be a disturbing thought. When Hasslein gets Zira drunk and surreptitiously records her, she lets slip that the Earth will be destroyed. Hasslein tries to convince the president that the revelation means that the chimpanzees are a danger. The president—whose core of decency is well projected by William Windom—is not convinced, but Hasslein gets his way when, in a secret session, the Commission of Inquiry agrees with him that the chimpanzees should be interrogated more fully.

During further questioning, Cornelius insists that the interlocuters not address he and his wife as "monkeys." "It is offensive to us," he explains. Dehn by way of Boulle (in the *Planet of the Men* script *monkey* is used as an insult) has neatly flipped Xan Fielding's translation faux pas on its head, making a virtue of turning the term into the equivalent of the *n*-word for black people. It doesn't quite make sense, though. Back in Ape City, simians would only ever have had it said to them by other apes, not by mute humans. It should also be noted that while Cornelius and Zira object to that slur, they see no contradiction in demonizing gorillas and orangutans for destroying the world, seeming to see them as a separate race to chimpanzees.

Pressed as to how apes came to dominance, Cornelius says that it was because of a plague back in their prehistory that killed cats and dogs and motivated humans to adopt simians as household pets. Those pets then became slaves. Within five centuries, they began to develop speech, rational thought, and resentment of their slave status. Prompted by the example of a chimpanzee named Aldo—the first of their kind to enunciate the word *no* to a human—apes mounted an uprising. Cats and dogs and Aldo excepted, the chronology is something adapted from Boulle, either from the pages of his book or through the Frenchman whispering in Dehn's ear.

When Zira won't admit that she started to use the word *dissect* in the inquiry, she is forcibly injected with a truth serum. The full horror of ape experiments on humans then becomes clear. However, Dehn refrains from making the Presidential Commission of Inquiry cartoon villains. In keeping with the writer's impressive procedural approach, they are depicted as fair minded in their reaction to the new revelations, recognizing that the fact of Zira performing experiments two thousand years in the future on humans who were dumb brutes cannot be looked on as the atrocities they would be perceived as in 1973. However, the commission cannot ignore the fact that apes may one day pose a threat to humans. It orders both that the expected baby be destroyed and that Cornelius and Zira be medically prevented from having any more children. Fearing that they will be killed, and infuriated by an orderly's use of the word *monkey*, Cornelius and Zira escape from the guarded facility to which they have been moved. The orderly is accidentally killed in the process. The film's early breezy tone has now decidedly evaporated.

Dixon and Branton go to see a circus owner named Armando, whom they know because Dixon recently delivered the baby of big-top chimpanzee Heloise. Armando (the delightfully flamboyant Ricardo Montalbán) agrees to their suggestion that when the circus moves on in a month's time he transport the chimpanzee trio to the haven of the Everglades. Zira gives birth at the circus to a male she names Milo. Armando's plan is disrupted when an order is made for zoos and circuses to be searched, necessitating that the chimps go into hiding. An apologetic Armando gives Zira a Saint Francis of Assisi medallion ("He was a holy man who loved and cared for all animals"), which Zira places around Milo's neck. Zira then insists on saying goodbye to Heloise.

The chimp trio take refuge on a derelict tanker. There, Zira states to Cornelius that she doesn't like humans, lamenting, "We've met hundreds since we've been here, and I trust three." It's an illogical conclusion, because they have been treated with far more kindness and indulgence than Taylor, Brent, and company were shown by simians in their own time. However, there's no disputing the villainy of Hasslein, who now proceeds to go rogue. Tracking down the couple, he confronts Zira on the ship's main deck. When Zira refuses to hand over the baby, he pumps her and her child full of bullets. From the upper deck, Cornelius—given a gun by Dixon so that, if it comes to it, they can take their own lives before humans do—shoots Hasslein. (That there is no plausible way he would have acquired such marksmanship skills is another blink-and-you've-forgotten-it Dehn plot hole.) Cornelius is in turn shot by arriving national guard and police. McDowall acts the death of Caesar well, emitting animalistic gasps before tumbling to the lower deck. Movingly, Zira—having thrown the baby's corpse overboard—crawls over to die on top of her husband.

It's yet another grim Planet of the Apes ending, but for the first time in the franchise it is leavened by a glimmer of hope, even triumph. The final scene shows that the baby in Armando's circus is wearing the Assisi medallion. In case we don't get the picture, it starts repeating the word *mama*. This means that, also for the first time, an obvious way has been left open to continue the series. After the success of *Beneath*, Fox and APJAC weren't going to make the same bridge-burning, planet-destroying mistake.

Escape from the Planet of the Apes, released on May 26, 1971, is a sometimes preposterous movie (right down to the baby enunciating a word it would barely, if ever, have heard). Yet it is also an amusing, thoughtful, moving, and powerful one. It nicely reverses the conceit of the first two movies. (This transposition whereby apes are broadly the heroes and humans mainly the villains would be maintained for the rest of the quintet). Another inversion the film proffers relates to the fact that—like Taylor and Brent in the first two movies—Cornelius and Zira are fish out of water. It also presents the entertaining proposition of beings from the future—and familiar fixtures of a fantastical franchise—trying to negotiate contemporary America, paving the way for *Star Trek IV: The Voyage Home* to do the same in 1986.

The film is more than all of those things, though. Much of its entertainment value derives from exploring and playing with its own mythos, something not previously possible in cinema because movies had never sought inter-film continuity. It is for this reason that, after viewing *Escape*, *Cinefantastique*'s reviewer Frederick S. Clarke marveled that the series was "not just three separate films, but one great work that has the promise of being the first epic of filmed science fiction."

~

One of the reasons the follow-up to the first Apes film was so successful, critically and commercially, is because new screenwriter Paul Dehn didn't merely engage in the easy option of one-dimensional ape-versus-human action but maintained the social commentary thread. Over the rest of the quintet, he would consistently exploit the low-rent environs of SF movies (as they were then perceived) to explore highbrow issues. "The second movie, it's very much on the nose," Rich Handley notes of a narrative in which the religious dogma and nuclear annihilation material is both overt and intertwined. "Christ is supplanted by a nuclear missile." As well as the mutants deifying the Alpha-Omega bomb in a parody of the store that Western superpowers placed in the nuclear deterrent, *Beneath* carried some other pointed passages. "I don't say all humans are evil simply because their skin is white," intones Ursus. Meanwhile, a shot of students chanting, "We want peace. Peace and freedom" is clearly a Vietnam-protest allusion.

The flipping of the franchise's premise in *Escape from the Planet of the Apes* doesn't much lend itself to allegory but does enable topicality. Animal rights was an increasing issue of concern and is alluded to when the disturbing fact emerges that Zira had performed operations on humans, and the point is conceded by the commission that this is no worse than what humans currently do to apes. An additional topical issue gets an airing when Zira gives a speech to a Bay Area distaff group, one that indicates she is sympathetic to what was then called women's lib. "A marriage bed is made for two, but every damned morning it's the woman who has to make it," she declares. There is also a message of—in Handley's words—"government gone crazy in an effort to protect the people." Dr. Otto Hasslein is a man whose scientific certitude tips over into complete lack of empathy and eventually into the usurping of the role of his elected masters. Eric Braeden may well have been cast purely on merit, but his perfect yet accented English couldn't help but put people in mind of another doctor, the current liberal hate figure Henry Kissinger, President Nixon's similarly German-born right-hand man.

That *Escape* appeared in the same year as *Diamonds Are Forever*, however, raises a point about the limits of Dehn's capacity for social commentary. That aforesaid James Bond film featured a pair of contract killers named Mr. Wint and Mr. Kidd. A homosexual couple, they are depicted in a mockingly pejorative light that now seems nothing less than shocking. As a gay man, Dehn would no doubt have loved to pointedly show a homosexual character in a positive way, but no mainstream Hollywood film studio would have allowed him to do that in the early 1970s or for many years beyond.

~

Whereas the novelization of *Beneath* was published by Bantam, the following three books to adapt Apes films were issued by Award. Yet though Award was a much smaller and less prestigious publisher, their books-of-the-film were all far superior to the Avallone work.

Jerry Pournelle was both a veteran of the space program and a coming name in the field of science fiction, winner of the John W. Campbell Best New Writer award and a president of the Science Fiction Writers of America organization. The year after the publication of his adaptation of *Escape*, he would issue with Larry Niven the epic *The Mote in God's Eye*, a totemic novel in the genre.

Pournelle's smooth-flowing style makes the *Escape* book a pleasure to read, as does his ability to impartially inhabit the heads of both humans and apes. Additionally, his knowledge of California, where he was resident and where the bulk of the film is set, enables him to offer geographical and topographical exactitude, the type of layering uncommon in books-of-the-film. Similarly, he takes the care to provide names for characters who in the movie are anonymous. More than that, though, he makes us privy to the thoughts of the president, Hasslein (here possessing the Christian name Victor), military men, and Lewis and Stephanie. To some extent, the apes even take a backseat. However, his rendering of the slayings of Cornelius and Zira has even more pathos than in the film, him omnisciently ramping up the poignancy by adding the observation, "That was how Lewis Dixon found her; and that was how they were buried, with the infant beside them."

6

LITTLE MONEY, MUCH INSPIRATION

Moving, thoughtful, and well-crafted *Escape* might have been—not to mention a component of the first filmed epic of science fiction—but it was also uncomfortably close to the region of commercial disappointment.

It would be completely wrong to describe it as a flop. It grossed around $10 million, second only to *The French Connection* as Fox's biggest hit of the year, and the studio was therefore happy to give the go-ahead to a fourth Apes installment. The profits, though, were not in the region of the first two Apes pictures, and APJAC was therefore further enmeshed in a catch-22 cycle: the money Fox made available to Jacobs and company for another sequel was incrementally lower than that provided for the previous picture ($1.7 million) on the grounds that the last picture had done less business than the previous one. In vain did APJAC point out that a bigger budget for the last one might have resulted in better box office.

Once again, Jacobs hired Paul Dehn to find more possibilities for the Apes property. Meanwhile, he placed in the director's chair the man he had wanted all along. London-born J. Lee Thompson had started out as a stage actor then pursued a career as playwright before, in the early 1950s, graduating to directing. Those inclined to assume a jack-of-all-trades-master-of-none scenario would have been given pause by the fact that, by 1957, he had a stone-cold classic under his directorial belt in the shape of gripping wartime drama *Ice Cold in Alex*. He added to that tally with *Tiger Bay*, *The Guns of Navarone* (for which he was Oscar nominated), and *Cape Fear*. Getting to direct the fourth Apes film was, of course, the end of something of a saga. "I rue the day that I came out of it," Thompson later admitted to *Cinefantastique*, a large part of his regret obviously down to the fact that he had missed out on a bonanza by selling his share in the property back to the producer in those early days of Jacobs prostrating himself at the feet of dismissive studio executives. Jacobs had subsequently asked Thompson to helm the second and third Apes films, but it wasn't until the fourth installment that the two men's schedules didn't clash. This time around, Thompson was felt to be particularly appropriate because *Conquest of the Planet of the Apes* was set to be an action piece.

Don Murray took the role of the film's villain, Governor Breck, a Fuhrer-like figure whose animus toward apes is the mirror image of Dr. Zaius's hatred of humans. "When I was cast, I made it my business to see the other films," Murray says. "It was really exciting. An extraordinary series of films. The first one with Charlton Heston, that was brilliant and there was never anything like that before. I think the quality held through *Conquest of the Planet of the Apes*." Murray found that the franchise entry in which he was participating was unprecedentedly grim and dystopian. "It's much too dark to be a family film," he says admiringly. The 1970s was an era in which many filmmakers felt that to be circumspect about bloodshed was a moral cowardice, which kowtowed to the precepts of a dying, reactionary order. In *Conquest*, APJAC Productions went with this trend.

They also ramped up the element of political subtext. *Escape*'s dialogue mentioned Aldo, the fabled first ape to say "No" to a human, but *Conquest* suggested that he could be seen as analogous to Rosa Parks, the woman who refused to obey the Deep South law that said a black person had to give up a seat on a bus to a white. This underlined the fact that *Conquest of the Planet of the Apes* brought to the fore a strain that some had always perceived in the series. Mort Abrahams recalled to *Simian Scrolls* that, shortly after the first film's release, black entertainer Sammy Davis Jr. had rushed over to him and Jacobs in a restaurant and enthused, "That film is the greatest explanation of the relationship between blacks and whites that I have ever seen." Abrahams admitted he was taken aback that Davis had "looked at it through a different eye." "It's a very curious thing that the Apes series has always been tremendously popular with Negroes who identify themselves with the apes," Dehn told *Cinefantastique*. "They are Black Power just as the apes are Ape Power and they enjoy it greatly." *Conquest* deliberately adopted the vision of that different eye. The squeamishness that attended the casting process of the first film was now forgotten as the filmmakers embraced the analogy of humans as oppressor whites and apes as subjugated blacks. The film drew parallels with the American civil rights movement, rooted in the 1960s but still an ongoing concern. "There was an analogy to the Watts riots," says Murray, referring to famous 1965 disturbances in Los Angeles whose black participants it so happened were compared by Los Angeles police chief William H. Parker to "monkeys in a zoo." To drive the point home, a black man was cast as Breck's assistant MacDonald so as to enable dialogue like the statement of lead ape character Caesar, "You, above everyone else, should understand: we cannot be free until we have power." The script also found Caesar insisting that apes have a "slave's right to punish his persecutors." "We wanted that film to be very angry," Dehn explained at the time.

Conquest didn't just reflect events in the real world but actually took the analogy to the next level. Whereas the civil rights movement had in real life resulted in gains obtained by democratic means within a societal structure that remained broadly the same, *Conquest* depicted the oppressed taking complete control—and doing so by brute force.

If anything, Murray's approach to his dictator character made the film even darker. His résumé thus far contained nothing similar to this role, having been a long series of upstanding and heroic parts matching his swarthy good looks. Was he slightly apprehensive that people might not take him seriously as a baddie? "I never thought of that at all," he says. Nonetheless, he did his homework as regards villainy. "Dictatorship makes you think right away of Germany, and I speak fluent German. So I translated the entire role into German and I learned it in German and rehearsed it in German. Then, of course, I did it in English. That's the only time I've ever done anything like that with a movie. It just gave me that feeling of a character that's used to his power and enjoys subjugating people."

There were, though, plenty of on-set laughs for Murray. "Roddy McDowall was a close friend of mine," he points out. "He made it comfortable for me." In one sense, Murray mischievously didn't reciprocate. McDowall was obliged by his makeup to only partake of lunch that could be devoured through a straw. "I'd go in with a big, juicy sandwich and eat with him."

As with all Planet of the Apes films so far, the picture is set in the future. This one, though, takes place not in the far future of the first two films or the immediate future of the last one, but 1991, in other words, nineteen years after the release date, and eighteen years after the time frame of *Escape*. Despite the futurism, though, it feels less SF than its predecessors, being the first Apes film to not involve traveling in time or space.

Behind the opening credits, we are shown processions of apes in boiler suits being shepherded across a concrete jungle by officials with truncheons. Armando and a chimpanzee on a chain arrive to distribute leaflets advertising Armando's circus. Ricardo Montalbán reprises the Armando role, a greying beard convincingly representing the passage of time. The chimpanzee is the son of Cornelius and Zira, no longer called Milo but Caesar. Some have suggested the choice was a tribute to Planet of the Apes nearly-man Edward G. Robinson, who after his participation in the makeup screen test didn't make the cut for the first film: one of his most famous roles was in *Little Caesar* (1931).

Proving that nuanced acting is still possible even under layers of hair and makeup, Roddy McDowall plays Caesar as more innocent than he did his poised father, a logical product of him being not just younger but also someone who has not grown up in an ape-dominated society. However, over the course of the film, Caesar transmogrifies into something far harder. Of course, McDowall's conscientiousness as an actor could be said to be undermined by the fact that there is no plausible explanation for the fact that Caesar has inherited an English accent from the father he barely met—if anything, he would have the same Latin accent as Armando. McDowall's career, though, had already proven that few cinemagoers dwelled on such issues. In any case, McDowall's presence was probably now as commercially valuable as Heston's inclusion had been to *Beneath*.

The circus ape carefully pretends to be mute. "There can be only one talking chimpanzee on Earth," Armando says as they traverse the walkways of the conurbation (actually, the plaza of the newly built Century City, the depersonalized, brutalist architecture of which was considered perfect for the film's timbre). "The child of the two talking apes, Cornelius and Zira, who came to us years ago out of the future and were murdered for fear that one distant day apes might dominate the human race. . . . The mere fact of your existence would be regarded as a great threat to mankind." Perhaps less time should have been devoted to the insertion of such clumsy exposition and more attention paid to explaining why the society described herein as "North America" is now very different to that part of it seen in *Escape from the Planet of the Apes*. Where the culture in that picture was essentially the same as existed in the year the film was made, this one has tumbled into something resembling a police state. The viewer is only vaguely invited to infer that it is the utilization of apes that has created this state of affairs: that with people disgruntled about simians depriving them of work, the government feels compelled to use draconian methods in dealing with social unrest. As though taking their cue from their hard-line government, the humans we see are almost uniformly terse with each other.

The ape makeup is noticeably inferior to that seen in the previous films. The hairlines of the chimpanzees—including Caesar—look almost like a human's bad toupee, and some faces are barely superior to a joke-shop mask. John Chambers is nominally still in charge in this department, but not even his Oscar-winning expertise can overcome the fact that the producers were now having to make do with a budget for the entire film not far off the money made available to Chambers's department alone in the first installment.

The police are none too gentle with uncooperative apes. In Caesar's sight, a chimpanzee is set upon by the forces of law and order (whose SS-stormtrooper-like uniforms are just as significant as the apes' prisoner-like jumpsuits). The chimp is listed as Aldo in the credits, a ghost of Dehn's original intention to make him the Spartacus-like ape of legend mentioned by Cornelius in *Escape*. Caesar mutters, "Lousy human bastards" and, as Armando tries to convince the police it was himself who spoke, flees the scene. Armando finds Caesar but realizes he can't take him back to the circus because that's the first place the authorities will look. Instead, he decides to report him as missing.

Armando is interrogated by Governor Breck, who doesn't believe Armando's story that it was he who spoke and that he said, "*in*human bastards." Breck is disturbed by the rising tide of disobedience in the city from apes and by their incrementally increasing IQ levels. His fear is that the simians are simply "waiting for an ape with enough intelligence, with enough will, to lead them. Waiting for an ape who can think. Who can talk." It's a somewhat unlikely dread to have been engendered by a few disobedient servants, but it's the perfect excuse for Dehn to create another villain in the mold of the previous movie's Otto Hasslein (and of Zaius and Ursus in the movies previous to that, albeit with the nature of the anomie transposed). When Armando fails to reappear, Caesar follows his prior instruction to hide among his own kind. He smuggles himself into an ape cage on a loading bay. From there, he finds himself transported to a training center, where he sees the brutal methods by which his kind are made into servants. We are also shown society's universal maltreatment of apes following their induction period, encompassing imperious housewives and bullying maître d's.

Caesar is put up for sale at auction. His preternatural intelligence causes Governor Breck—unaware of who he is—to instruct that he be purchased for his own department. This means that Caesar winds up working at the ape-hater's headquarters. So does a pretty chimp named Lisa with whom he has previously exchanged flirtatious looks. (By submitting to the rigors of the makeup chair to portray Lisa, Natalie Trundy becomes the only actor in the series to play human, mutant, *and* ape.) In turn, this means that when Armando throws himself from Breck's window rather than submit to the truth-finding powers of a device called an "Authenticator," Caesar quickly gets to hear of it.

At this point, all credibility follows Armando out of that window. Simply as a consequence of being in the seething presence of Caesar, apes start disobeying human instruction, arming themselves, and plotting violence against their masters. Apparently, a nod or an encouraging look from Caesar suffices in lieu of their lack of a common means of communication. In the blink of an eye, Caesar is organizing the chimpanzees and gorillas. (Orangutans are thin on the ground, although we do for the first time see a female example of such.)

When Breck discovers that his new chimpanzee purchase was oddly originally found in a consignment of orangutans ("there are no chimpanzees in Borneo"), he orders him to be located. MacDonald—played with nobility by Hari Rhodes—is reluctant to go along with Breck's paranoid theories and brutal methods. He leads Caesar away from danger. "I wish there was some way we could communicate, so you'd understand," muses MacDonald aloud, at which point Caesar demonstrates that the circulating story of a talking ape is not myth. "But I will tell you something that is," says Caesar. "The belief that human beings are kind. . . . They won't learn to be kind until we force them to. We can't do that until we are free." Apes will gain this freedom, he says, "by the only means left to us—revolution."

MacDonald lets Caesar go, but the ape's grand plans are delayed when he is recaptured. He is subjected to torture to make him talk—literally. When he does, and the threat he represents is thereby made explicit, it's pointed out that as he is already wired up to a shock table, an extant order for him to be destroyed can be carried out instantly. However, MacDonald has gone to the control room to turn off the table. Caesar apparently intuits this and plays possum.

Caesar overcomes the functionary who has been left to dispose of his body and goes off to round up his rebellious army. Their first port of call is the Ape Management building. The police adopt a shoot-to-kill policy. The now armed apes in turn are merciless in their revenge mission, and scenes of carnage follow.

By means of an acetylene torch, Caesar and crew force their way into Breck's command post. When Caesar asks the now helpless governor why apes are different to the cats and dogs his kind once loved, Breck gives a speech that is like the rationale provided by Zaius to explain his anomie toward humans crossed with the sort of pretentious and unpersuasive metaphysical theorizing in which Pierre Boulle specialized: "Man was born of the ape and there's still an ape curled up inside of every man. The beast that must be whipped into submission. The savage that has to be shackled in chains. You are that beast, Caesar. You taint us. You poison our guts! When we hate you, we're hating the dark side of ourselves."

MacDonald pleads with Caesar to end the bloodshed, but in an unwise choice of words asks him to show "humanity." The speech that Caesar proceeds to make in return has a touch of the demagogue about it. "What you have seen here today, apes on the five continents will be imitating tomorrow. . . . From this day forward, my people will crouch and conspire and plot and plan for the inevitable day of man's downfall. The day when he finally and self-destructively turns his weapons against his own kind . . . I will lead my people from their captivity and we shall build our own cities in which there will be no place for humans, except to serve our ends."

It takes another implausible occurrence to stop him in this absolutist intent. Just as Breck is about to be battered to death by multiple rifle butts, Lisa—who has been seen regretfully shaking her head on the peripheries of the violence—makes an extraordinary evolutionary leap to enunciate an entreaty that resembles the word "No!"

Caesar backs down, saying, "If it is man's destiny to be dominated, it is God's will that he be dominated with compassion and understanding. So, cast out your vengeance. Tonight, we have seen the birth of the Planet of the Apes!" In another extraordinary evolutionary leap, the ape army apparently now understands human language and starts whooping enthusiastically.

Dark as it is, this ending is considerably less brutal than the one originally shot. Dehn's script dictated that "Breck's twitching body finally falls limp and motionless under the leash." Test-screening audiences were repelled by the sight, and McDowall was summoned to a soundstage to overdub dialogue—there wasn't sufficient money for reshoots—in which his original bloodthirsty rhetoric was toned down by that addendum inspired by Lisa's distress. "I preferred the ending where my character was killed," says Murray. "I think it was very logically a dark movie."

The franchise's production and marketing was by this point handled with almost scientific precision: shooting had started in December in order to ensure the final print was issued to distributors by May 7, a significant date in the American calendar because the children on their summer break, hungry for diversion, were a market supposedly worth an additional $2 million. Ironically, though, this film was the least child-friendly installment thus far. Jacobs is known to have once proclaimed that he would never issue a film that didn't have a "G" rating, but he had to go back on his word and on its release on June 14, 1972, *Conquest* became the first "PG" Apes movie. However, Thompson asserted that it would have been an "R" had the changes not been made. Despite excluding from its demographic unaccompanied children, however, *Conquest* performed better than any other Fox picture that year.

Yet, this time some must have felt that the film's commercial performance was irrelevant. The story purveyed in *Conquest* meant that the franchise's overarching narrative had circled back on itself. Additionally, the juncture in that loop at which it had stopped provided a resolution. The apes were now in charge, explaining the society in which Taylor had found himself back in the first film. Logically, that epic of filmed science fiction about which *Cinefantastique* had enthused had reached its final installment.

Author John Jakes specialized in sword and sorcery, epitomized by his manqué Conan character, Brak the Barbarian. While he might have seemed too fantastical a choice for writing the novel adaptation of

Conquest, he acquits himself perfectly well when it comes to description, combining functionality with lyricism. He deftly depicts the apes' uprising in all its ambiguous righteousness. He also makes it more believable than in the film, showing the fine detail of Caesar's plotting that the movie failed to furnish.

Conquest being the Apes picture that changed most between shooting script and final edit, Jakes's narrative is consequently significantly different to the one cinemagoers saw. In his telling, Caesar doesn't pull back from the brink of his vengefulness. His ending, though, is superior not just because of the greater pathos inherent in such a conclusion but because it gives full vent to his dramatic style:

> Cries of animal fury filled the plaza. Governor Breck's twitching body finally went limp. The screeching of the frustrated apes grew louder as they searched for new targets for their unleashed resentment. . . . They raced toward the growing crowd of human prisoners in the holding area.
>
> Firelight. Gleaming eyes. The sound of truncheons. And apes screaming their blood-mad rage . . .
>
> Almost pityingly, Caesar said to the black man, "Do you doubt me? Why don't you answer, Mr. MacDonald?"
>
> But MacDonald had closed his eyes as the silent tears ran down his face.

7

NOT SO FAST! BATTLE COMES AFTER CONQUEST

"Arthur Jacobs said he thought this would be the last so I fitted it together so that it fitted in with the beginning of Apes 1, so that the wheel had come full circle and one could stop there quite happily."

So said Paul Dehn to *Cinefantastique* upon the release of *Conquest of the Planet of the Apes*. However, he also admitted that the true answer to the question of whether this was the end of the line was, "Wait and see how much money this one takes." As *Conquest* took a healthy $4.5 million, it meant that there was another Apes motion picture to be teased out of the shell.

"They decided to bring the character back," says Don Murray of Governor Breck. "But what they didn't do is they didn't ask me if I wanted to do the character." Although he says of *Conquest*, "I was very happy to have that part of my film history," he declined the offer of participation in a follow-up and never had any regrets about doing so. "I just didn't like the idea of repeating a role in another film. I didn't think that was an interesting thing to do." From his point of view, he may have dodged a bullet. "That was the last good one, in my opinion," he says. "*Battle for the Planet of the Apes* I don't think had nearly the quality, the production value and clarity, as the rest of the series did." He is not alone in this viewpoint.

As a consequence of Murray's non-involvement, *Battle* has a new governor in the shape of Kolp, a character who in the last movie had been a bearded, heavyset assistant to Breck responsible for interrogation. He is once again played with creepy menace by Severn Darden. Also failing to reprise his *Conquest* part was Hari Rhodes, who wasn't available. However, there is a character called MacDonald who answers to the man who has assumed Breck's mantle. Yet—fatuously—it is MacDonald's brother, who—even more fatuously—happened to have worked in the same building as his *Conquest* sibling. In lieu of APJAC doing the logical thing by simply casting another actor as the first MacDonald, Austin Stoker was brought in to play this one.

Dehn also told *Cinefantastique*, "I'm getting a very strong feeling someone else ought to do the Ape screenplays from now on." Ironically, he got what he wanted—and then wished he hadn't. Dehn agreed to write the fifth Apes film and provided a sixty-eight-page treatment (a screenplay in shorthand format). When ill health prevented him completing a full screenplay, the script work was taken over by married writing team John William & Joyce Hooper Corrington. The pair had recently won acclaim for their 1971 postapocalyptic movie *The Omega Man* (starring, as it happens, Charlton Heston). However, they, by Joyce's later admission, had never seen any Planet of the Apes films. Dehn did a final polish of the Corringtons' work, including—according to Jacobs—writing almost 100 percent of the dialogue. In contrast to Serling being relaxed about his joint credit for the first film's screenplay, Dehn was infuriated to only be awarded a "story" attribution by the Writer's Guild of America, whose verdicts are not infrequently a bone of contention, not least on another of Dehn's films, *The Spy Who Came in from the Cold*.

J. Lee Thompson took the director's chair again, becoming the first person to helm two Apes movies. The film would have a very different tone to his previous effort. *Conquest* had been the apotheosis but also the effective end of the APJAC films' social critiques. "It gets a little muddy with the fifth one," notes Rich Handley of *Battle*. "Because of budgetary limitations, the fifth movie is kind of watered down and doesn't really introduce that many new themes. It just plays on the same theme as in the previous four." He could also have pointed out that, with the relative box office underperformance of *Conquest* felt to be attributable to its dark timbre, there was a deliberate intent to rein back on the politics.

The film begins in tranquil style in 2670 AD with a peroration by an authoritative orangutan, played by, of all people, John Huston. Although getting the legendary director to appear was a coup, it can't help but be noticed that while the series continues to attract big-name talent the production values go on declining: the lips of his muzzle don't meet properly when he speaks.

By way of a quiet address to an unseen outdoor audience he brings the viewer up to speed on what happened after the events of the previous Apes movie: "The surface of the world was ravaged by the vilest war in human history. The great cities of the world split asunder and were flattened. And out of one such city our savior led a remnant of those who survived in search of greener pastures where ape and human might forever live in friendship according to divine will. His name was Caesar."

We are then transported back to a point in time not long after the events of *Conquest*, no year stated, but clues furnished in the fact that ape and human have been at peace in this area of North America for twelve years and an orangutan named Mandemus has been keeper of the Ape City armory for twenty-seven years. Caesar and Lisa are now married. After having played the character as a callow turned vengeful soul in the previous film, McDowall is now required to portray Caesar as a poised regent and father of a prepubescent son.

These days, Ape City constitutes a settlement (significantly, it's also referred to as a "village"). Such small scale made sense in the first two films, in which it was vaguely conveyed that simians were restricted by nuclear radiation to a small corner of the world, but it is less logical now that Earth history has "changed lanes." The latter phrase comes from the theory about multiple alternate realities articulated by Hasslein in *Escape* and is here repeated by an orangutan named Virgil, who—despite his know-it-all demeanor—has no logical means by which to be aware of Hasslein. It's an example of what might be termed *franchise echo*: the way that reverberations, inversions, and repetitions of the series' established themes and details are now multiplying, consciously or unconsciously, logically or illogically. Another example is the fact that nearby New York is referred to as the "forbidden" city because of its radioactivity.

On the other hand, the fact that apes live in treehouses amid iron-age culture but have access to firearms manufactured before the war neatly clears up the clashes of technology seen in the first two Apes movies. If only we could be sure that Dehn and/or the Corringtons intended this.

Apes and humans live in friendship to an extent, but they are not equals. Humans aren't allowed in "council" and have to ask permission to augment an ape-oriented vegetarian diet with animal meat. (In fact, in real life chimpanzees are omnivorous, and even hunt and devour a species as close as monkeys.) An ape may say the word *no* to a human, but—because it was the word apes were conditioned by torture to fear—a human may never say it to an ape. Although this society is more peaceable than the old human-run culture (children are forbidden to play war games), it's not exactly democratic. Caesar takes his name literally and is a king with an anointed successor in the shape of son Cornelius (Bobby Porter).

In terms of intellect and professions, the apes have fallen into the roles they had in the first two films: the chimpanzees are reasonable souls, the gorillas are boneheaded military men, and the orangutans are pompous intellectuals. Franchise echo: they're also, for no rational reason, dressed in the exact same color demarcations of the first couple of films. All apes are shown as being able to speak fluently even though barely enough years have passed since the events of the last film for even a new generation to have come of age, let alone the vast stretches of time necessary for evolution to do its business.

General Aldo objects to even the limited harmony in which man and ape are living. He is not as good a gorilla villain as Ursus, being implausibly hotheaded for someone in his elevated position. Moreover, in another example of the deteriorating makeup quality, his face looks slightly plasticky. The lack of psychological nuance and facial flexibility, however, doesn't stop Claude Akins playing Aldo with bristling, harrumphing finesse.

It's confusing as to why the general has been given the name of the legendary first ape to say "no" to a human. However, a sort of inside-out version of that fabled incident crops up here when Aldo attends a mixed-age literacy class helmed by a human named Abe (Noah Keen). The class is learning how to write "Ape shall never kill ape." (Franchise echo: a sacred law adopted by the new society even though there's no way for it to have acquired the knowledge that it was the mantra in the future world from which Caesar's parents came.) Aldo starts to screw up an example of exemplary schoolwork submitted by young Cornelius. Worried about the reaction of Cornelius's father, Abe makes the mistake of saying, "No, Aldo!" and then has to run for his life.

After Caesar defuses the situation—accepting that the teacher was responding to provocation—he and his assistant MacDonald engage in philosophical debate. It's Caesar's contention that only when apes "grow to know and trust" humans can they be equals. He also believes that the world's future is safer in the hands of simians. MacDonald knows that the latter is not necessarily the case and invokes the testimony on the subject from Caesar's own parents, which he points out can be accessed on film under the dead city (i.e., the recordings made for the Commission of Inquiry in *Escape*).

Caesar, MacDonald, and Virgil (the latter played impishly by songwriter Paul Williams) duly head for the Forbidden City. Before they do, though, they have to—in one of the best scenes in the movie—negotiate with Mandemus. He's an amusing character (with an even more amusing fringe), played with a twinkle in the eyes set beneath his elaborate brows by Lew Ayres. Mandemus's typically orangutan pretension doesn't rule out interesting observations ("I really don't hold with knowing the future, even my own. . . . I mean, if we knew for a fact there was an afterlife, and that the afterlife was bliss eternal, we'd all commit suicide in order to be able to enjoy it"). He is not just keeper of the Ape City armory but also of Caesar's "own conscience." He takes said roles very seriously and makes the three jump through intellectual hoops before issuing them with firearms and a Geiger counter.

Franchise echo: despite their heavyish equipment, the trio do not use the horses at their disposal but go on foot to the Forbidden City. One suspects that the motive on the part of the filmmakers is to create a vista of figures stumbling across an unfamiliar horizon redolent of scenes in the first Apes movie when the astronauts left their spaceship.

The Forbidden City is a mixture of skillfully distressed props and slightly comical matte paintings. Locating the tapes, the trio plays the section where Cornelius recounts the incident of the first ape to say "no" to a human. (The script has to leave out the fact that his name is Aldo to avoid confusing the viewer.) When he learns from the tapes that gorillas will in the future destroy the planet, Caesar suddenly sees man's reason for fearing apes. Leaving aside awkward logic and continuity issues—this information related by Zira in *Escape* was never knowledge she could logically have come by, and it was technically Taylor who precipitated that act of destruction—it's an example of the way this script strives for even-handedness, as opposed to the black-and-white morality of *Conquest*.

Another example is the fact that there are both pacifists and warmongers among the subterranean humans who are revealed to be living in the remains of 1990s New York. Radiation-deformed and weirdly costumed, these are the ancestors of the mutants seen in *Beneath*, although Dehn's intention of making this explicit was not fulfilled. Kolp sees the interlopers on one of the security cameras dotted around the shadowy corridors. (As well they might, the subterranean humans are surprised to find that an ape besides Caesar both talks and possesses discernible intelligence.) One of Kolp's underlings objects that if they do harm to the three strangers it will destroy twelve years of peace. "Yes, it has been rather boring, hasn't it?" Kolp responds.

Under attack, Caesar's crew defend themselves with a water hose before making their escape (APJAC's decision to make this a categorically family picture presumably explaining why they don't employ the guns with which they have taken the trouble to equip themselves). On the pretext that they might come back and kill them, Kolp orders that the apes be pursued and killed. Meanwhile, Caesar—on the assumption that they are all warlike because of the reception they provided—prepares to make war on the humans of the Forbidden City.

When young Cornelius follows his escaped squirrel through treetops—one of the few times the series has shown any arboreal facility on the part of apes—he comes upon a secret meeting of militant gorillas led by Aldo. The gorillas are disgruntled by Caesar's recent decision to allow humans to attend council so as to glean man's insight into the unexpected outside menace. Aldo incites those present to "smash the humans," although his encouragement to "smash Caesar" as well meets with less enthusiasm. When Cornelius is discovered, Aldo—fearful of what he may have heard—cuts the branch on which he's sitting, and the child plummets to the ground.

The subterranean humans proceed toward Ape City in a ragtag procession comprised of outlandishly dressed foot soldiers and vehicles that include rusting cars, an old school bus, a Jeep with mounted machine gun, and the odd motorcycle. (One suspects that the future makers of the Mad Max movies were taking mental notes.) While Cornelius holds vigil over his dying son, MacDonald discovers the embers of the fire of the gorilla plotters and the slashed tree bough above it.

When a warning is sounded about the advancing convoy, Aldo takes advantage of Caesar's distracted state to assume command. He declares martial law, locking up all humans. The apes line up at the barricades, including orangutans, the first time they have been depicted in the series in an action role. However, the outgunned apes have to beat a retreat. With Cornelius having passed away, Caesar joins the fray. His brainpower proves crucial when he pretends to be at bay so as to enable the apes to encircle and overcome the invaders.

Aldo orders that the corralled humans in Ape City be killed. Caesar tries to reason with him, but Aldo's gorilla soldiers back up their leader with their guns. It is at this point that Virgil intervenes to point out (admittedly, without definitive proof) what MacDonald has hinted to him: that Aldo has broken the "Ape shall never kill ape" edict by murdering young Cornelius. The crowd turns on Aldo, who retreats to the branches of a nearby tree. A seething Caesar follows him. When Aldo pulls a knife on him, Caesar grabs his wrist, and Aldo loses his balance. The fatal fall to the ground that the gorilla proceeds to suffer is as implausible as young Cornelius perishing from a similarly short drop, but the accidental death handily means that Caesar technically hasn't broken the golden rule himself.

When Caesar orders that the corralled humans be released, MacDonald points out that their lack of gratitude is perhaps due to them being freed into a world in which they are second class. This—along with the fact that Aldo, the most evil being in their midst, was an ape—engenders a change in mind-set in Caesar and, hence, among his subjects.

In the newly fraternal atmosphere, the city's armorer wants all the weapons destroyed, but Caesar declines, saying, "The greatest danger of all is that danger never ends." Cut to Huston. It is now made clear that his character is the Lawgiver, the all-knowing orangutan of whom we have heard so much during the quintet. It is clear that this Lawgiver is not the judgmental, human-hating voice of the Sacred Scrolls and that, in turn, this fact is due to Caesar. The Lawgiver's lesson is not only taking place six hundred years after Caesar's death but also, we now see, in the shadow of said chimpanzee's statue. The orangutan is teaching Caesar's philosophical legacy to a rainbow nation of children: black, white, ape, and human.

What would be a reasonably affecting series finale is somewhat ruined by the fact that the statue of Caesar is seen to shed a tear. This was a change wrought by Dehn to the Corringtons' script, one which Joyce said "turned our stomach." The Corringtons' preferred ending involved human and ape children fighting each other in a playground. Dehn's technique was clumsy, but his intent was the same as the Corringtons. He stated in a memo to Jacobs that the tear was a "forecast of Earth's destruction in *Beneath*," which he felt necessary for "the series to be linked consecutively in the form of a 'saga.'" In other words, ape-human harmony was impossible because the events laid out in the first two films were set in stone. Both the Corringtons and Dehn could be posited as wrong: it was surely logical to believe that future events had been altered by Cornelius, Zira, and Caesar, enabling a future in which humans and apes lived in peace and thereby ensuring that the events of the first two films never happened. It would also have mercifully given at least one installment of the franchise a happy ending.

Battle for the Planet of the Apes, released on June 13, 1973, is an efficient adventure yarn. However, it's another Apes movie that is both short in length (like *Conquest*, not much longer than an hour and twenty minutes) and slight in concept and execution. Its budget was actually marginally higher than that of *Conquest* but still inadequate to its objective. Handley says, "I love *Battle*—it's a really good film—but the budget prevents it from living up to the name. It's called *Battle for the Planet of the Apes*, but is it really? Or is it a battle for three tree houses? And they're [defending] against a school bus." He also points out that an earlier draft of the script powerfully depicted Caesar stricken by the effects of the radiation poisoning to which he'd been exposed in the Forbidden City. "It becomes a point that Aldo is making: 'You're becoming more human,' because he's starting to become hairless due to radiation exposure. I wish they had left that in. It would have been a great visual and it would have given the fifth movie a little more profundity, a little more depth. . . . I don't think they could afford to do the ever-changing look of Caesar's face 'cos it would have involved money." Oddly, gravitas- and length-adding scenes depicting the beginning of the Alpha-Omega bomb cult were actually filmed but excised from the film. They were later restored for a Blu-ray release.

Battle's end-of-the-road ambience seems to have been recognized by the filmmakers. The movie's poster sold the film as "The Final Chapter."

~

So good had the second and third Apes reverse adaptations been that it's something of a mystery why each time Award Books didn't simply place the novelization with the incumbent writer. Whatever the reason, for the book of the fifth movie they decided to change scribe yet again.

David Gerrold has recalled that he got the *Battle for the Planet of the Apes* novelization gig because Award was located in the same building as *Galaxy Science Fiction* magazine and the publisher asked the publication's associate editor Judy-Lynn Del Rey if she could recommend someone. Gerrold's SF credentials were impeccable. His first writing sale was the iconic and unusually humorous *Star Trek* episode "The Trouble with Tribbles." He had subsequently written for *Star Trek: The Animated Series* and had had several novels published.

The process into which Gerrold was plunged epitomizes the task of the novelizer of the era: he was given two weeks to turn out a sixty-thousand-word manuscript. He sportingly rose to the challenge, adjudging it interesting and a lot of fun. He also felt that it wasn't such an onerous task: as the script ran to 110 pages, he merely had to expand each page into three. A few in-jokes and an innuendo about the size of a villain's missile helped up the word count. Gerrold even employed the fact that there wasn't a great deal of money involved as leverage to get himself work as an extra in the film. His three hours in the makeup chair (McDowall was asleep in the seat next to his) and his training in how to lope like an evolved chimp resulted in a single wide-angle shot during the scene in which the school bus breaks through the barriers.

For some reason, the cover of Gerrold's book featured not a still from *Battle* but *Conquest*. Something else not boding well is that, following the Lawgiver prologue, Gerrold's opening chapter starts: "Aldo the gorilla knew how to save his people. Aldo the gorilla had a plan. It was a good plan. It was right. He knew it. He smacked his lips in anticipation as he thought of it. Yes. Apes should be strong. Apes should be masters. Apes should be proud. Apes should make the Earth shake when they walked. Apes should *rule* the Earth." Thankfully, things do improve after this passage's almost comical sentence-to-sentence relay of phrases and leitmotifs. However, his minimalist writing style would have seemed a step down for those who enjoyed the floridity of Jakes's adaptation of *Conquest.* Even so, his swift, movie-like pacing means the reader can get swept up in action if not ever detained by lyricism.

The included material absent from the finished movie doesn't take the form of anything quite so dramatic as the diametrically opposed tone of the ending of the *Conquest* book compared to the film, but it does provide a layering absent from a relatively one-dimensional movie. It also makes for a darker narrative than to be found in what was a consciously family-oriented picture: the scenes here of Caesar being tortured with a flamethrower by Kolp and the mutant invaders being massacred by gorillas are strong stuff.

Moreover, Gerrold's ending is somewhat more satisfying—and optimistic—than the film's close: "The rapt faces of ape and human children stared back at him. Chimpanzees, orangutans, and gorillas, blacks, Orientals, and Caucasians. All together."

~

In 1973, Arthur P. Jacobs had big plans, including screen adaptations of *Dune* and *Oliver Twist.* Those big plans naturally required big money. To finance them, he sold APJAC Productions, and his interest in the Planet of the Apes property, to 20th Century-Fox, surely the final proof that he now considered Planet of the Apes an exhausted franchise.

Despite founding a new production company named APJAC International, Jacobs would never get the chance to use the financing he had obtained. Exactly two weeks after *Battle*'s unveiling, he died of a heart attack. He was just fifty-one. Although Linda Harrison says she was shocked to hear of his demise, she also notes, "He never stopped working. He worked around the clock." Indeed. Less than two hours after his May 1968 marriage to Trundy, Jacobs was reported to have been conducting a business meeting. By all accounts he also smoked and drank around the clock, and this all took its toll. By the time of the shoot of the first Planet of the Apes film, when he was only in his mid-forties, he had experienced his first heart attack.

The Planet of the Apes films overshadowed Jacobs's other productions but did not outnumber them. It's difficult to assess how great or otherwise a producer he was. None of Jacobs's non-Apes films are considered a stinker but none a sensation. Aside from *What a Way to Go!* and *Doctor Dolittle*, he was responsible for 1969's *Goodbye, Mr. Chips* and *The Chairman* aka *The Most Dangerous Man in the World* (the latter as executive-producer); Woody Allen's 1972 comedy *Play It Again, Sam*; a 1973 multiple-Oscar-nominated musical adaptation of *Tom Sawyer*; 1973 Roddy McDowall—featured TV pilot *Topper Returns* (as executive producer); and—posthumously—*Huckleberry Finn*, a 1974 sequel to *Tom Sawyer*. The notion that Jacobs was really an executive producer who left the grunt work to subordinates seems to be supported by a recollection of Harrison, who says of her two Apes films that it was Mort Abrahams, not Jacobs, who was "on the set every day." She adds, "Arthur was probably doing the publicity part. That's where he was so good." The idea that Jacobs took credit for subordinates' hard graft seems supported by something revealed by Frank Capra Jr. to author Brian Pendreigh. Capra said that he acted as producer on *Tom Sawyer* but that Jacobs refused to officially list him as such because "this is way too good." This act could perhaps be generously put down to the instincts of an inveterate publicist (or a "kind of Barnum and Bailey showman" as Zanuck described Jacobs to Pendreigh). However, in his published journals Charlton Heston wrote of a deeper moral malaise, asserting, "Arthur Jacobs is so difficult and slippery a character to deal with, I hardly know where to begin."

Outside of movie industry circles Jacobs's name was never that well known even in his lifetime and, approaching half a century after his death, is now almost forgotten. Yet whatever the exact nature of his work, Jacobs is undeniably the Planet of the Apes "Without Whom," the man who made it all possible. He pursued the idea of adapting Pierre Boulle's novel to the big screen in the face of considerable obstacles and setbacks. That he got the picture into theaters at all is extraordinary; that he ensured it was a sophisticated and innovative experience is almost miraculous.

8

PLANET OF THE PRODUCTS

That *Battle for the Planet of the Apes* looked shop-worn and threadbare is usually put down to the parsimoniousness of 20th Century-Fox and the loss of writer continuity. However, there might also have been an issue of wholeheartedness about the enterprise. Capra later publicly lamented an aura of aimlessness and end-of-days attending the production process.

This can't have been helped by ridicule. By this point in time, the shamelessness with which the franchise's success had been milked was being widely mocked. Takeoffs can be affectionate, but when in March 1973 the long-running humor title *Mad* ran a comic strip in the run-up to the release of the fifth installment, there was a certain bite to it. Its title was "The Milking of the Planet That Went Ape," and its opening panel read, "There's a wise old expression that goes: 'Leave well enough alone!'" It continued, "It seems that everyone in the world has heard the expression except a certain movie studio that gave us a brilliant science-fiction epic a few years back . . . and then proceeded to give us sequel after sequel, each one more tiresome and boring than its predecessor. And it doesn't look like there's any end in sight." It was a long way from the days of the franchise being hailed as "the first epic of filmed science fiction."

This perception of flogging a dead horse was challenged, however, when *Battle* proceeded to become a surprising commercial success. That perception was then undermined further when CBS gave the first three films their broadcasting debuts from September 13, 1973. They topped the weekly American TV ratings, achieving a 57 percent audience share. A still greater transformation in the perception of Planet of the Apes as a defunct property was provided when 20th Century-Fox decided to cash in at the movie theaters on the continuing interest that those TV ratings had confirmed.

Rather than conventional rereleases, the studio opted for film marathons. "20th Century-Fox wants you to . . . go ape!" declared publicity posters that featured a picture of a gorilla jabbing a finger at the public, Uncle Sam style. The 1974 proposition for which people were being asked to sign up involved not the army but something not much less grueling: watching all five movies one after the other, albeit for the price of one. (Some theaters made up for what they theoretically lost on the discount via two daily showings of each marathon.) In other words, an experience lasting so long—more than the average person's working day—that the popcorn consumed during the first movie might well have been digested by the time the opening titles of *Battle* appeared. Audiences weren't in the least put off by the idea, though. The campaign was not just highly successful but also newsworthy, even if we can possibly put down to media exaggeration reports of near riots when disappointed patrons had to be turned away from full cinemas. These marathons coincided with the first usage of the term *Apemania*, although it was coined to describe a phenomenon that was a manufacturing, not a media, one.

The biggest moneymaker for the Apes franchise transpired to be neither film nor TV, but something that had previously been considered by the entertainment industry an adjunct to its activities that was financially gratifying, but of no intrinsic importance. The world was about to be awash with Planet of the Apes merchandise. Afterward, the entertainment industry would never be the same again.

Tie-in product was not new. Tarzan merchandise went back to 1922 when the ape-man's creator Edgar Rice Burroughs granted permission to New York manufacturer Davis & Voetsch to market toy simians with the character's name attached. Tarzan's name and/or loinclothed image would subsequently appear on commercial products in unquantifiable numbers. From 1929 onward, Mickey Mouse was appearing on writing tablets, soap, ice cream, bracelets, and much else. During the Christmas period of 1934, kids were pestering their parents for the Buck Rogers 25th Century Rocket Pistol. The die-cast Corgi model of James Bond's Aston Martin DB5 was the retail sensation of 1965's Yuletide season. The original 1960s *Star Trek* TV series spun off model kits and (belatedly) action figures. Moreover, even adults regularly bought tie-in product in the form of the novelizations and soundtrack albums by which films would routinely be accompanied.

Yet even by the 1970s, the full potential of merchandise had yet to be grasped. Marty Abrams was president of Mego, an American company that specialized in action figures and accompanying playset environments. In 2019, he explained to Lauren Orsini of *Forbes* the mind-set of owners of intellectual property rights that prevailed in the 1960s. "The only thing that was being licensed at that time was Mickey Mouse. At that time, Paramount, Fox, Universal, none of them had their own in-house licensing departments. They worked with outside agencies."

Arthur P. Jacobs had not been unaware of the potential that merchandising offered moviemakers for both additional profit and promotional cross-fertilization. He ensured that when *Doctor Dolittle* appeared in the cinemas, toy shops and grocery stores were offering *Dolittle* balloons, watches, notebooks, jigsaws, cereals, crackers, and a list of other items numbering three hundred or so. Had the movie been more successful and thereby created a demand for this tie-in product, Jacobs would have been lauded for his prescience. Instead, the masses of unwanted returned stock plastered with Rex Harrison's face made the producer look a presumptuous chump. It's almost certainly this fact that explains the paucity of Planet of the Apes merchandise released to tie in with the 1968 movie.

In fact, the first Planet of the Apes film had precisely one example of child-oriented merchandise attached to it (the de rigueur soundtrack LP was aimed at adults)—namely, a set of forty-four Topps trading cards featuring scenes from the film. (There were, of course, tie-in reissues of Boulle's parent novel, but as well as not being particularly child oriented they were not something requiring licensing from Fox.)

Despite the extraordinary success of *Planet of the Apes*, and despite the series of sequels it begat, Apes merchandise didn't become any more abundant. *Beneath* was accompanied by a comic book adaptation, but no card set; after *Beneath*, there were no comic books, card sets, or even soundtrack LPs attending the APJAC films. It's an almost unbelievable fact that the Planet of the Apes merchandise boom occurred not during the five years in which the movie series was on its first run in theaters, but after that series had been brought to an end due to the conviction that its market had shriveled to almost nothing. In other words, the Apes merchandise tsunami could have been even bigger than it was—which is saying something.

The first stirrings of Apemania came in the wake of those spectacular viewing figures for the films' first television broadcasts. Those stirrings were tentative. In this respect, the little guys actually stole a march on the giants. While the names of the Addar Plastics Co. and Pressman are not iconic in manufacturing lore, it was these modest outfits that in late 1973 were the first to invest in the idea that Planet of the Apes could be a merchandising moneymaker.

The inaugural Addar Apes product was hobby kits, starting with Cornelius and Dr. Zira. Snap-together plastic character sculpts on dioramic bases, they were hit-and-miss in terms of both quality (poses were stiff) and accuracy (Cornelius was shown against the backdrop of the remains of New York City from *Beneath*, which he had never been seen visiting). Once constructed and painted, though, they would have been a pleasing addition to a child's bedroom shelf or chest of drawers. Even the products' colorful boxes would be gratifying to a young mind, particularly as they bore—as would so much of the merchandise—the distinctive Planet of the Apes film-poster logo with its stylishly upward projecting *L*, conjoined *ET*, and melded *ES*. The model-kit series was very successful. The line ultimately expanded to take in ten characters, including Dr. Zaius, Caesar, General Ursus, and General Aldo. Addar also branched out into Planet of the Apes kit-in-a-bottle dioramas.

Pressman's Spin 'N Color set was for ages three to six. "Fun to learn numbers: colors" was the strapline of a product involving players spinning a card wheel then coloring the pictures of the ape faces it specified.

While this might well have been true for some people, others would have preferred the more mindless entertainment offered by Ben Cooper "rubber dangle figures" (or "jigglers"), even though these generic clothed apes on a string—which appeared at the end of '73—were only really identifiable by paper nametags that would have quickly become detached in young hands.

The following year, the big boys decided to get a slice of the action that was being promised by Fox's film marathons. The Go Ape! pressbook distributed by the studio to exhibiting theaters included among its "exploitation" suggestions a page listing Planet of the Apes–related toys and merchandise that would be "in stores throughout the nation in time for your engagement." It advised, "Tie in with local merchants for contests and promotions to help your town go ape!" Although there is a suggestion that some of the licenses were still in negotiation and may not ultimately have been granted or else were awarded to different companies who bid higher for the rights, and although some of the terms employed are generically vague, the list provides a revealing microcosm of what was about to engulf Western culture. The list also demonstrates the truth of the adage that licensed merchandise doesn't have to make conceptual sense to be attractive to its demographic but has to merely have some notional relation (amounting in some cases to an illustration and a logo) to a current obsession. Hasbro Industries was planning paint- and pencil-by-number sets; the Milton Bradley Company a boxed game; Ben Cooper Planet of the Apes variants of the costumes and masks for which they were famous, as well as PVC figures and a makeup kit; and Mattel were making toy guns branded as the "Planet of the Apes Arsenal." After a six-year hiatus, Topps Chewing Gum was getting in on the ape action once more with Planet of the Apes–branded stickers, posters, decals, gum, confectionery prize boxes, and, of course, trading cards. H-G Toys could offer puzzles and Noble & Cooley produced an Apes drum kit. Pressman was making a ring toss game, an educational coloring toy, skil [*sic*] balls, a cartoon creator, and a maze toy. Pilgrim Sportswear was stitching girls' and boys' sweatshirts, T-shirts, and polo shirts. Kites and pencil sharpeners were Durham Industries' thing. Well Made Toys were putting together Plush Dolls. The Chemtoy Corporation was offering modelling dough and a movie viewer. Miner Industries was purveying playsets and target games.

The two biggies on the list were Azrak-Hamway and Mego, manufacturing giants whose logos are embedded in the soul of every Seventies American child. (Their products are known in other countries via their sub-licensees, for instance, Mego product might appear in the United Kingdom as merchandise from the—for Britons—equally iconic Palitoy.) Azrak-Hamway was planning Planet of the Apes frisbees, plastic inflatables, water guns, wind-up mechanical figures, miniature mechanical horses and figures, battery-operated remote control figures, and vinyl finger puppets. Their parachute with miniature figure attached transpired to be the "Official Planet of the Apes Sky Diving Parachutist"—plastic, rifle-wielding simians attached to a bell of red-and-white striped cloth. Anyone who knew anything about Planet of the Apes was aware that the simians therein had not mastered flight and that Dr. Zaius (one of the figures) was unlikely to be seen with a gun about his person. Those children capable of perceiving this as traducing the franchise's mythos were unlikely to care as they waited for the figure to complete its delightful descent.

Mego (pronounced "Mee-goh") were preparing dressed articulated dolls, ape tree houses, plastic horses, riding vehicles, carrying cases, stuffed rag dolls, money banks, and hand puppets. Marty Abrams actually outbid Azrak-Hamway at the last minute to obtain the rights to the dressed articulated dolls, or action figures as their largely male demographic would no doubt prefer to call them. Like Azrak, the company cannily produced figures of characters from both the film series and TV series. However, they were unable to produce a specific action figure of Taylor because Charlton Heston had not signed away his likeness. Consequently, the human they manufactured to pal up with Cornelius and do battle with Zaius was a generic "Planet of the Apes Astronaut." Of course, likeness rights are not an issue with actors hidden behind ape makeup, enabling the company to purvey the franchise's simian characters—as figures and in illustration—to its corporate heart's content. This may go some way to explaining why Planet of the Apes specifically caused the merchandising dam to break. Once it did so, even heavyweight motion picture actors were amenable to trading likeness rights for the considerable remuneration that had now been proven to be available.

Christopher Sausville is an Apes merchandise collector and author of the book *Planet of the Apes Collectibles*. "A lot of it was kind of hokey," he admits of Apes merchandise. "There's floats for pools. There was Fuzzy Feet. There was some stuff that came out that was just way over the top. . . . The inflatable stuff I always thought was kind of weird. . . . The radio was weird: there's an AM/FM radio with a picture from *Escape* on it of Cornelius and Zira and Milo. . . . I just think it was a money-making machine and they were pretty happy to give out the license to anybody who wanted it. There was even a Planet of the Apes [ice] lollipop. A guy that I know actually has one in the package."

Yet, for Steve Clement, who wrote a feature examining the Apes merchandising phenomenon for Marvel Comics' *Planet of the Apes* magazine, hokeyness and over-the-topness did not prohibit some kind of quality control. "The pleasant surprise was that, as far as I could tell, most of the materials were worth what the manufacturers were charging," he stated. The only exception he saw was a punch-molded rubber Cornelius on which the workmanship seemed careless. He was particularly impressed by playsets for Mego's action figures, including Treehouse, Action Stallion, Battering Ram, Catapult and Wagon, Fortress, and Forbidden Zone Trap. Although priced noticeably higher than most other products, he adjudged them to be well designed and creatively stimulating, "as if somebody actually *cared* what the kids might end up playing with."

The Mego Treehouse was a "giant sized headquarters for all Planet of the Apes 8-inch action figures." Lucratively for Mego, the latter were not included. Even more lucratively, the set was not designed from scratch. There was a reason the Treehouse only vaguely resembled the arboreal home of Caesar in *Battle for the Planet of the Apes.* Sausville points out, "The Mego treehouse and the jail and the village . . . all those accessories, they were knockoffs from other things. They just called it 'Planet of the Apes.'" Yet, if they knew about it, kids didn't care that Big Jim and Action Jackson molds and designs had been repurposed. The October 1974 issue of trade magazine *Playthings* said of the Treehouse that it was "outselling comparable toys 20 to 1."

"Some of it was cheesy, but some of it was really good," Sausville admits. In particular he cites Addar's "Stallion & Soldier" model kit—a rifle-hoisting generic gorilla on a galloping steed. "It's a beautiful figure."

This, incidentally, is not to be confused with Mego's Action Stallion, a battery-controlled horse which not only could accommodate on its back a Planet of the Apes Mego action figure but could also be used to pull the same company's Apes Catapult and Wagon.

Had it been the case that, post-Apes marathons, the merchandise tidal wave was in danger of receding, the fact that from September of the same year a Planet of the Apes TV series was being transmitted every week into millions of homes emphatically forestalled that eventuality. In November 1974, *Cue* magazine was estimating there to be "300 different kinds" of merchandise items on sale related to Planet of the Apes. New York merchandiser Selwyn Rausch told the magazine, "By the end of this year we estimate $100-million gross sales in all kinds of Ape-related merchandise. Why anyone would want a Planet of the Apes wastebasket I don't know, but they're selling like crazy."

9

APES ON THE AIR

The new owners of the Planet of the Apes live-action rights clearly had a property of continuing viability, but how to capitalize on it? A new movie was never really in the cards. The sort of spectacle audiences expected from SF fare was ruled out by the kind of budgets 20th Century-Fox would be prepared to shell out for a sixth cinema outing. There was now only one obvious solution.

A Planet of the Apes TV show had been mooted as far back as 1968. In the early 1970s, Jacobs had been actively preparing for the TV transfer and had only altered his plans when *Conquest* did better box office than expected. Television had long been a big part of Fox's production business, with their small-screen smashes including classic TV such as *Batman*, *Lost in Space*, and *Peyton Place*. The CBS network readily agreed to air their putative Planet of the Apes program.

Encouragingly, Stan Hough was appointed as the show's producer. Hough had a deep history with the Apes franchise, having been a production executive on all five installments of the film series. Despite this good omen, though, it has to be noted that the very act of transferring the property to the small screen constituted a step down, at least in the United States. Nineteen-seventies American television was a much inferior beast to the same country's cinema offerings. The country's small-screen action was lowest-common-denominator stuff, synonymous with formulaic, bland storytelling punctuated by both simplistic moralizing and incessant commercials.

Defenders of the honor of American TV, though, could always invoke some gems from its history, prominent among which was *The Twilight Zone*. That thought seems to have occurred to 20th Century-Fox. The services of Rod Serling were engaged on a Planet of the Apes project yet again.

At the outset, the intention was to carry onto the small screen the continuity for which the Apes films were celebrated: Serling's pilot episode featured a pair of astronauts who go looking for a missing astronaut called Taylor. However, the commitment to this continuity seems to have been rather loose, what with plot turns that would have made the narrative incompatible with the events depicted in *Beneath*. Before too long, the TV series became what was then not called a "reimagining." (A later Apes director would coin that term.)

In Serling's vision, two human astronauts crash onto a planet ruled by simians, which they realize is their own future world. They are hunted by an intellectual orangutan named Zaius and a gorilla soldier called Ursus but assisted by a friendly chimpanzee named Galen. Serling's ideas were cherry picked rather than used wholesale: Art Wallace ended up scripting from this template the first two agenda-setting episodes, supervised by series developer Anthony Wilson.

The human heroes were ultimately Peter Burke and Alan Virdon. James Naughton (born 1945) played Burke. He was both an award-winning theater actor (for *Long Day's Journey into Night*) and a fairly seasoned TV actor (he had been a regular in 1973–1974 detective series *Faraday and Company*). "I think I might have seen a film," he says. "Maybe the original one. But I hadn't studied it." Ron Harper (born 1936) took on the part of Virdon. He was a familiar face on American television dating back to 1961 when he appeared as Detective Finn in *87th Precinct.* He had since appeared in comedies *Wendy and Me* and *The Jean Arthur Show*, as well as the *Dirty Dozen* knockoff *Garrison's Gorillas.* Harper was more *au fait* than Naughton with the franchise, including the Boulle novel.

"There was a blond—that was me—and one was a brunette—that was him," says Harper of the differences between the two principal humans. That facetious delineation may not be as irrelevant as it sounds, as will be discussed later. More seriously, Naughton says, "Burke was more of a freewheeling kind of single fellow. Virdon had been a family man." As such, Virdon is hopeful of returning to his wife and son in his own time, while the more flippant Burke is resigned to his fate.

Chimpanzees, gorillas, and orangutans are demarcated by the same temperaments, professions, and dress as they were in the films. Urko, as the gorilla was renamed (played by Mark Lenard) is distinguishable from the second film's murderously belligerent Ursus only by the second syllable of his name, and Zaius (Booth Colman) has to try to quell his impulses. However, Zaius is a slightly different proposition to his namesake predecessor. A "councilor" of the ruling orangutan class, he knows that humans were the dominant species before they destroyed civilization and is determined to suppress this fact, but he also wishes to capture the fugitives alive so as to glean information that will enable him to better deal with any others who might materialize.

As the common factor in 80 percent of the films, it might be assumed that Roddy McDowall had been a shoo-in as the ape lead, but he actually had to petition for the Galen role. Marvin Paige, the show's casting director, told Marvel's *Planet of the Apes* magazine, "We had begun looking at actors for that role, never feeling that Roddy would be interested . . . or that a feasible situation could be worked out. Then Roddy, kind of through his representatives, approached us and indicated that he would certainly be interested in discussing the situation." Paige added, "I think he's a tremendous asset to the series. And he's playing a character that's really different from the other characters he's played in the features." A recent graduate (we first see him angling for a job as Zaius's assistant), Galen was nominated by McDowall as his favorite of the three Apes characters he played. "Galen was larky," he explained in *Planet of the Apes Revisited*. "He had a wonderful sense of humor and a great sense of the childlike." The chimpanzee comes to throw in his lot with the astronauts after beginning to question received ape wisdom and then accidentally killing a gorilla. His name originated from the first Apes movie, where Galen was the handle of an obstreperous young assistant to Zira. For his part, Naughton says of McDowall, "I was surprised, actually, that he would want to do it. They were terribly hot, very difficult days in that monkey suit. It was like a three-hour makeup job. He'd have to start at four o'clock in the morning if we were going to start shooting at seven." In contrast, Harper notes, "Jim and I, we'd be in and out in half an hour."

Harper and Naughton had to go through the same peculiar process to which every thespian in the Apes movies had become accustomed. As Harper puts it, "We had to adjust to pretending to finally accept that it was normal for an ape to talk and wear a costume. After the first one or two episodes, we got used to it, and then they just become characters."

The *Planet of the Apes* producers intercut franchise greatest hits that they couldn't afford to shoot themselves, for instance long-shots from the APJAC movies of Ape City. They also sometimes proffered exteriors that were patently studio sets. With mild acidity Naughton notes that the "days out in the country" on the Fox lot in Malibu Canyon beat "being on a mock-up in a soundstage." For all this, though, the show by its nature brought a touch of Hollywood production values to television. Each episode cost a then astronomical $250,000. "We had plenty," says Harper. "I mean, the uniform, the costumes and everything were there. We had to have at least a half a dozen apes [per episode] or more." The high production values were brought home to Naughton when he first saw the crashed spaceship that had brought the astronauts to this strange place. "They went to some trouble. They had a trough that the ship supposedly would have dug in the ground as it landed. And we shot inside it and getting out of it. That was pretty intricate for a TV show at the time." Naughton also says, "Part of the reason it was so expensive was they had the best makeup men in Hollywood. And there were lots of them."

Although John Chambers and Tom Burman had moved on to fresh fields, the baton had been passed to the appropriate person in the shape of Dan Striepeke, who—unlike either Chambers or Burman—had seen the APJAC movie quintet through to the end: Burman left Fox during the making of the third film, while Chambers worked on the first three films and merely supervised the mold making and technician hiring on the final two. "When they called me to do the series, I told Fox that the only way I'd have anything to do with it was provided they maintain the quality of the movie features," Striepeke told Marvel. "So far they've kept the quality; we haven't used any 'short cuts,' so I've been pleased with everything." Whatever unhappiness Striepeke was feeling was due less to quality than the tight schedules of small-screen productions. The films had a forty-to-fifty-day shooting schedule, but the TV series shoot involved months at a time without rest. This could lead to semi-farcical situations. The day before the first episode was to be filmed, actor Woodrow Parfrey (Galen's cousin Veska) picked up an eye infection. After much deliberation and a certain amount of panic, the problem was quasi-inanely solved by giving his character an eyepatch.

Lenard and Colman were highly respected actors. Similar tilting for respectability was evident in the engagement of the services of Lalo Schifrin, responsible for, among other examples of sonic iconography, the unforgettably slinky theme tune to *Mission: Impossible*.

Certainly, the opening titles of the first episode of *Planet of the Apes*—screened on September 13, 1974—augured well. Schifrin's alarming, discordant music was married to shots that were quite chilling: the two astronauts running away from horse-mounted apes seen against a high sun, the silent action creating a dreamlike, oppressive air, especially when it culminated in a shot of a monstrously nostrilled gorilla with rifle held aloft. Unfortunately, the show itself never got quite as good as that.

In opener "Escape from Tomorrow," Virdon and Burke crash-land in the same type of stylish but implausibly miniscule craft seen in the first three films. From weird sightings, strange interactions, and perusing a tattered book, Virdon and Burke realize that they have ended up back on Earth a thousand years after their launch date. In this Apes iteration, humans are not the pelt-swathed mutes of the first two films but living in crude housing, wearing sewn clothing, and able to speak. They are analogous to medieval peasants, confined to settlements by the ruling apes and permitted to fulfil roles only as laborers, farmers, and servants. The change has been made to better facilitate plots: dumb, primeval humans wouldn't lend themselves to nuanced conflict.

When the vacated spaceship is discovered it has the upper echelons of the ape world aflutter. It is quickly realized that should it become widely known that humans are capable of a technological expertise beyond apes it will threaten the society's ecosystem, something particularly alarming to simians because they perceive humans as innately violent. (This rationale is a little undermined by the fact that in this society "Ape Shall Not Kill Ape" is not a golden rule, as demonstrated by the death sentence handed down on Galen when he is mistakenly thought to be a murderer.)

Such things as a reference by Zaius to another crew of human astronauts having materialized ten years previously have led Planet of the Apes aficionados to try to shoehorn the TV show's continuity into that of the films. Such considerations were of no relevance to children of the era, many of whom didn't even know there had been Apes movies, and it was the kids who made the series, for all its commercial and critical failures, a financial sensation. People are often astonished to learn how briefly the *Planet of the Apes* TV series was on the air: such was the tsunami of publicity preceding it (including a modified "Go Ape!" poster with a strapline reading "On CBS TV Fridays"), and the tidal wave of merchandise that flowed from it that the majority impressionistic memory is that it was not a flop but a phenomenon. In fact, the show lasted just thirteen weeks.

Its short existence may have been dictated by the very expectations of success that surrounded it from the beginning "They figured—and I did too—that it would last at least five years," notes Harper. So sure was CBS of the series' viability that, unusually for American TV of the era, the program was not kicked off by a pilot designed to attract sponsors. "I guess it was to the credit of the producers that they actually got a commitment from the network to go right for the series," says Naughton, although he does add, "I guess too, because there was an awful lot of expense in trying to make all that stuff work and all the makeup and costumes and everything, it might have been more expensive to do a pilot and then have to wait."

Mediocrity, though, played its part in that truncated lifespan. In the opening episode, the premise is set up inordinately quickly, and the stranded astronauts' bewilderment and despair is rather perfunctorily drawn. "It might have helped if we had taken the time to have a two-hour TV episode," reflects Harper. "That could have been more of an introduction into where we were going with it. . . . But I guess the network didn't want to spend that much money in case it didn't work." Not that the writing got any less pat and simplistic after that, something surely not assisted by the fact that the scripts were provided by no fewer than fifteen people. The three fugitives would wander from town to town and encounter humans, and sometimes apes, in various kinds of trouble. They would do their best to help them, while in the meantime try to avoid discovery by their simian pursuers. When the issues were wrapped up—sometimes via the men from the more advanced society finding a solution beyond their temporary companions, including quinine and fishing nets—they would move on.

Sprinkled into this *Fugitive*-like formula were the de rigueur action set pieces. "I spent a lot of my time running at guys dressed up in monkey suits, leaping up in the air and kicking them and then falling on the ground," recalls Naughton. Indeed, that Burke and Virdon were astronauts with an apparent incongruous knowledge of martial arts technique made some suspicious that the show was attempting to cash in on the David Carradine *Kung Fu* series. Both actors, however, deny the claim. Harper: "A human couldn't wrestle a gorilla and win. We had to do something trickier." Meanwhile, Naughton relished the action sequences as a way to stave off the tedium of shooting. "When you're doing a TV show, it's day-in, day-out, and on a show like that it's very long days," he says. He recalls that each episode "would take us about eight shooting days" and that "we were working five or six days a week." He reasons, "So you try to make it as enjoyable as possible."

Hough could be found bragging to Rowland Barber of *TV Guide*, "We can reveal truths and show things we could never otherwise get away with, make social statements about the violent side of human nature, about the horrors of the police state, about the blindness of prejudice." However, both actors are in agreement that few of the series' episodes had the social subtexts of the Apes movies. Naughton: "That was really what I think the worth and success of the films was. That there were those kinds of social issues that were being illuminated. There was a certain amount of that in the series, but not an awful lot." Harper: "A fourth of them maybe would hit an issue, but mostly it was just such a routine: one of us would get captured by the apes, the other would rescue them, bom, bom, bom." Moreover, both actors feel that *Planet of the Apes* was unusually deficient even by the bland American

TV standards of the time. "Its stories were not as exciting as they could have been," says Harper. "[It needed] a little bit more variety. . . . You have a whole different world that you can use than regular Western good guy / bad guy." Mark Lenard opined to Marvel at the time, "The apes are the interesting ones. . . . I would like to see them investigate the ape culture more, the apes character, and abandon this whole idea of the astronauts saving the poor apes with their technology and their wiliness." McDowall later publicly agreed with Lenard, although did feel this problem was starting to be addressed as the series went on. The latter may have been a consequence of Harper articulating his grievances. Harper recalls, "I said to the writers, 'It's not a reality show—apes don't really talk or wear costumes or shoot guns. We can do more creative stuff. Otherwise, it's going to be a routine.' They said, 'Oh, we're working on it.' . . . Stan said, 'We can maybe try and add some things to clarify it a little bit better.'" However, he adds, "I think it was more than just what *they* thought. I think they were thinking in terms of the network: what do they want to see on an hour action show once a week? . . . It's very hard to convince the executives to do something other than what they wanted to do."

There were other script problems. The most notable one was the disappearing McGuffin. Initially the show revolved around a "magnetic disc" retrieved by the astronauts from their wrecked spaceship. "[It] was the way we were going to be able to find our way back," Naughton points out. Yet the quest for a means to play the disc—and thus enable Burke and Virdon to use its navigational data to retrace their cosmic and time-continuum steps—was not mentioned after the first brace of episodes. Wryly notes Naughton, "I don't know if they just didn't have an answer for that or if it just didn't tickle the fancy of whoever was writing the show. It's interesting how they set that thing up and then they just didn't follow through." Harper: "Maybe they had it in reserve for the second or third year. But we never got that far." Possibly, even, it was forgotten about because the person who thought of it—Serling—was no longer in the picture. Whatever the truth, the upshot was that the show was rendered essentially aimless.

Naughton does point out, "There were a couple of shows that I felt were really quite good." He cites the quality of the third episode, "The Trap," the story line of which was based on a suggestion in Serling's notes. "Urko and I wound up in an old subway station," Naughton recalls. "There was a collapse and we were underground and it was the most imaginative show where this ape had to actually be faced with the proof that there had at one time been another civilization where man was on top and the ape was not. It challenged everything he knew, and it was a fascinating way to explore the differences that we as humans have to deal with: different kinds of cultures and races and all those big questions." Another unusually thoughtful episode was "The Deception," which has a Ku Klux Klan plot strand in the shape of a vigilante mob of apes randomly taking revenge on humans for the murder of one of their kind.

With CBS itself publicly describing the ratings as "poor," *Planet of the Apes* abruptly departed the airwaves. "It was about a half a season," says Naughton of the thirteen-episode guillotine. "In those days, it used to be about 26 episodes for the season. . . . They came in and made the announcement while we were working. . . . I don't think it was a surprise. I don't know how much of what I'm telling you about the formulaic nature of the show was on my mind at the time or if it's just in retrospect, but looking back it seems that that's what caused it. [Plus] the cost of it. We were also in competition . . . *Sanford and Son* and *Chico and the Man* were both pretty successful shows. They ran back to back right against us."

Ironically, an unbroadcast fourteenth episode was one of the few that boasted the type of adult-oriented social commentary endemic to the Apes films. In the hard-hitting "The Liberator," Burke and Virdon stumble upon a town where a cult leader wants to drop gas bombs to rid the world of apes. Originally intended to be episode 13, it was pulled because CBS was nervous that allegories about the then-ongoing Vietnam War might be read into its discussion of toxins as a battle tactic.

There were several episodes already written that weren't filmed. Asked if he had learned the lines for those, Naughton says, "No. I don't know that I had seen them either." Fox did provide a fatuous and belated resolution to the series in 1980 when that year the studio eked out a last bit of profit from the show (at least until new media came along) by splicing episodes to form TV movies to be sold for syndication. These artificial feature-length creations were originally bookended by newly filmed segments featuring an older-looking Galen (played by McDowall) speaking directly to the viewers. At the close of the last of the five pseudo-films, *Farewell to the Planet of the Apes*, Galen revealed that Virdon and Burke had "found their computer in another city and disappeared into space as suddenly as they arrived"—an explanation pretty much in keeping with the series' pat spirit.

There were two possible responses to the situation in which Harper and Naughton found themselves: disappointment at the loss of a job and relief to get out of a situation that wasn't working. "I felt both of them," says Harper. "I think both of those things are true in my case," echoes Naughton. The latter adds, "The check was really nice to get, and I enjoyed the people I was working with. And when you're engaged in a community endeavor like that, there's a comradeship, so that when you get the word that you're a failure and [the] show's been cancelled, that's disappointing. On the other hand . . . my whole life I hadn't been wanting to be an action figure. So it sort of came out of left field. But I did the best job I could. . . . There were other things down the road that I was looking forward to doing, so it was like, 'Okay, what's next?'"

What was next for Naughton was, as he puts it, "a varied career," much of it involving directing and trilling. "I think of myself as an actor who sings," he says. Among his Broadway musical success is the long-running *Chicago* and *City of Angels*, the latter of which was Tony festooned.

Harper continued his career of jobbing actor and became a regular face in soap operas. When he was cast as Virdon, many was the journalist who had fun with the fact that he had graduated from *Garrison's Gorillas* to *Planet of the Apes*. They were given further assistance in such linkage by the fact of him being domiciled in Tarzana, the Californian district named after the Edgar Rice Burroughs character raised by simians.

For all its lack of success, the Apes live-action show seems to have made quite an impact on television production. Over the next few years, American TV would be full of buddy series in which the lead characters were two men, one of whom was blond and one brunette, with personalities as contrasting as their hair. Whenever viewers of a certain age caught sight of publicity photos of *Starsky & Hutch*, *The Dukes of Hazzard*, or *CHiPs*, many of them were left wondering, "Where's Galen?"

Moreover, the writing was the only department in which the *Planet of the Apes* television show lacked excellence. As Naughton points out,

"They had a lot of talent around there. . . . We had a lot of really wonderful, accomplished actors in the show. . . . All the principal ape characters were being played by some really distinguished actors. . . . Sondra Locke was a sort of love interest for Ron Harper. Just after we did that, she wound up making a couple of movies with Clint Eastwood. . . . I think in terms of makeup and stuff like that they did a very good job. . . . The music was one of the singularly best elements in the show."

Moreover, the show is fondly recalled by many. Naughton: "I have to tell you I'm just astounded at how many people seem to remember it. I get stuff in the mail a couple of times a week, asking for autographs and pictures and all that stuff. I'm [surprised] at how much staying power the show has had. . . . We must have been doing something right for some of those people."

~

As noted, the flop of the *Planet of the Apes* TV series was at odds with its cultural ubiquity. The show's novelizations were part of this disproportionate visibility. There were no fewer than four of them—as many as there had been movie-sequel novelizations.

Award remained the publisher, and, again, there was a change of author under their Ape auspices. This particular wordsmith at least wrote all four of the books, thus providing a continuity that the TV show, with its revolving door of writers, certainly couldn't boast. George Alec Effinger was both a prose writer (he'd published novels *What Entropy Means to Me* and *Relatives* and short story collection *Mixed Feelings*) and comic book scripter (he was a Marvel "Bullpenner" even if he wrote lesser-known fare like *Gulliver of Mars* rather than any of the marquee characters). Award's cover blurbs for his Apes books were disingenuous to say the least. Encomiums like "A fascinating phenomenon!," "Superior entertainment—masterful adventure!," and "The most popular science fiction series since *Star Trek*!" may well have genuinely come from the pages of the attributed *Galaxy* and *If* magazines. However, they certainly weren't referring to these books, or even this particular strand of the Apes franchise. Honest blurbs would simply have stated that Effinger made a surprisingly good fist of the circumstances in which he found himself.

In addition to the fact that the scripts he is adapting were bland and cumulatively repetitive, the author is slightly undermined by the fact that each of his Apes books actually adapts two of the series' episodes (said pairings, moreover, being apparently arbitrary). This format of two novellas in one book works to highlight the inconsistencies in the source material caused by the show's multiplicity of writers. Third volume, *Journey into Terror*, adapts the episodes "The Horse Race" and "The Legacy," and there's little Effinger can do about the fact that in "The Legacy" Robert Hamner depicted Galen as an ingénue while David P. Lewis and Booker Bradshaw's "The Horse Race" portrayed Galen as a rather more poised figure. Moreover, for some reason, none of the eight episodes Effinger was instructed to translate to prose was the premise-explaining series opener "Escape from Tomorrow" (which didn't stop Award creating an apparently deliberate assonance by titling the series' second book *Escape to Tomorrow*).

However, some deft exposition in volume 1 brings the reader up to speed on the overall concept. Effinger then sets about efficiently telling the stories as broadcast while providing his own surprisingly detailed but unobtrusive augmentation in the form of omniscient explanation of motive, backstory, and interior life. (He perhaps takes things a little too far when he opens the adaptation of "The Deception" with the point of view of a squirrel.) He is impressively even-handed with apes and humans.

Although volumes 1–3 of this series (*Man the Fugitive* was the first) are easy to come by, judging by its scarcity *Planet of the Apes #4: Lord of the Apes* had a much lower print run. The fourth volume would seem to have been commissioned as a consequence of the success of the first three: its differing cover design betrays the fact that the previous, uniform-looking trio were published in one separate batch. A striking fact is that the juncture at which volume 4 appeared—1976—did not coincide with the live-action *Planet of the Apes* TV series, but with reruns of the subsequent animated TV series *Return to the Planet of the Apes*. The latter demonstrated that even despite the flop of the live-action show there was still life in the Apes franchise.

"I personally think they pulled the plug too soon," says Rich Handley of the live-action series. "I think it would have caught on because I know so many people who were crushed when it ended. Sequels earn diminishing returns. It may be that Fox said, 'We're still making money but if we extrapolate this out, we're probably better off launching something new.' I know that 1970s studios were not big on having long-running film franchises in general. That sort of thing came later. Somebody may at the top have decided, 'I don't like *Planet of the Apes*. I don't want to be associated with this.' Because in the seventies science fiction was not cool. Even though movies were doing well, it was the kind of thing people made fun of you for watching."

Those who detect the whiff of fan paranoia in Handley's claims are referred to the fact that the live-action *Planet of the Apes* TV series was a smash all around the world, not least in the United Kingdom, where it topped the ratings, was repeated (the British term for *rerun*), and even spun off successful stage shows. Moreover, after the program was taken off the air, demand for Planet of the Apes merchandise—in the United Kingdom, the United States, and elsewhere—continued unabated.

10

COMICS OF THE APES

The Marvel Comics *Planet of the Apes* magazine that carried Steve Clement's article about Apes merchandise was, of course, itself part of this product tsunami.

While it carried text features on the television series, Marvel's publication did not feature a comic strip adaptation of it; yet while it adapted the films into comics, it was unable to use actors' likenesses. Once again, kids didn't care about the inexactitude, although the fact that the publication was rather classy, no doubt, helped in this respect. Comic books, in fact, have proven to be a surprisingly rich and inspired section of the Planet of the Apes universe.

That said, the first Planet of the Apes comic books were unprepossessing. In 1968, Japan's Akita Shoten issued an adaptation of the first Apes movie, written and drawn by Jôji Enami. While there doesn't seem to be a record of said publisher adapting *Beneath the Planet of the Apes* into that format, in 1970, American company Gold Key fulfilled that brief with a book illustrated by Alberto Giolitti, writer unknown. There were further Manga Akita Shoten Apes comics in 1971 and 1973 when Minoru Kuroda and Mitsuru Sugaya, respectively, wrote and drew adaptations of the first movie again and *Battle for the Planet of the Apes.*

All these publications were creatively hampered in that they condensed entire movies into one-shots. Gold Key specialized in TV and movie tie-ins, but the glamour of their subject matter was always undermined by the suffocating staidness of their creative approach. Akita Shoten's Manga Apes books were hardly more elevated in quality, even if staidness is one thing they can't be accused of. "They're weird," says Rich Handley, who has read and analyzed every Planet of the Apes comic ever published. "They're very, very strange in that they add scenes that don't make a whole lot of sense. Like the fact that there's a fifth astronaut in Taylor's crew, or the fact that they encounter dinosaurs. The fact that the apes seem to be doing things like experimenting on people and creating weird two-headed monsters."

After this inauspicious start, however, things picked up. There have been through the years more than two hundred issues from numerous publishers of licensed Planet of the Apes comics. The strictures that go with a licensed property—depicting universes devised by other hands and being overseen by outside parties with their own corporate and artistic agendas—has not prevented writers and artists producing some superb comic books that have genuinely served to enhance the franchise.

Just how much potential there was for great comics in the Planet of the Apes property was proven by Marvel less than a half decade after that first American Apes book from Gold Key. The home of Spider-Man et al. had lately become amenable to the idea of licensed comics following the phenomenal success of *Conan the Barbarian*, their sword and sorcery title based on the pulp novels of Robert E. Howard. "*Planet of the Apes* had played on TV—the original movie—and had gotten this huge, huge audience," says Roy Thomas, then Marvel's de facto editor in chief, of the impetus for a Marvel Planet of the Apes publication. "It was considered there was going to be a Planet of the Apes phenomena." Marvel's Apes publication was not a standard-sized color title but one of the company's magazine-format publications with black-and-white interiors. This line, initially published under the Curtis imprint, had a certain kudos because magazines were not subject to the strictures of the Comics Code Authority and could take a more mature approach to content. "Which is why we had truly horrific mutants with melted faces and so forth," Handley notes of the Curtis adaptation of *Beneath the Planet of the Apes*. Adding to the patina of class was the fact that the magazine format enabled longer stories and fully painted covers.

With Tony Isabella appointed editor, writing duties on the *Planet of the Apes* comic book were handed to Doug Moench, a man in his mid-twenties who had recently graduated to Marvel from Warren Publishing, which—perhaps not coincidentally—specialized in monochrome, magazine-sized comics. The publication would essentially become Moench's baby. Although it would feature a variety of artists, he wrote every single one of the comic strips that said illustrators were given to draw. "I was Old Reliable," says Moench. "The editors loved me 'cos I was never, ever late. And then some of them would be nice and say, 'And it's good, too.'"

The debut issue of Marvel's *Planet of the Apes* was cover-dated August 1974 (an on-sale date of May or June). It featured the first installment of a six-part adaptation of the first Apes movie. Ultimately, the book would run comic strip versions of all five APJAC films. These adaptations were something Moench found almost ridiculously easy. "I didn't much like the adaptations of the movies, but boy, was it a way to rack up money," he recalls. "I'd just mark up the screenplay and then retype parts of it. . . . I ended up doing one chapter of that a week for a couple of years."

As his comment indicates, his scripts were not, strictly speaking, adaptations of the movies. "I used the screenplays for all five to do my adaptations," he says. "In those days, there were no VCRs . . . Your average comic book writer could not demand a screening." Moench thereby rapidly became aware that what appears even in a shooting script is not necessarily what ends up on the screen. With the translations of the first two movies, he says he found himself thinking, "Wait a minute, I don't think this little bit was in the movie. Oh, well, I'll just put it in anyway. Maybe I'm remembering wrong." The penny dropped when it came to the later adaptations. In a comment that may shock many, he reveals, "I had only seen the first two movies." It's doubtful that someone so detached from a property as to have not bothered to take in three-fifths of it would be allowed to helm such a licensed title today. In any case, his version of *Battle for the Planet of the Apes* contained significant elements not included in the finished film, including the sight of Caesar losing his hair through radiation poisoning and the fact of its human villain being Governor Breck, not Kolp. "I got all this mail about how dare I change the movie," Moench recalls. "The screenplay I got was radically changed after the fact and I had no idea. The editors proofread it and sent it to the printers, so they didn't have any idea apparently." For Handley, the fact that Marvel's Apes-film adaptations were progressively different to the parent movies is actually part of their appeal. "Because back in the days of pre-internet, it was almost impossible—unless fans just happened to go to the right convention—to find unused scripts," he says. "It's so cool to see these earlier versions of the movies playing out visually instead of just the script for them."

In any case, the adaptations of the films paradoxically were not the heart of the Marvel publication. Each issue led with Planet of the Apes stories of Moench's own devising, ones in which he was helping to invent the concept now known as "expanded universe." It was an exercise he found far more fulfilling than the screenplay adaptations. His original series "Terror on the Planet of the Apes" started life as one page of notes by Gerry Conway, the writer who had originally been assigned the book before having to pull out. The notes concerned a human called Jason and a chimpanzee named Alexander, friends in a world that would seem to be the one seen in *Battle for the Planet of the Apes*. Moench built it from there. As a pivotal device, he turned the characters into children because he felt kids to be less hung up on differences than adults. He ensured to work in some of the social subtext common to the Apes films, noting, "You couldn't live in America at that time and not be aware of this stuff." The first installment, for instance, featured a gorilla group who were the equivalent of the Ku Klux Klan.

Moench was assisted in his high-minded ambitions by the evocative and stylish art of Mike Ploog, which was a notable contrast to the merely serviceable rendering by George Tuska of the adaptation of the first film. In fairness, Tuska was handicapped by the fact that there was destined to be a jarring visual dissimilarity between film and comic book versions. Roy Thomas revealed that the artwork for the opening episode of the adaptation of the first Apes movie had to be redone because the central hero as drawn was thought to resemble too much the likeness-owning Charlton Heston.

In terms of story, whether adaptations or originals, Moench encountered no objections from the rightsholders. "I never was asked to rewrite a single thing," he says, although does concede a certain self-censorship:

"Obviously, you can do all kinds of radical things in that universe, but you can't alter the basic reality." Roy Thomas, though, considers a writer of licensed-property material to have more leeway than might be imagined. "We are making up new stories, and isn't that what we're doing if we write Spider-Man or any other character we didn't create?" he reasons. "Doug Moench really threw himself into it and had a lot of fun with it."

One would imagine so by glancing at some of the Moench-devised Apes narratives. One was the Jason and Alexander story in issue 26, "North Lands!," which proffered horned-helmeted Viking apes. Moench also devised the series "Future History Chronicles," of which Handley notes, "The apes were living on vast city ships that sailed the oceans and [it had] just such gorgeous, gorgeous artwork and well-written stories. It basically took Planet of the Apes and put it in a world of fantasy and sorcery." Similarly out there was the medieval-set "Kingdom on an Island of the Apes" and its sequel "Beast on the Planet of the Apes." Perhaps wildest of all was "Terror on the Planet of the Apes," which was brimming with outlandishness that included apes riding giant toads, mutants with heads like mushrooms, talking brains in jars with the syntax of Chicago gangsters, and Daniel Boone–like frontier apes. Enthuses Handley, "It is ridiculous, it is silly, and it is perfect."

There was also material that was marked by impressive thoughtfulness such as "Quest for the Planet of the Apes," a two-parter set between the fourth and fifth movies. Explains Handley, "Aldo challenges Caesar for rulership of Ape City. The two of them have to travel to a Forbidden City and find 'The Best Thing' and bring it back to the village. Whoever finds the best thing will be the leader. Aldo comes back with guns, which is why there's an armory in the fifth movie, but

Caesar comes back with knowledge and, in very typical Planet of the Apes fashion, the knowledge is more important than the guns. It's a great story, thematically it totally fits the movies, and it bridges the gap between the fourth and fifth movies by showing the early days of that fledgling Ape City."

The irony of all this is that this quality and singular vision would seem to have been a result of the fact that Moench didn't give a toss about Planet of the Apes. Handley muses, "Doug's Planet of the Apes is a corner of the Planet of the Apes that seems to have been LSD infused. (I'm not saying Doug was LSD infused.) I think it could only have been written by a guy who said, 'How can I have fun with Planet of the Apes and not have to pore over the movies?'"

It should be noted that, whether adaptations or original stories and regardless of quality, much of this content befuddled many 1970s youngsters. This is because it did not resemble the only experience they had of the franchise—namely, the live-action television series—which started airing a few months after the Marvel comic book's debut issue and which surely boosted its sales figures. "None of it had anything to do with the TV show," says Moench. "I don't remember that having been mentioned at all when they asked me to do the book." In one of the last issues, number 27, then-editor John Warner explained, "We are not going to adapt the TV series. . . . We don't have the rights nor the source material we would need." Nonetheless, the magazine couldn't ignore the live-action show, not least because it had several text pages to fill each time out. It therefore published several interview features with the cast and crew. For all that, the fact that the publication's success was not predicated on the interest of fans of Burke, Virdon, and Galen is underlined by it outlasting the TV series by two years.

Those text features were the filling in the sandwich of the two comic strips and meant the entire publication was an undiluted immersion in Planet of the Apes world. As well as articles on the TV show, the magazine carried features about the films, many of them highly informative and knowledgeable. The first issue alone included an interview with Rod Serling about his work on the first Apes picture, an article on the film series' makeup, and a surprisingly critical overview of all the movies. Features in succeeding issues ranged from a lengthy review of Boulle's novel to an interview article about a couple who had obtained a license from 20th Century-Fox to appear at public events in Cornelius and Zira makeup.

Over in Britain, Marvel's UK division began a Planet of the Apes comic in October 1974. As with Marvel's other British titles, it was published weekly and composed of American-originated material. However, unlike most other Marvel reprint titles, severe problems soon arose with shortage of material. Notes Rob Kirby, British author of a forthcoming history of Marvel UK, "They launched that weekly only months after the American title, and that was monthly, hence you got Apeslayer after a few weeks." *Apeslayer*, which debuted in March 1975 in number 23 of the British Marvel Apes title, will live long in infamy. It repurposed a Marvel strip called *Killraven* that had taken place in the continuity of H. G. Wells's *The War of the Worlds*, changing its titular hero's Martian enemies to simians by means of superimposed hairy heads and doctored text. "I laughed out loud when told of it by a friend who was working in production," recalled Isabella to *Simian Scrolls*. "I wonder what would have happened if they had run out of *Killraven* material as well." Fortunately, the world never got to find out. After eight excruciating installments, *Apeslayer* was discontinued.

"They needed after the Apeslayer debacle to make sure they had enough material," says Kirby. "So poor old Doug Moench was driven absolutely barmy doing all the film adaptations as quickly as possible and then all these other back-up strips, just to give the British comic enough material that it wouldn't run out. In fact, at one point we were printing the film adaptations two or three months ahead of the Americans, so actually it's the American magazines that are reprints, not the British ones." Moreover, the British strips were often longer, featuring panels not included in the US versions. The British title lasted for 231 issues, before declining sales saw it—as was the British custom—absorbed into another comic, in this case *The Mighty World of Marvel*, where it was a featured story for another fifteen editions.

In the second half of 1975 came yet another Marvel Apes publication in the shape of *Adventures on the Planet of the Apes*. This American comic book reprinted the film adaptations from the Curtis title but was aimed at a younger demographic, being in the conventional American comic book format of thirty-two four-color 6.5-by-10.25-inch pages and with a much lower cover price than the black-and-white magazine. *Adventures on the Planet of the Apes* was cancelled after eleven issues, following the conclusion of the colorized reprint of the adaptation of the second movie.

The B&W book lost one-third of its pagination with issue 14, with a commensurate drop in price, and by issue 29, the movies had all been serialized. Yet, although Marvel did not possess adaptation rights to the live-action television series or (Warner also revealed) the subsequent animated Apes TV show, Marvel seems to have been happy to carry on publishing the title. In issue 27, Warner vouchsafed, "We will be creating a third new series, which we don't have a title for yet. It will feature

Derek Zane (from our KINGDOM and BEAST original stories), but the story-line will be completely different from what he's been involved with before." Two issues later, the editor clearly had no idea that this was the last time he would be addressing Apes fans: he was encouraging readers to write into the letters column.

The reason for his publication's abrupt disappearance from the shelves was that 20th Century-Fox had decided to slit their own throats. "Doug Moench told me that when the Marvel series ended it wasn't because of low sales," says Handley. "The reason it ended was because Fox upped their licensing fees." With comics being not only, in Moench's words, "a nickel and dime" industry but also one in serious decline due to kids increasingly spending their allowances and time on other diversions, the hike made it untenable for Marvel to agree to a more expensive deal. Handley is scathing about Marvel "unrealistically" raising their fees in the aftermath of the abject failure of both the live-action TV show and its animated successor. "They had a good thing going with Marvel and they jettisoned it."

Of the black-and-white comic book's twenty-nine-issue, two-and-a-half-year lifespan, Moench notes, "That's quite a long run for something like that." Moreover, the publication's stories have been revived by more than one other comics company, most notably Boom! Studios. "They reprinted all of my stuff in these beautiful, huge hardcover things," says Moench.

In the short run, Planet of the Apes merely provided Marvel Comics multiple successful publications. In the long run, the franchise may have been profoundly more beneficial both to the company and the industry in which it operated. Apes comics had proven to Marvel the commercial viability of licensed titles based on live-action media. As such, when Marvel was shortly approached by the makers of a new science fiction motion picture called *Star Wars*, they agreed to publish a comic book version. *Star Wars* #1 appeared in April 1977 (cover-dated July), about seven weeks before the film's debut. It became the first American comic for a generation to sell more than a million copies. A company that had been on the verge of bankruptcy was transformed. Says Thomas, "That particular series of six issues that got reprinted and reprinted and reprinted in different formats, and then the *Star Wars* book after that, practically ensured Marvel's survival."

~

While Marvel didn't have the rights to print adaptations of the live-action Apes TV series, that doesn't mean such rights didn't exist. Comic strip adventures featuring Burke, Virdon, and Galen were certainly issued, albeit in some of publishing's more obscure backwaters.

The United Kingdom's Brown Watson released three Planet of the Apes annuals in successive years. These A4 (roughly letter-size) hardcover books focused not on the films but the live-action TV show, whose massive popularity in Britain is demonstrated by the fact that the last of these books was published in 1977, long after the series had been cancelled. The seven strips to be found across the three Brown Watson annuals are not credited, although that might be a blessing to the creatives concerned. "I have a fondness in my heart for the Brown Watson books," says Handley, but admits, "They're really simplistic."

The Apes film comic adaptations to be found stateside in 1974 in Peter Pan / Power Records book-and-record sets weren't much better. In fact, there is a suspicion that the reason that *Conquest* was the only picture not adapted in this line is because it was too mature for the intended audience. The Pan/Power packages contained seven-inch vinyl records with accompanying twenty-page color comics of the same size, the discs' ten-minute condensings of the films exactly following the comics' panels and speech, with the only difference being the accompanying music. The creative credit borne by these sets is the corporate line "Arvid Knudsen and Assoc."

There were other comics based on the TV show, but they were unlicensed. Seven Spanish-language issues, written by Jorge Claudio Morhain and illustrated by Sergio Alejandro Mulko, were published in Argentina. Although not related to the TV show—and barely to the film series—there were also bootleg Apes comics in Indonesia from Maranatha, again in the native language. Amounting to six in number, they were written and drawn by Harry Mintareja. "It was a pretty big market in both those countries for unlicensed comics because there was no way to go after them due to a lack of copyright laws," says Handley. "Although in Argentina there might have been more legal grounds because the company that produced those seven comics actually had to change names at one point." Budapest-based Youth Newspaper Company–MOKÉP published an unlicensed 1981 adaptation of Pierre Boulle's original novel written and illustrated by Zórád Ernö, itself a reprint of a serialization in Hungarian crossword puzzle magazine *Füles*. All, on one level, were artistically negligible and morally dubious but, on another, symptomatic of the way the comics medium retained faith in the Planet of the Apes franchise at a point in history when all other industries appeared to have lost it.

11

DEVOLUTION

Considerable vainglory had surrounded the *Planet of the Apes* television series. It had been hubristically commissioned without even the benefit of a pilot, and there had been much trumpeting of its arrival. Following its ignominious, mid-season cancellation, then, it was symbolically appropriate that the franchise moved quickly to what was in those days almost a formal acknowledgment that an intellectual property was in its death throes: an animated Saturday-morning children's TV series.

With the merchandise still selling in droves, it certainly made sense to continue the franchise in some way and, specifically, with a project oriented toward kids. However, the very fact that 20th Century-Fox gave the go-ahead for the TV cartoon *Return to the Planet of the Apes* was a measure of the franchise's falling stock. Although 1970s Saturday morning American television was awash with animated versions of illustrious franchises—Gilligan's Island, The Hardy Boys, Star Trek, Tarzan—those franchises were being pimped out for pennies. As Robert Kline, who worked as a storyboard supervisor and artist for Filmation—the kings of such fare—candidly conceded, "It's kind of the last gasp of a property. [The rightsholders] wouldn't put it on Saturday morning as a limited animation TV series until they figured, 'Well, we can't really do much else with this.' . . . [They were] extinct properties."

Not that all such fare was trash. Trekkers consider the scripts of Filmation's *Star Trek* series (1973–1974) comparable in quality to those of the original live-action series. However, while good teleplays could be proffered because they were no more costly to commission than bad ones, children were never going to be offered high-grade, high-expense animation. The trademark of Saturday morning cartoons was lack of visual richness and almost comical overuse of the "stock" shot.

The presence of the original actors on the soundtrack to Filmation's *Star Trek* added to its unexpected feeling of authenticity. Had Roddy McDowall been engaged for *Return to the Planet of the Apes*, his distinctive tones would have been a similar boon, but the only voice actor hired for the Apes cartoon with any association with any previous filmed Apes fare was Austin Stoker. The man who played MacDonald in *Battle for the Planet of the Apes* was cast as the voice of Jeff Allen, one of the trio of astronauts whose turn it was to be doubly astounded at having been catapulted forward in time and onto a strange world that is actually their own. (The journey this time is from 1976 to the 3970s.)

If the absence of McDowall was a worrying sign, the fact that *Return* was produced by DePatie-Freleng Enterprises was, to those in the know, equally perturbing. The company run by David H. DePatie and Friz Freleng had always jostled for 1970s Saturday-morning cartoon supremacy with Filmation and Hanna-Barbera but, up until now, their modus operandi had been—like Hanna-Barbera—the creation of new properties. Not only were DePatie-Freleng inexperienced in adapting existing franchises, they specialized not in adventure but humor.

For all that, though, in several ways *Return to the Planet of the Apes* was high minded and high quality, starting with the lineup of that astronaut trio. Bearing in mind that only a half decade previously the credits of *Beneath the Planet of the Apes* had billed Don Pedro Colley, one of the telepaths, as "Negro," it wasn't necessarily inevitable that the Allen character be black. Moreover, at a time when all astronauts were linguistically and literally "spacemen," another of the trio was one Judy Franklin, voiced by Claudette Nevins. Additionally, unlike the first movie's Stewart and Dodge, these characters are not introduced when already dead or shortly before being killed and stuffed. In this context, one could even merrily suggest that the fair-haired Bill Hudson (played by Richard Blackburn and Tom Williams) was the token white man. Meanwhile, Dean Elliott's eerie, discordant music—very reminiscent of that of the first movie—provided an oddly sophisticated accompaniment to crunched Corn Flakes and sibling squabbles. Furthermore, in marked contrast to its live-action small-screen predecessor, this was a series with a discernible through-line. The show's nonepisodic, arc-driven nature was particularly unusual in kids' cartoons, which specialized in contrivedly self-contained installments.

Credit for the macro-orientation goes primarily to producer/director Doug Wildey. A former comic book artist, he was responsible for, among others, the mid-1960s Hanna-Barbera sci-fi series *Jonny Quest.* Wildey wrote the premise for all thirteen *Return* episodes. In this mapping-out process, he decided to take a different approach to the subjugated humans, who had often been a side-issue in previous Apes product. He told Russo, Landsman, and Gross, "My idea was they would be animals at the beginning and slowly evolve." This evolution comes about because of the arrival of the three sophisticated versions of their kind.

Larry Spiegel was the main one of the five writers chosen to bring Wildey's idea to life, penning six of the episodes, including the opening brace. Curtain-raiser "Flames of Doom" introduced the Simian Council that ran the society/country/world (by now, the aficionado understood that they're pretty much the same thing in Planet of the Apes fare). This parliament is discussing recent rumors that "humanoids" have learned how to talk. Gorilla General Urko (voiced by Henry Corden) wants humans exterminated. Chimpanzee behavioral scientist Cornelius (Corden and Edwin Mills) wants them captured and studied. In the absence of conclusive evidence, the council—led by orangutan Zaius (Richard Blackburn)—decrees that treatment of humans shall remain the same as it currently is (hunted for sport, used for menial labor, and kept as domestic pets) but that should proof of speaking abilities emerge they will be destroyed. The perils the astronauts face in the episode following the crash-landing of their ship are, though, not ape related but natural (a grueling desert trek) and supernatural (roving desert fireballs, the ground suddenly forming canyons). These sections are highly reminiscent of the oppressive scenes in the first movie when the astronauts are walking barren landscapes.

The trio are presented with their first clue that they are not on an alien world when they make contact with primitive humans. A young woman turns out to be wearing the dog tags of an astronaut named Brent, who was born a hundred years before the trio entered the space program. Humans can indeed speak and appear to have been doing so long enough to, if not have mastered conjunctions, give themselves names: the woman (also voiced by Nevins) explains that she is called

Nova. The humans scatter when they hear the approach of "borrogoss," their name for apes. When Hudson gets captured and taken to what is formally called "Ape City," it is revealed that these apes live in gleaming, sophisticated metropolises.

The astronauts encounter a disfigured group of humans called the Underdwellers. Although reminiscent of the Alpha-Omega mutants in the *Beneath* film, they worship not a bomb but a prophesized female savior named "Oosa," so called because of the letters *USA* at the base of a sculpture of her. In a neat twist, this bust is of Franklin, struck in her honor when back in the 20th-century Earth lost contact with her and her colleagues.

The series' semi-classy mash-up of Pierre Boulle's book, Arthur P. Jacobs's films, and the live-action TV series makes for an interestingly lateral addition to the Apes canon. However, *Return to the Planet of the Apes* has major, even fatal, faults. Some drawbacks simply go with the territory. The apes wield only large weaponry like tanks because the television authorities forbade the more logical rifles, handguns, or even blunt instruments on the grounds that they could provoke copycat behavior among the show's tender demographic. Similarly, we have to take on trust the fact that the Underdwellers have deformed faces because they are never seen lest they scare the watching kids. The fact that violence, the suggestion of violence, or the use of words like *death* were also verboten unavoidably contributes to a stilted aura.

Yet there are deficiencies unnecessary even in the context of 1970s kid stuff. The literature-savvy darkness is juxtaposed with childish buffoonery such as the sight of a simian version of the Mount Rushmore carvings, a reference to a playwright named William Apespeare, and the mention of a painting called the *Apa Lisa*. Urko wears a bright orange outfit and sometimes sounds like Fred Flintstone. The anger and bewilderment that the astronauts would have experienced at being flung beyond the lifespan of loved ones is barely touched upon. Perhaps only the more intelligent child would have recognized stuff like the latter, but few, however immature, would have been impressed by the artwork. The animation is very crude and flat, with only the background paintings exhibiting any luster. It's also almost laughably undynamic, often consisting of a slow parade of still illustrations. It being the case that animation constitutes a procession of images shown so quickly as to create the illusion of motion, this could almost be said to be anti-animation.

Return to the Planet of the Apes was transmitted on NBC starting on September 6, 1975. Wildey wanted a coda of three episodes in which the story lines were wrapped up to the extent that the humans' increasingly dexterous conflict strategies prompt the apes to engage in an uneasy truce with them. When the network rebuffed him, it saved him addressing the problem of how he was going to depict a pitched battle leading up to the truce if explicit conflict was out of the question.

While *Return to the Planet of the Apes* had its own novelizations, oddly they were all issued after the animated series had finished its run. Not that they should be assumed to be redundant. These three books marked a franchise first: Apes novelizations that were superior to their source material. Of course, this is a relative matter. However, it can be confidently stated that the authors made even more with slim pickings than had George Alec Effinger.

In contrast to the live action series' endless tie-ins, these books were the only merchandise specifically related to the DePatie-Freleng show.

This couldn't be readily discerned from their covers, however. The first volume, *Visions from Nowhere*, features not an animated-series character but Aldo from the *Battle* film; *Escape from Terror Lagoon* and *Man, the Hunted Animal* display scenes featuring Urko, Zaius, and Galen from the live-action Apes show, the first two of whom appear in the cartoon but in different iterations, the third of whom doesn't appear at all.

The franchise's books had now moved over from Award to Ballantine, who—though more prestigious—went the low-rent publisher route in deploying a pseudonymous house name to represent multiple authors, in this case William Arrow. Volumes 1 and 3 were actually the work of William Rotsler, and fellow rising SF prose star Donald J. Pfeil provided volume 2.

The books adapt episodes 1–9 sequentially, although that logical approach is somewhat undermined by the final four episodes being left unadapted. This time around, disparities between what is seen on screen and what is presented on the page are to do with something more than the writers having access only to scripts. That *Return* episodes were only a half-hour long was a big enough issue when it came to filling nearly two hundred pages, even though all the books adapted more than one episode, but there was an additional problem in that the television scripts themselves were aimed at younger children and, therefore, hardly weighty or wordy fare.

Rotsler tends to be more faithful in his representation of the episodes he is adapting while Pfeil opts for a more impressionistic approach. That there is indeed much slaughter is indicative of just how big a market existed for novelizations at the time. These *Return* books were no doubt often read by children, but it's doubtful that they were their intended audience: death by gunfire, crocodile, landslide, and blunt instrument is lasciviously recounted. Many kids would probably have enjoyed such stuff, but would have been turned off by the reams of dialogue added to pad out the narrative. Yet although filler in that sense, such material also constitutes an enrichening. In all three books, there is much ape-world history and detail—presented in both dialogue and authorial voice—not present in the show's episodes. Conversely, and oddly, chunks of the show's plots are sometimes jettisoned. Both writers include a character called Mungwort, a chimp/gorilla half-breed who is dismayed by the slaughter with which he is tasked. Although present in the series, he is never named therein.

As with the live-action show, the last novelization in this series is harder to find than the others. Also as with the live-action show, some Apes fans actually prefer the novelizations to the broadcasts they are based on.

Whatever its worn-out nature, that *Return to the Planet of the Apes* was commissioned at all demonstrated that there was still life in the Apes franchise. That was a fact, though, of which merchandise manufacturers were perfectly cognizant.

A legal tussle occurred in 1974 when Azrak-Hamray issued "Action Apeman" figures that did not feature the standard imprimatur notice "APJAC Productions." These generic clothed apes with rifles slung across their backs seemed to be the manifestation of grievances the company bore about being outbid for the franchise's action-figure license. The product clearly constituted passing off and provoked a joint lawsuit from Mego and 20th Century-Fox. Azrak-Hamway agreed to discontinue the product and pay damages.

Those who imagined that this suit constituted parties fighting on a battleground that was rapidly disappearing beneath their feet would have been mistaken. That Steve Clement article on Apes merchandise appeared in issue 25 of Marvel's magazine, cover-dated October 1976 (on the stands a couple of months before that). By this point, it had been more than three years since the release of the last Apes movie, two years since the flop of the live-action Apes TV series, and a year since the flop of its animated, small-screen successor. Yet when he conducted a trawl of two stores for Apes product, Clement in no way found that he was writing about a dying phenomenon. In a "large metropolitan department store," his exploration of the toy section aisles unearthed eighteen individual items. He then moved onto a "large inter-urban toy store." Besides carrying almost 90 percent of the items to be found in the previous store, this toy shop carried eighteen further individual pieces. Clement also pointed out that some merchandise wasn't available in stores but was readily purchasable via mail order. "There is still a terrific demand for Apes trademarked products," he concluded.

Like all crazes, though, it eventually did come to an end. "Probably late seventies," Christopher Sausville says. "That's when my age-group kind of headed toward high school, grew up a little bit, weren't into toys. Moved on to other stuff." By then, though, it had been comprehensively proven to movie studios that there was no limit to what would sell if it was branded with the logo and/or images of a popular movie or television show. "Apes merchandise was . . . the most profitable merchandising ever up until *Star Wars*," asserted Roddy McDowall to Russo, Landsman, and Gross. "It was gigantic; staggering." He could have added that its long-term effect on the entertainment industry was incalculable.

George Lucas—who was preparing *Star Wars* just as Western culture was in the grip of Apemania—certainly seems to have been taking notes. He successfully requested the merchandising rights to his movie series. It's said that he has made even more money from the tie-ins to the adventures of Luke Skywalker and company than he has from the films themselves.

The point when even the merchandise began to lose its commercial appeal marked a curtain for Planet of the Apes. The franchise gradually retreated from the public consciousness. There were of course sporadic movie showings at small theaters, television broadcasts of the films, syndicated reruns of the live-action series, and reprints of Boulle's novel, but it was now understood that this constituted "The Past." From the 1963 Boulle novel onward, the Planet of the Apes phenomenon had had a great dozen-year run, but it was clearly over.

12

MISSING LINKS

When in 1990 American publisher Malibu Graphics / Adventure Comics started a Planet of the Apes line, it seemed an odd juncture at which to revive the franchise, in this or any medium. That year was not far past the midway point in a twenty-five-year period in which new Planet of the Apes fare was entirely absent from screen media.

Rich Handley suspects that it was in fact due to the Apes franchise being moribund that the Malibu comics came about. "The license was probably not expensive," he says. "Planet of the Apes was largely a dead franchise. That probably was attractive to what was basically a young company." Another benefit of the fact that Planet of the Apes barely showed on the radar of 20th Century-Fox was the creative freedom experienced by Malibu's various writers, the most prominent of which was Charles Marshall. It's quite true that Marvel's Doug Moench never experienced interference from the studio, but times had changed, and rights owners were taking more seriously—and getting more proprietorial about—expanded-universe material. "In those stories they go in some truly unusual directions," Handley says of Malibu. "Things like having apes based on the Monkees, or apes based on American Indian tribes, or apes that speak Spanish. I'm actually a big fan of Malibu for that very reason. It has some duds along the way. I thought the Ape City mini-series set in Europe was kind of goofy. But for the most part, I thought that Malibu did a better job than people give it credit for. It's the forgotten stepchild of Apes comics."

Adding together their monthly title and various one-shots and miniseries, Malibu's Apes line lasted three years and a total of fifty-one issues. "Which was twenty more than what Marvel did," points out Handley. "So they were successful. I don't know who they were marketing to. I can remember ads in the back for what looked like comics aimed at kids, but at the same time they also had *Alien Nation* and that was not aimed at kids. So maybe they were going for an all-ages thing." The Malibu miniseries in which the worlds of Planet of the Apes and movie-turned-TV series Alien Nation came together was the first Apes franchise crossover of any kind, but by no means the last. (The first crossover could actually be said to be the *Apeslayer* strip, but only on the narrowest of technicalities: due to sloppy editing, several references survived to *Killraven* and hence the strip's H. G. Wells / *War of the Worlds* hinterland.)

Some of the franchise's fans might cite an additional plus-point about Malibu's efforts: for those three years, they were the only people in the world keeping the Planet of the Apes flag flying.

~

That for twenty-five years after 1975 there was no new Planet of the Apes screen media does not mean that no one was interested in creating such. The period was one in which Fox displayed occasional willingness to revive what had after all once been a huge moneymaker for them.

Moreover, filmmakers weaned on the franchise had now come of age and were keen to put their own stamp on the property.

At some point straddling the end of the 1970s and the beginning of the 1980s, another animated Apes TV series was proposed. Put forward by the Ruby-Spears production company, this one was based on the live-action show, logically enough considering that Joe Ruby and Ken Spears had written for it. The pair even took the trouble to commission concept art by famous Marvel Comics illustrator Jack Kirby. The specific reason that their efforts foundered is not known, but the instinctive assumption must be that such a blend of the two previous Planet of the Apes TV series—both failures—can't have seemed a prepossessing concept.

When it comes to the comatose Apes cinematic franchise, it wasn't until 1988 that it began displaying any fresh signs of life. This was the year that Fox—bought by Rupert Murdoch in 1985—invited Adam Rifkin to pitch ideas for a new movie. It was an odd choice. Rifkin is now a well-known writer-director but was then in the foothills of his career. Some of his ideas sound intriguing, including full-blown internecine warfare between the different ape species and an ape civilization modelled on the Roman empire. However, he doesn't seem to have had much of a grasp of the series' history. This sequel was to have depicted one Duke, son of Taylor and Nova, brought up by the exiled Cornelius after Taylor's execution by an ape dictator, with the adult Duke leading an uprising against the apes. This putative sequel to the 1968 film has to pretend that the events of *Beneath* never happened.

Nonetheless, Fox was sufficiently enthused to give the project a green light. Names like Tom Cruise and Charlie Sheen were said to be interested in playing Duke. Whether this would have made for an artistically or commercially successful venture was all rendered moot, though, by a change in the Fox top tier on the very cusp of shooting. The new regime was less simpatico, and amid recriminations about demands for rewrites, the project came to naught.

While some diehard Planet of the Apes fans won't have lost sleep over the demise of that project, many will have been caused "if-only" feelings by a putative Peter Jackson project. In 1992, the New Zealander wasn't yet the directorial behemoth he has since become, but the Apes treatment he pitched with Fran Walsh that year dripped with love for the franchise. He proposed what was essentially part 6 of the APJAC story line, and although it was to be set centuries after *Battle*, he was insistent that Roddy McDowall should play one of the simians. Admittedly, nobody outside the Jackson household or the Fox studios has ever seen this treatment, but few Apes fans would suggest that it doesn't sound promising. Sadly, though, it fell victim to yet another changing of the guard at Fox.

Another changing of the guard brought Peter A. Chernin to the top of the Fox tree. In 1993, he authorized Oliver Stone to executive-produce and cowrite a new Apes film. As writer-director, Stone was responsible for some of the most exciting and thoughtful cinema of that or any era, including *Platoon*, *Wall Street*, and *JFK*. Stone's chosen collaborator was Terry Hayes, the screenwriter responsible for transforming the Mad Max concept from a parochial and staid police revenge drama into a postapocalyptic phantasmagoria, itself notably similar to that of at least one Planet of the Apes film tableau. The result of this exciting combination turned out to be *Return of the Apes*, in which two scientists, discovering that deteriorating DNA constitutes a threat to mankind's existence, travel back in time to inject an evolution-changing cure into early humans, then find themselves stranded in the past in the midst of a war between man and talking apes.

The concept clearly doesn't have much in common with the premise of the previous Apes films and wasn't meant to. "I watched the original movies again a couple of nights ago, and they were *awful*," Stone announced at a production meeting. Even so, with Arnold Schwarzenegger set to star, for all we know the film may have turned out to be as exciting as Arnie-led SF projects like *Predator*, *The Terminator*, or *Total Recall*. However, all speculation about potential was once again rendered irrelevant by Fox pulling the plug, this time supposedly because the studio was worried that the picture would be too dark to be family friendly.

Schwarzenegger remained in the frame for male lead when it came to the next mooted Apes project, this one to be directed by Chris Columbus and written by Sam Hamm. In this script, mankind's existence is once again threatened by disease, but one that has been deliberately induced, and furthermore by apes. Said simians are the dominant species on a distant planet named Orbis Terrae. Noting that Earth has space programs, they are worried about the possibility of human contact. A group of Earth astronauts follow to its source the vessel that has brought plague to their world. Once they land, of course, the traditional Planet of the Apes fun starts. After that, a couple of the crew make it home only to discover that Earth is now run by simians. While the latter might be a twist straight out of Boulle, a strain straight out of the Seventies Apes cartoon is juvenile humor wherein Burger King becomes Banana King and *Penthouse* magazine *Apehouse*.

When in 1995 Fox rejected Hamm's ideas, Columbus departed the picture. James Cameron entered it the following year. His role was producer when most people would probably have preferred him to be director because of his fine work on *Aliens* and the Terminator franchise. A succession of putative directors slipped from Cameron's grasp. First was Roland Emmerich (*Independence Day*, *Godzilla*), who turned down his overture. Next was Peter Jackson, whose previous pitch was now back in favor but who declined to sign on because he felt his vision might be incompatible with that of Cameron and the still hovering Schwarzenegger. Peter Hyams (*Capricorn One*, *The Star Chamber*, *2010*) was next. When Fox nixed that choice, both Cameron and Schwarzenegger decided they'd spent enough time on this apparently permanently dormant project.

Fox commissioned a new screenplay from William Broyles Jr. Writer on the classy likes of *Apollo 13* and *Cast Away*, Broyles entered into his work with almost frightening zeal. In 1999, he submitted a first draft titled *The Visitor*, subtitled *Episode 1 of the Chronicles of Ashlar*. An accompanying twenty-page document went into fine detail about the relevant ape planet's culture and geography. His expansive vision, though, was to be only partially fulfilled.

"They were going through Cameron, all these directors, and then they faded out and finally Tim Burton came aboard," says Linda Harrison. As a consequence of attending a function at Fox's famous Commissary, the female lead in the very first Apes movie found that she had a ringside seat, and possibly a pivotal role, in the resuscitation of the franchise. "All these people wanted to have lunch with me and the head of the studio came over to me and shook my hand and said, 'We just hired Tim Burton to do the movie.' And I said, 'Well, I hope he gives me a part.'" It so happened that that evening Harrison attended a family birthday dinner at which were present her ex-husband Richard

D. Zanuck, the latter's wife Lili, and Zanuck and Harrison's two sons. Harrison related the Tim Burton anecdote to the gathering. She recalls, "Dick said, 'Well, did you tell him you were my wife?' I said, '*They* knew I was your wife.' The next day, the man that came over to see me called Dick and he said, 'We want you to come in as producer.' So somehow my boys think that meeting sealed his deal."

Since leaving 20th Century-Fox in 1970 in some rancor, Zanuck had switched professions from studio executive to independent producer. As such, he was now fulfilling the role Arthur P. Jacobs had on the original *Planet of the Apes* film. It was a pleasing piece of symmetry, perhaps the only major one possible in light of the fact of the impossibility of participation by either Jacobs or Roddy McDowall, the latter having passed away in 1998.

Tim Burton, the director with whom Zanuck was working, ordered wholesale changes to Broyles's script, so much so that the writer's original vision became yet another iteration of Planet of the Apes that exists only in an alternate reality. The important fact was, though, that the Planet of the Apes franchise's quarter-century coma was over.

13

EVOLUTION FALTERS

It tends to be forgotten now, but the retention of Tim Burton to bring Planet of the Apes out of that coma occasioned considerable excitement. To many SF-film fans, he was a god, having consistently and impressively helmed projects right up their alley including *Batman*, *Edward Scissorhands*, and *Sleepy Hollow*. Meanwhile, pertinent to those not necessarily into SF was the fact that Burton's stewardship of *Ed Wood*, biopic of the titular movie garbagemeister, indicated a facility with brushstrokes subtler than those seen in the aforesaid broadly drawn blockbusters. All that excitement, though, would ultimately turn into disappointment, some of it bitter.

The title *The Visitor* was jettisoned. Burton's simian film was given the exact same title as the 1968 *Planet of the Apes* lodestar picture. Remakes had been around since just after the dawn of cinema, but often their purpose was functional (i.e., silent movies being redone as talkies). In recent years, though, they had tended to inherit only a title and broad concept from the film they were supposedly based on. In the early twenty-first century, the word *reboot* hadn't quite yet crossed from computer terminology to motion picture parlance, so instead

Burton—or someone in his camp—invented for this Apes project the word *reimagining*.

Just as budgetary concerns lay behind some of the changes Michael Wilson wrought to Rod Serling's vision, so Broyles Jr.'s screenplay was subjected to an economy-minded polish by the team of Lawrence Konner & Mark Rosenthal, who had written *The Jewel of the Nile*, *Superman IV: The Quest for Peace*, *Star Trek VI: The Undiscovered Country*, and the 1998 remake of *Mighty Joe Young*. Despite this Apes film bearing no resemblance to the '68 picture, oddly—but not ungratifyingly—its credits would go out of their way to give a shout-out to the writers who kicked off the whole franchise, carrying as they do the line, "1968 *Planet of the Apes* theatrical motion picture adapted by Michael Wilson and Rod Serling."

Makeup artist Kazuhiro Tsuji was pleasantly surprised by a director who came with an enfant terrible weirdo reputation. "He was [a] nice person," he says of Burton. "I was expecting him to be much more eccentric, but he was pretty normal." Fellow makeup man Jamie Kelman was impressed by Burton's creativity. "It was a thrill to watch him pace around the set, all the wheels in his head spinning," he recalls. "He'd stop and silently look at something, get an idea, and have the entire shot changed and reframed." When Kelman saw the impressive Ape City set that Burton had commissioned, it seemed to auger well for the movie's quality. For a start, it was so big that Fox's own lot couldn't accommodate it. "It was built within the largest stage at Sony studios," explains Kelman. "We all worked there for a couple of weeks, and there was always more details to discover."

That the film begins with a pair of simian eyes opening to fill the screen with a malevolent stare serves notice that the franchise is returning to the days when apes were the villains. The narrative begins in 2029 with a deliberately disconcerting scene involving a space-suited chimpanzee piloting a ship. It transpires that this is just a test module and that the chimp is a baby named Pericles, one of many aboard the massive USAF space research station *Oberon*, which uses trained simians for flights. His handler is Captain Leo Davidson, who is significantly seen striding past a sign reading "Caution Live Animals." That Davidson is played by Mark Wahlberg is an odd, but subliminally quasi-logical piece of casting: Wahlberg himself has admitted that he has simian-like features.

The changes in Planet of the Apes land are not restricted to the fact that the hyphen is these days gone from what had been "20th Century-Fox." The film's outer-space scenes, for instance, demonstrate that technology has shifted profoundly in the twenty-eight years since the last Apes film. The non-ape special effects here—courtesy of Bill George—possess a seamless, utterly convincing beauty that make the matte paintings and back projections of the APJAC era seem almost prehistoric.

The *Oberon* is threatened by an electromagnetic storm. True to the station's policy of using apes as coal-mine canaries, Pericles is placed at the controls of a space pod that is sent to investigate. Contact is promptly lost. Davidson—a less-than-benign character, belligerent with his commanding officer and prone to teasing the apes by falsely offering treats—hotheadedly defies orders and launches a pod in pursuit of Pericles's craft. Although he briefly makes visual contact with the other pod, he loses it again. As his colleagues back on base receive a strange video mayday whose meaning is less clear than its tone of terror, Davidson's craft is buffeted by turbulence that sends it tumbling to an unknown planet. He has to hastily evacuate as the pod sinks to the bottom of a lake. No sooner has he escaped this peril than he is facing danger from far less explicable means. Raggedly dressed humans dash past him. They are being pursued via both tree branch and horseback by terrifying humanoid apes in quasi-battle dress and coned headgear.

The Burton film's ape makeup was the work of Rick Baker. "There was an early thought that they should be CG because that's the modern way of thinking," Burton admitted to journalist Mark Salisbury. "But Richard and I felt very strongly that part of the energy of this material is the good actors behind it." New York–born Baker had first come to wide attention in 1981 with *An American Werewolf in London*. The agonized transformation he engineered of lead character David Kessler from civilized human to long-fanged lycanthrope garnered him the inaugural regular Academy Award for Best Makeup. His apes in Hugh Hudson's 1984 Tarzan movie *Greystoke* were unnervingly lifelike and incredibly detailed (for instance, yellowed fangs on the elders). His work on *Gorillas in the Mist* (1988) is unlikely to have done him any harm either. Eddie Yang, part of Baker's Cinovation makeup crew on the 2001 *Planet of the Apes*, notes of Baker, "He is very well respected because he actually is such an accomplished artist himself. There are many people who hire other artists to do a bulk of the work, but Rick is just as excited about doing it himself and he always has such a great way of approaching a design. He has a very sharp eye and makes you kind of nervous when he views your work."

Kelman found that the director had firm ideas about the makeup. "I remember him coming to visit the trailer while I was making up his then girlfriend, Lisa Marie." The latter was playing the chimpanzee trophy wife of orangutan Senator Nado. "He quickly scribbled a drawing of what he wanted her facial hair to be like." The requirements for the female apes would in fact prove to be a rumbling issue during production. Yang recalls Helena Bonham Carter's makeup as Ari to be "quite a challenge." The director and producer had decided that this Apes film would be a departure from the franchise's tradition of male and female apes being mostly only distinguishable by their comparative heights and voice timbres. The fact that Burton's female apes have elaborate hairstyles instead of hair brushed uniformly back off their foreheads is merely the start of it. As Yang muses, "It is tough to take a chimp and make it look attractive, or even feminine for that matter." Tsuji: "I sculpted Helena's piece. . . . It was a hard issue. In the nature, female chimps get bald much faster than male. They don't look attractive at all." He recalls "a lot of different directions" being taken before the final distaff design was arrived at. "I didn't totally agree with that design. They even had eyebrows."

Tsuji was responsible for the design, sculpture, and application of the makeup for the seething chimpanzee character Thade. Initially, he wasn't too enamored by the casting of Tim Roth in the role. He recalls, "We begged the production to hire [an] actor with a small nose and they hired the actor with the biggest nose!" However, he says, "I think the design turned out good. He is a mean character, which enabled me to put more of a beast look to it. I also put this stylized hair on the ear to make it look pointy. [Roth] had these beautiful eyes that worked well with makeup. He is [an] amazing actor. He really made that makeup a lot better. He was really easy to do makeup on, too. He just slept during the makeup application. The biggest problem was the costume. It was so hot—he sweated a lot—so every day I tried a different way to apply the makeup so that it would last longer."

Cinovation member Mark Alfrey feels that pressure of time created less-than-optimum conditions. "Sculpting was taking place for several months before shooting began, but most of the sculpting was done for mid-range and background characters because the main cast was selected very late in production," he says. "By the time it came down to creating their makeups, the process felt a little rushed." However, Kelman insists, "Thanks to Rick Baker's high standards, time was not a pressure for me. I recall always having a proper amount of time." At the start of the shoot, the time frame for individual application of ape makeup was around four hours, but he says, "Most of us got it down to two and a half-hours by the middle of the show." He adds, "I found it to be a very happy set. Everyone felt they were working on something that would be special."

In some senses, Baker's crew were using the same techniques that prevailed in the days of John Chambers. Glues and paints may have been different, but it was still foam latex and human hair being applied. Fred Blau would no doubt have been the one most *au fait* with this. Having worked as Roddy McDowall's makeup man on the television series, he was also engaged on the new iteration. However, Kelman points out, "Makeup appliances have improved, especially now with silicone appliances. The foam latex in 2001 was so much better movement-wise than in 1968, because it wasn't Muppet mouths." In the APJAC films, camera angles had to take into account whether an ape actor's teeth would be visible beyond the choppers provided by makeup, even though said real teeth were painted black as a precaution. Yang: "The original had the teeth sculpted into the appliance, a few inches away from the actor's face, and having no independent lip movement. The ones done for the new film were actually the actor's lips stretched over dentures that pushed out the muzzle. This gave you movement in the [ape] lips, articulated by the actor's lips." Yang remembers that the transformation in voices caused by the dentures briefly became an issue. "They were going to re-dub," he says, "but Rick was saying that if they had large teeth like that, their voices would really sound the way it is."

Meanwhile, contact lenses had changed a great deal from those used in the original film. Makeup staffer Cristina Ceret notes, "They are soft now and can stay in the eye much longer than before. Back then, the actor could only wear the lens for eleven, twelve hours and then [they] came out for one hour to rest the eye. Not very practical for movie making."

Another important difference was a greater variety in background ape faces, a legacy of a young Baker having been puzzled by the sameness of appearance of the franchise's nonspeaking simians.

Once the makeup artists had finished their work, the actors themselves added the final element. Alfrey points out, "The makeups were foam latex but they were quite thin and soft. Each actor spends time in front of a mirror gauging how well his acting shows through and compensates."

The upshot of all this was makeup on another plateau to that seen in the original quintet. In the APJAC films, there was always a suspicion of plastic rigidity to the ape muzzles and often a feeling that viewers looking hard enough might see artificial hairlines. Baker's apes look so real that they make the viewer aware of the fact that every previous Apes vehicle was to a small extent predicated on a gentleman's agreement between filmmaker and audience whereby minor deficiencies are overlooked. His simian faces move utterly fluidly and naturally, while his fur looks completely genuine, not least because it constitutes an entire gamut of condition, including greying, molting, and receding. For those who imagine that this observation is intended as a putdown of John Chambers and colleagues, it should be noted that Baker was working in a period equidistant between the primitive-ish makeup techniques of the first films and the methods of computer-generated imagery (CGI), which have dispensed with prosthetics almost completely. No doubt Baker's efforts will in time seem, like those of Chambers, impressive but limited.

Complementing Baker's effects is the fact that much attention has been paid to a fully rounded depiction of simians. Although the convincing representation of humanoid apes was taken seriously enough in the original quintet that the actors walked in a stooped and bowlegged manner and occasionally interspersed their dialogue with hoots, chatters, and snarls, by the twenty-first century filmmakers could step up the realism, partly because a modern studio wasn't going to baulk or even laugh at the idea that actors should go to ape school. The Burton film's simian cast were given expert, six-week-long instruction in how real apes behave. Demonstrating both that modern creators think through more thoroughly the logic of the universe they are creating and that there are far fewer technological barriers to fulfilling their ambitions, these apes don't only walk but also bound at high speed on all fours, swing agilely from tree branches, and leap onto high objects when frightened. They are also quad-handed, employing their lower extremities as comfortably as their higher ones as they perform tasks like writing letters, playing cards, or handling weapons. Gorilla teenagers beat their breasts, and chimpanzees *umph* in the faces of people with whom they're arguing. Nor do the ape voices sound merely like human tones transposed to an ape, but rather rumble from deep inside chests the way that one imagines talking simians' would. The apes also project an immense power and presence. For the viewer to observe their dense, looming, growling forms is to instantly understand why they have dominance over the planet's smaller, hairless apes.

As with all previous Apes adaptations, the simian species are restricted to chimpanzees, orangutans, and gorillas, although Alfrey does reveal, "There were designs for a rogue gang of baboons, but that idea was dropped." However, the demarcations among the species set by Boulle, and hitherto always previously adhered to in adaptations, no longer apply. The hunter apes whose appearance so startles Davidson are both gorillas and chimpanzees. While the orangutans remain non-combatants, they are not the high-minded types of previous movies: it transpires that the slaver who buys the hunters' human bounty is an orangutan, while Bornean orangutan Senator Nado oozes decadence. The different ape species also intermarry.

It's not just the apes that are properly thought through but also the world they inhabit. Although once again there is no sense of this being a "planet" (are there other countries? continents? cities?), detail is not otherwise compromised by expediency. The apes live in stone and wood buildings, but ones that have vines and branches running through them. Moreover, there is none of the technological inconsistency of the movies where preindustrial apes had somehow developed guns: here, the apes' most intricate weapon is a starfish-shaped flying blade.

On the minus side, whereas the first two films' cast of characters was well balanced between villainous firebrands, temperate goodies, and Machiavellian schemers, a disproportionate number of Burton's apes simply seem like variations on Ursus. Vicious gorilla soldier Colonel Attar (Michael Clarke Duncan) is hardly counterpointed by his simmering commanding officer General Thade, a military man with designs on both power and the affections of the senator's daughter Ari, and whose hatred of humans is so deep that he is incandescently angry if one so much as looks at him. Things are not exactly helped by over-acting. Tim Roth's screen debut was on British television in 1982 when he played skinhead Trevor. He seems to be invoking Trevor's thuggish ghost in a grimacing, hoarse-voiced performance for which the description "hamming it up" seems inadequate.

At the quarter-hour mark, Burton gets out of the way the inevitable in-joke when Davidson—at the moment of his capture—grabs the ankle of Attar and is met with the response, "Take your stinking hands off me you damn dirty human!" Of course, it would have been symmetrically perfect if this line had been delivered by an ape played by Charlton Heston. However, Heston does appear—briefly, uncredited, but powerfully—as Thade's sickly father. (His name—in the mash-up tradition of Apes adaptations—is Zaius. Nado's trophy ape wife, incidentally, goes by Nova.) Heston gets a line of equal resonance for long-term Apes fans. "Damn them!" he says of humans. "Damn them all to hell!" Heston's leading lady from the 1968 film makes an even briefer appearance, Linda Harrison wordlessly playing "Woman in Cart."

Among those captured with Davidson are Karubi (Kris Kristofferson, largely wasted in a small role). Karubi has a blond, center-parted hairdo similar to that of his daughter Daena (Estella Warren), even if the latter has a blue-eyed, pert-lipped beauty that contrasts to his grey beard and grizzled mien. The captured humans are taken to trader Limbo, a sleazy, peeling proposition played by Paul Giamatti. Limbo's avarice and cowardice provide the film's comic relief. Its conscience is offered by Ari, a chimpanzee who leads (or possibly constitutes) a human rights movement, whose title is literal. Bonham Carter's incongruous and illogical English accent is, of course, another Apes tradition. (Roth somehow manages to sound neutral.)

As in the TV series, the humans are subjugated but can talk and reason. Humans are hot-branded by apes, but their slave status—and the casual cruelty done to them—is demonstrated even more horrifically when teams of men are shown pulling carriages even though the apes have domesticated horses. Layering is added to the notion of the services humans provide apes when it is revealed that they sew the simians' clothes. (It would have been superb if someone had thought to state that this is because of the fully opposable thumbs issue.) When Ari disrupts the branding process of the new arrivals, Davidson implores her to help him. An exchange follows that runs, "This one seems different" / "How could he be different? You can't tell one from the other." While that is a reasonably agile way of inserting another Apes tradition/in-joke, it's shortly followed by a disappointingly clumsy piece of dialogue when Davidson demands of Daena, "How the hell did these monkeys get like this?" and she replies with the hackneyed, non-naturalistic "What other way would they be?"

The film's fast pace is exhilarating. However, it sometimes backfires, for instance, the absurdly quick and easy way that Davidson breaks the lock on his cage. When he frees Daena too and she insists that they must rescue her family, the process by which they do so feels less like a terrifying venture into unknown, hostile territory than a stroll in the park crossed with taking candy from a baby. The escapees enlist Ari's help to guide them out of the city. In return, Davidson promises to show her something that will change her world forever, a reference to his spaceship and its technology. That it hasn't properly been established yet that apes don't have such technology is another example of the drawbacks of fast pacing.

General Krull is a former soldier reduced by Thade's vindictiveness to servant status in the household of Senator Sandar, Ari's father. Krull throws in his lot with the escapees, although remains ambivalent about the worth of human life. His equidistance between belligerence and thoughtfulness is perfectly conveyed by Cary-Hiroyuki Tagawa, whose white-eyed glowering is actively disconcerting. The character is also employed to address the issue of the *m*-word. *Monkey* is used indiscriminately by the ape handlers on the *Oberon*, who might be expected to know better. Just as the viewer is lamenting the ignorance of the screenwriters, however, the matter is clarified in a quite perfect way. Davidson reflects to Krull, "Talking monkeys can't exist." Krull pounces on him to issue the snarling correction: "*Apes*. Monkeys are further down the evolutionary ladder—just above humans!" It's far more logical than Cornelius's implication in *Escape* that the misuse of the *m*-word is a long-standing ape grievance.

Davidson takes the party to the lake in which his craft sank, much to the whimpering consternation of Ari, who is shown as being afraid of bodies of water, as indeed apes—dense-boned and nonbuoyant—are in real life. Davidson retrieves from his ship a kit bag containing various gizmos including a gun and a device to contact his ship. The group is tracked down by Limbo, anxious about his "property." The orangutan ends up a reluctant member of their party.

Thade visits his dying father who tells him that in the "time before time" apes were the slaves and humans their masters. Zaius counsels his son that he must not let the humans get to the forbidden area known as "Calima," which holds the secret to the apes' true beginnings. This scene should have taken place before one wherein Thade kills two gorillas who take him to where forest branches bear evidence of the descent of Davidson's pod. The chimpanzee's desire to silence them doesn't quite make sense without him being told how dangerous humans are. Come to think of it, the Zaius scene should also have been used to provide a justification for Thade's hatred of humans, which seems to have no logical root.

Disturbing-looking scarecrows line the way to Calima, placed there by apes to scare humans off the sacred area. Calima is exalted because it's the site where the Almighty supposedly breathed life into the fabled first ape Semos, who in turn created all apes in his image. The "Holy Writings" state that Semos will one day return to this place to bring peace to his children. Davidson, though, is heading for the area because his device tells him that it's the whereabouts of his crew, who have clearly come to look for him.

What he finds is devastating. The remains of the crash-landed *Oberon* are thousands of years old. Davidson's pod had been pushed forward through time by the electromagnetic storm. As the *Oberon* had only ventured into the storm to look for Davidson, it means that he is responsible for its crew's fate. There are further revelations. The site's name transpires to derive from the now partially obscured sign previously glimpsed on the *Oberon* ("CAution LIve aniMAls").

Davidson glumly charges up the ship's power source—being nuclear it lasts for an approximate forever—to access its visual log. It yields a message made by the *Oberon* crew after the research station landed on what was an uncharted and uninhabited planet. The message relays the fact that their apes were a lot smarter and stronger than they imagined. Led by one named Semos, they have gone out of control and attacked them. This is the same panic-stricken video that the *Oberon* crew had seen when the storm had originally hit, only then it was being flickeringly bounced back through time.

The apes that dominate this planet, Davidson realizes, are the descendants of the ones that rebelled on the *Oberon*. It naturally follows that the world's humans are the successors of the *Oberon* crew. This would certainly explain why everyone speaks English, although it hasn't occurred to Davidson to wonder. In this film it doesn't feel like an issue: his character is such a knucklehead that he would probably think nothing of it.

Chatter has spread about the man who is defying the apes. Humans congregate at the forbidden area wishing to throw in their lot with Davidson. Meanwhile, at the campsite of the pursuing ape army, Thade viciously rejects Ari's overtures after she debasingly offers herself up in return for the safe passage of the humans. Davidson blows up the fuel cell of his ship in order to incinerate the first wave of ape soldiers and unnerve the remainder. He then leads the newly assembled human army in attack. Allegiances change on the battlefield. Krull follows in Limbo's footsteps by joining forces with the hairless apes. Ari saves Daena's life, and the latter, noticing the brand that Thade has spitefully burned into her hand, drops her previous hostility.

Just as Thade is about to dispatch Davidson, a mysterious bang emanates from the sky, followed by the descent of a pod just like the one Davidson arrived in. It's Pericles, thrown forward in time like his master. To all the apes present, though, an ape in a flying craft descending to Calima can only be the promised Second Coming of Semos. Their awe only lasts until the point when Davidson explains to them that the real Semos destroyed the peace that once existed between ape and man and makes them realize that everything they ever believed in is untrue.

Not only are humans and apes now at peace, but Davidson has—courtesy of the pod's unexpected arrival—a way of getting off this upside-down world. He says his farewells to Daena, but the scene has no real resonance as feelings have not been established between the two of them but, rather, between Davidson and Ari. It has been implied that the latter rescued Davidson from the slaver because she had the hots for him. Their meaningful glances culminate in Davidson kissing Ari on the lips as he hands her Pericles and climbs into his ride home. It's all the culmination of an unmistakable thread of bestiality running throughout the franchise starting with similar scenes between Mérou and Zira in the Boulle novel and continuing through such things as an ape-human hybrid child proposed (and makeup tested) at the planning stages of *Beneath* and the live-action TV series episode "The Deception" in which a blind female chimpanzee falls in love with Burke.

Finding the coordinates of the storm that brought him here, Davidson plunges into it. He gets back to planet Earth in an apparent five minutes, which is handy considering the small amount of oxygen such a miniscule craft could possibly hold. He crash-lands in Washington, DC, adjacent to the Lincoln Memorial. His unexpected arrival prompts the scrambling of police. The cops who level their guns at him across the hoods of their squad cars are all simian. The memorial, it turns out, is not for the sixteenth president but for General Thade. This climax is largely redolent of Boulle, albeit with an element of the original film's ending in the inclusion of a piece of iconographic American stone.

It comes across as a finale with no rhyme or reason other than smart-aleckry. Nonetheless, it doesn't detract too much from the picture. It would be easy to quibble that it would have been preferable if the apes on the *Oberon* had been shown to be treated more cruelly than merely being subjected to Davidson's mild teasing: his colleague's advice that pretending he has food in his hand makes them "confused, even violent" is hardly the stuff to lead to bloody rebellion. One could also complain about the plot being bereft of the sort of philosophical and sociopolitical subtexts found in the previous films: this is a slam-bang action-adventure movie with only token interest in such high-falutin' stuff. Overall, though, Burton's *Planet of the Apes* is an enjoyable, breathless romp.

It's also underrated. Media critics panned it. Hard-core fans of the franchise hate it. For his part, Rich Handley says, "The human characters, right across the board, were really boring. When you watch the original movies, Taylor and Brent and Hasslein and the MacDonald brothers, you can relate to them. You can watch the movie and you become interested in what are these characters going through. There's not a single human character in the Burton film that I gave a shit about."

Certainly, some of the film's crew were left wondering what had happened to their initial high hopes and optimistic feelings. Mark Alfrey reflects, "I went in thinking it would be an exciting event and I left feeling like it was just another job. The finished film was a disappointment." Kelman identifies what he feels is a flaw in Burton's abilities. Pointing to the disparities in the results achieved in the likes of *Edward Scissorhands* and *Sleepy Hollow* compared to *Mars Attacks* and *Planet of the Apes*, et al., he offers, "It seems like Tim Burton handles a town-sized movie better than a whole global world-sized movie." He adds, "I think the approach was all wrong anyway. They didn't say anything new. The context of the times of the sixties was so tumultuous, there was so much to say. Our remake felt hollow because it was just rushed corporate product."

Yet for all its detractors, both inside and outside the production, the two-hour film—released on July 27, 2001—was a commercial success, the eighth most successful picture of the year domestically, the ninth worldwide. With a budget of $100 million and $368 million in takings, it had without question economically justified a sequel. Some detractors like to believe that the lack of a follow-up is a sign of the power of the disapproval of fandom, but in fact it seems to be down to lack of enthusiasm on the part of Burton.

"I couldn't give a shit about sequels," Burton told Salisbury. His antipathy to follow-ups may have been accentuated by his Planet of the Apes experience. His issues with the project included his budget suddenly being reduced, the bad taste left in his mouth by the allegations (which he insists were false) that he had an on-set affair with Bonham Carter who later became his wife, and the fact that—as he admitted—he was more intrigued by the concept of the film than the actuality of it. "It's the first project I've been involved with where I knew it was . . . not a mistake as such, but that it was the most dangerous," he said. That danger, articulated to Salisbury, was disobeying an old maxim: "Don't try to remake a classic. If you're going to remake something, pick something that was bad, so you can make it better."

It's widely rumored that both Roth and Bonham Carter did not want to do a new film if Burton wasn't involved as director. Whatever the truth, the long-awaited revival of the Planet of the Apes franchise was dead in its tracks.

Although the Cinovation team express little enthusiasm for the finished film, there is almost universal disgust among them that the picture failed to garner even an Oscar nomination for its stunning makeup, let alone an award. Alfrey offers, "They probably didn't think it was innovative. Admittedly, the process was standard practice. Nothing new." His colleagues are less philosophical. Kelman views the situation as "a plain travesty." He has strong opinions as to the whys and wherefores. "There was a real Rick Baker backlash at that time," he asserts. Baker had by now picked up six Academy Awards, plus three nominations. "All the other makeup people were tired of being ignored. But the fact of the matter is that . . . you can't compete with that level of incredible quality and large scale that Rick provides every time. I literally heard people involved with the Academy saying, 'Enough with the rubber heads already! How about paying attention to some real makeup!' Of course, this is a ridiculous statement, but there are plenty of makeup artists who don't or can't do prosthetics who would love to win a Best Makeup Oscar for a nicely applied beauty makeup. So many people have no clue how far beyond lipstick and blush a job like *Planet of the Apes* goes. Rick is a master-level artist. A bunch of petty, lesser makeup applicators who don't classify as artists will never be able to take that from him."

After 1976, Planet of the Apes books, like their parent screen action, went into a long hibernation. During that hibernation, the market for them changed beyond recognition.

In the new millennium, recording of TV broadcasts was now technologically, financially, and legally possible for the mass of the public. Moreover, many motion pictures were available to rent or buy on video cassette and its successor DVD. Added to that, movies now appeared on television after a considerably shorter time than they previously had.

Consequently, people weren't much interested anymore in the "Book of the Film." In the year of the release of Burton's *Planet of the Apes* film, the *New York Times* was reporting that "only about two dozen movies are novelized each year."

Yet while the reverse-adaptation market may have shrunk, it had also expanded sideways. Nineteen eighty-four saw the first novelization of a video game. There also came the growth of Junior/Young Readers novelizations, which were sometimes published side by side with the adult equivalent. On top of that were original stories taking place in the fictional world of the relevant intellectual property. This type of "same universe" story had been popularized by Bantam's "New Star Trek Adventure" series inaugurated by James Blish's *Spock Must Die!* (1970) and, although originally intended merely as a self-contained moneymaker, became an important plank in a strategy to keep the public interested in a property when it wasn't currently in theaters or on TV screens. Moreover, the reverse-adaptation market was centered on science fiction, whose fans tended to invest more (emotionally and financially) in a property than "general" audiences and often bought novelizations as much to satisfy their completist impulses as to obtain aesthetic pleasure. Accordingly, then, the Planet of the Apes library continued to grow.

William T. Quick—author of the acclaimed cyberpunk/nanotechnology *Dream Trio* (1988–1990)—was commissioned to both novelize the Broyles Jr./Konner/Rosenthal script of the Burton film and to write two novels exploring backstory discussed or alluded to in it. Quick's two Apes prequels are actually more highly regarded than his rather perfunctory novelization. Partly, this wasn't his fault: his book of the film doesn't have the shock "Ape Lincoln" ending because the secretive

Burton refused to make available that information. However, it's also partly because he commits the cardinal sin of repeatedly choosing to use in his authorial voice the term *monkeys*, and this despite the script's explicit denunciation of the term. He also too often lunges for omniscience when the good novelization merchant understands that the format frees him to represent individual points of view. Moreover, he writes rather pulpily ("Across the buttons . . . a long hairy finger! Tap. Tap-tap. Tappity-tappity-tap! Digital patterns, a web, a path across the stars. Tap-*tap*!").

The Quick prequels are another matter. "They were such well-written novels," says Rich Handley. "They were the story of the USS *Oberon* and how it crashed. They take place after Leo Davidson has departed. So Mark Wahlberg's character is not in it, but the rest of the crew is and they're excellent. Those novels far outshone the light of the movie."

Released simultaneously with Quick's novelization of Burton's *Planet of the Apes* film was a junior novelization by John Whitman. Whitman also wrote two junior prequel novels, *Force* and *Resistance*, which were wrapped in child-friendly brightly colored covers. While such a multimarket approach might seem a shrewd idea, its success in this instance seems to have been limited. Two further books in the junior series—*Planet of the Apes: Rule* by J. E. Bright and *Planet of the Apes: Extinction* by Whitman—were cancelled before publication.

When it comes to the other main reverse-adaptation market, Dark Horse secured the license for comic books based on Burton's film. Following both an adaptation of the 2001 movie (*sans* the shock ending that Burton kept to himself) and miniseries *The Human War*, the company embarked on a monthly title set two decades after the film. The latter featured General Thade's evil granddaughter and depicted a search for Ari, who had gone missing. The first three issues were written by Ian Edginton, the next three by Dan Abnett. "It was excellent," says Handley, adding, "It got cut short." Although Burton's movie did as well as Dark Horse would have naturally hoped, as with the novels, not many people seem to have left the cinema thinking that they needed to know more about its universe.

Dark Horse was also responsible for another crossover in the form of miniseries *Tarzan on the Planet of the Apes*, a collaboration with Boom! Studios. A five-parter written by Tim Seeley & David F. Walker and drawn by Fernando Dagnino, it depicted *Escape*-era Cornelius, Zira, and Milo traveling back not to the United States in the 1970s but to late nineteenth-century Africa, where they discover a young white boy—Tarzan—whom they adopt and bring up as the stepbrother of their son Caesar.

Dark Horse's publishing campaign was ultramodern and multiplatform, their cumulative twenty issues including a Toys 'R' Us Collector's Comic, a serialized comic strip in *Dark Horse Extra*, and an e-comic (*Planet of the Apes Sketchbook*). Most physical issues were published with multiple covers.

Books and comics—and, come to that, film—were old media. There was a new kind on the block.

The Planet of the Apes Chad Valley Picture Show Sliderama Projector is a piece of Apes media that defies categorization. A 1975 product, it constituted a plastic projector that came with 224 color slide pictures on sixteen film strips. Each strip contained two stories (creatives uncredited) adapting episodes from the TV series (although, oddly, the tribunal scene from the first movie also featured). Another uncategorizable product from the Apemania era is the Planet of the Apes audio tales released by Power Records, the same company responsible for comic book and LP adaptations of four of the movies. The audio tales came on seven-inch, 45 rpm records and provided three completely new story lines featuring the characters from the live-action TV series. A fourth was added for an LP compilation.

In the 1970s, the idea of a product with an in-built light that threw a sequence of still pictures onto a bedsheet or of listening to audio adventures of characters normally seen in filmed media were intrinsically exciting. They provided a way to revisit a film or TV series at will in the absence of any other method. They are products, though, that could only have been appreciated by youngsters who never knew a world where every household had access to computer technology. In other words, they have been rendered comical and obsolete by video games. It should be stressed, though, that Planet of the Apes video games specifically have had a difficult, halting history.

A far less communal experience than cinema and disproportionately consumed by the young, video games sometimes resemble a secret annex of the entertainment industry. However, they are vastly profitable, and tie-in games sometimes more so than the cinema property of which they are nominally the ancillary merchandise. In an arresting contrast to the franchise's pioneering in other areas of merchandising, Planet of the Apes has rarely succeeded in exploiting this vast new revenue source.

Things got off to a bad-cum-false start on this score in the shape of the *Planet of the Apes* video game intended for the Atari 2600. It depicts Taylor evading orangutans and gorillas (chimpanzees are neutral presences) across landscapes like ape villages, forests, rivers, deserts, and caverns. His objective is the Statue of Liberty, which oddly here serves as a sanctuary, at least in the sense that reaching it completes the game. That the product was scheduled for release in 1983 during Planet of the Apes' quarter-century hiatus indicated a touching faith in the franchise's viability. However, it was all for nothing because a crash in the industry that year led to the game's cancellation.

It's a sign of the speed of the evolution of video games—even faster, you might say, than the development of simians between the third and fourth APJAC Apes movies—that when in 2002 the abandoned Atari *Planet of the Apes* was rediscovered by games enthusiasts on a mislabeled cartridge, nobody could initially work out what it was. It consisted of pixelated matchstick figures doing battle on a sideways-scrolling screen to the sonic backdrop of the tinny bloops and plasticky explosions familiar from the era's arcades. It could have been anything. Even allowing for the fact that programmer John Marvin had only developed the game to the prototype stage, it was a sobering reminder that, until embarrassingly recently, video games operated on a pitiful gentleman's agreement whereby the consumer bought into the idea that what they were playing was connected to a particular franchise simply on the basis of the title and the box it came in.

For what can only have been nostalgia's sake, in 2003 the company Retrodesign licensed the rights to issue the rediscovered *Planet of the Apes* game. Perhaps significantly, its name was changed to *Revenge of the Apes*, and the cover illustration was dominated not by a simian but a rifle-toting human. By now, video gameplay had progressed through sideways scrolling, platform, first person, and first-person shooter. It could also encompass one player or multiples of players. Meanwhile, the visuals had been transformed from a bunch of garish, four-color pixels to something approaching cinema-level realism. Fox presumably didn't want the embarrassment of overt association with the creaking, outmoded technology seen in the Atari 2600 game.

In any case, a video game titled *Planet of the Apes* had been released by UbiSoft on multiple platforms across 2001 and 2002. Visiware was the developer for the PC and PlayStation iterations, Torus Games for Game Boy Advance and Game Boy Color. The release date was dictated by the Burton film, but the game and movie were unconnected: the developers had been working in preparation for a James Cameron picture. However, there seem to be few clues as to what Cameron's take on the franchise would have been as the ninety-minute game seems narratively modelled on Boulle's novel (the central character's name is Ulysses) and sartorially on the APJAC films (its characters are clothed in the style of the Jacobs quintet). Already a misbegotten, redundant product, the single-player, third-person, action-adventure game did not take good advantage of the latest technology, lacking pace and intuitive gameplay, and was as poorly received as the film to which it was theoretically linked.

The quarter-century wait for the resuscitation of Planet of the Apes had resulted in a derided film, compromised book and comic tie-ins, and a mediocre video game. The future for the franchise in the new millennium looked rather bleak.

14

IF AT FIRST YOU DON'T SUCCEED . . .

Although the Planet of the Apes film franchise entered another hiatus after the Tim Burton effort, this time it didn't last a quarter of a century. More important, when the phoenix ascended from the ashes it remained in glorious flight. *Rise of the Planet of the Apes* (2011) was a critical and commercial success that inaugurated a new Apes film series that took both special effects and believability to new heights.

Before that, there came a modest but worthy amount of activity surrounding the franchise when, in late 2005, Metallic Rose Comics (Mr. Comics) entered into the Apes picture. The American publisher only released six issues, but for Rich Handley the contents' narrative arc shares with Doug Moench's "Quest for the Planet of the Apes" the status of his favorite-ever Apes comics story, and for the same reason: it came off "like the lost movie." The miniseries *Revolution on the Planet of the Apes*, mainly written by Ty Templeton, revived the characters from the original quintet. It took place between the events of *Conquest* and *Battle* but showed the story that the films never depicted: the rise of the ape society following the Caesar-inspired revolution. Each issue was divided between the main ongoing story arc and backup stand-alone same-universe tales. Along the way, it sought to find rationales for discrepancies in the APJAC films. "It made sense out of things that didn't make sense," says Handley. "Like how is it that the apes in *Conquest* are suddenly so much smarter than modern apes that they can do things like take your order at a restaurant or shine shoes or find books at a store or prepare your hair for a hairstylist? *Revolution* has an interesting explanation for it, which is that it plays off the idea that Caesar is divinely inspired, which is something we're told in the other movies, but it also plays off the whole idea at the end of *Conquest* that tomorrow the same thing will be playing out on the other continents for the same reason an emperor moth can reach other moths from miles away. Caesar somehow seems to have affected, by his very presence, all apes. That's the reason the apes start looking at him as he passes and suddenly have this desire to rebel. I love that idea."

That would certainly appeal to someone who views such things through the prism of a pronounced interest in continuity, but Handley emphasizes, "I think it's an extremely well-drawn comic. . . . It was one of the most fascinating things ever done in comics. It's cinematic in a way that Apes comics often are not."

Sadly for fans of the series, MR went out of business and a planned sequel, *Empire on the Planet of the Apes*, never appeared.

Rise of the Planet of the Apes was the first production by Peter Chernin, previously most well known as president and chief operating officer of News Corporation and as chairman and CEO of the Fox Group. In 2017, Chernin explained to Daniel Loria of Box Office Pro, "I always felt that out of all the classic sci-fi franchises, Apes was the one that lent itself best to an update because its social message remains extremely timely. Ironically, I ran Fox some years back, and it was one of the first films I started to develop. . . . Ultimately, the version that eventually made it on-screen a number of years later was the one directed by Tim Burton. I came back to the project around 2009, developing a script with Rick Jaffa and Amanda Silver."

Jaffa & Silver were the second husband-and-wife team to work on the Apes series after *Battle*'s John & Joyce Corrington, with the societal changes wrought by the intervening passage of time reflected in the fact that it was no longer considered de rigueur for a woman to take her spouse's name. Jaffa-Silver also acted as producers, along with Chernin and Dylan Clark. (By now, Pierre Boulle's credit is reduced to his book having "suggested" the "premise.")

In 2011, Jaffa & Silver spoke to Zaki Hasan of the *Huffington Post*. "Rick had cut out these articles that fascinated him about chimps being raised as humans in homes," said Silver. "And what invariably happens in all these instances is that the chimp grows into an aggressive, powerful animal and things go awry. . . . The chimp is always put . . . in some sort of facility and traumatized by that. . . . He had that crazy lightbulb epiphany, and he said, 'Oh my God, this is a great way to reboot *Planet of the Apes*.'" Of the overture to Fox, Jaffa explained, "They were not looking to reinvent or re-present *Planet of the Apes*. But the reaction to the pitch was very, very strong. . . . A lot of people got pretty excited right off the bat. 'Oh, wow, this is something new, and it's original,' and so let's take a shot."

The identity of the person given the job of directing the resurrection of the Apes franchise was unexpected, even though Rupert Wyatt was in the parlance of his native United Kingdom a "likely lad"—a young man of obvious potential. Born in 1972, he had directed and cowritten the acclaimed 2008 prison-breakout movie *The Escapist*, which, he modestly notes, "had done quite well at Sundance." However, recognition at that prestigious film festival didn't make an independent filmmaker with a limited curriculum vitae an obvious candidate for helming the resurrection of a multimillion-dollar franchise. "I was very surprised," Wyatt admits of his appointment by Chernin Entertainment to helm what was then titled *Caesar: Rise of the Apes*, although adds, "It didn't come out of nowhere."

Wyatt decamped to Los Angeles to reap the professional dividends of the reception to *The Escapist*. "For a lot of Hollywood producers, I was quite appealing 'cos they knew that I was able to tell a cohesive genre story and do so in an economical way. So I was one of the early first-time directors who then make this big step into studio filmmaking." Not that Wyatt was snatching the hand off every major that offered him a project. "*Sherlock Holmes* had come my way. I wanted to alter the script quite radically. That was my first lesson. Studio filmmaking, 'specially with younger directors, they like to separate 'church and state': screenplay and the actual directing. So it became clear to me that that film was going to be made with a script that I didn't necessarily envisage. So that didn't work out. So I started to read other scripts." Wyatt developed a relationship with Peter Kang, an executive at 20th Century Fox who'd liked *The Escapist* and who showed him the Jaffa/Silver script for the prospective new Apes movie. "I loved it. I thought the story was just terrific. So I threw my hat in the ring. But I came from the perspective of, 'I'm one of fifty.' . . . It was a long process of audition and meetings. There was a gradual whittling down of contenders . . . Tom Rothman, who ran Fox at the time . . . and Peter Chernin I think saw me as somebody that knew how to focus on aspects of stories such as in my first film. That was the bedrock of the Apes story in many ways: escape from the sanctuary. So Peter became a champion. He essentially was the one that persuaded Fox. Everyone had concerns that I was going to be able to pull it off, but Peter Chernin really put his weight behind me." However, even when this hurdle was cleared, it was still not entirely clear that the film would be made. "We had to go through a three-, four-month development process. Start working with Weta, get the budget to the right level, all of that."

Wyatt says he'd watched the previous Apes films when growing up but wasn't a fanatic. "So coming on to it, it allowed me to get much deeper into the mythology than I had before." Said mythology was being added to by the fact that the Jaffa-Silver script had an intriguing conceptual aspect. "Their plan from the get-go was to tell an origin story of sorts." The effect of this approach—using a contemporary time frame to create a segue into the narrative of the APJAC films—meant a reversal of the apes-as-villains premise proffered the last two times the movie franchise had commenced. "The draft that we started work on [was] very much Caesar's story. . . . That was key for me because then to be able to explore all of the contemporary aspects of society that evokes—whether it be the civil rights movement, whether it be animal vivisection, whether it be any notion of oppression or apartheid or anything like that—was a story that I was really fascinated with telling."

The fact of Wyatt not being a believer in the separation of creative churches and states meant that adding to and reshaping the mythology was something of which he was actively a part. "Rick and Amanda wrote the screenplay. I read their draft. We then shaded it and restructured it, created aspects. Created scenes like when Caesar drew the window of his home in chalk on the cell wall." Another director-added scene was one in which a character named Dodge Landon allows a pair of young women access to the ape sanctuary where he is an orderly. "I'd just watched *One Flew over the Cuckoo's Nest*. I remember that scene with Billy Bibbit when he brings two girls back to the asylum. We were inspired by that. So there was a lot of evolution. I was driven by the studio as well of course, and Peter and Dylan, the producers, but it was very important that I was able to isolate the story that was always there and then just elevate it as much as possible. So I did a couple of uncredited drafts, for sure." Of his lack of formal credit for his screenwriting contributions, Wyatt shrugs, "Filmmaking is a collaborative process."

Another of the ways that times had changed since the original Apes series is that sequels were no longer either unusual or sneered at. Surprisingly, though, Wyatt says, "The studio certainly wasn't talking about any planned trilogy at the time." He elucidates, "It's often considered bad luck to talk about sequels before a film comes out. . . . I'm sure there was always an ambition. There was an ambition on my part of course as well. But we would never officially talk about it. . . . I think, frankly, there was an unknown question that the studio asked themselves, which is, was there still an audience for Planet of the Apes?"

That the lead ape character is named Caesar is apposite for a film that resembles *Conquest of the Planet of the Apes* more than any other Apes movie. Andy Serkis was the man chosen to play this ape revolutionary. Although a big-name actor, Serkis is visually anonymous because in his biggest roles he has always been hidden behind digital "performance capture" methods. He was the wizened, stunted Gollum in Peter Jackson's Zeroes Lord of the Rings trilogy and the titular gorilla giant in the same director's 2005 remake of *King Kong*. In fact, some will have jumped to the conclusion that Serkis being recruited to play a simian by Wyatt and company was lazy casting. (Others may have subconsciously wondered whether it was decided that the series should cleave to the tradition of an English actor playing the most sympathetic ape.) In fact, Serkis was recommended to Wyatt by Joe Letteri of Weta, the aforementioned company responsible for *Rise*'s special effects.

Wyatt: "He said, 'He's extraordinary. He understands motion capture.'" It so happened that as well as having seen Serkis's acting buried beneath digital magic, Wyatt had witnessed it au naturel, specifically in the 2006 British television drama *Longford* in which he played murderer Ian Brady. "I knew what he could do as an actor. But Joe said, 'Look, it takes a very particular kind of actor to understand the degree of performance one needs to give, especially in a nonverbal role. Andy has the ability.'" Wyatt could ultimately only concur. "He's a very physical actor. He's got great timing. He's got an amazing ability to exude or to emphasize the right moments in a physical performance. You need that with a character like Caesar. You need to be able to define those bigger movements but also still retain the more subtle ones."

Caesar's chimpanzee ally Rocket was played by Terry Notary, who also served as what Wyatt terms "our movement expert." Notary had helped run the "ape school" for the Burton movie. "I know Terry was in the running for playing Caesar as well in the early stages of the film," says Christopher Gordon, who took the role of Koba, a mean-spirited bonobo who also allies with Caesar, albeit more ambiguously. This has a certain irony, for Gordon reveals that in many instances where the viewer is looking at Caesar, they're actually seeing Notary. "A lot of that was done as Terry playing the character as his stunt double."

No suggestion of lazy or obvious casting attends Maurice, an ape who assists Caesar in his quest to improve the lot of his fellow simians.

The role of this squat, molding, grizzled Bornean orangutan was given to a hollow-faced woman in her late forties. *Rise* was shot in Vancouver, where the theater-oriented actress Karin Konoval was based. "It became clear to me because of budget constraints and such that the supporting roles—and back then Maurice hadn't become the big character that he became in the trilogy—[needed to be] cast locally," notes Wyatt. "I found the theater actors in Vancouver really strong, especially in physicality. They were able to block and move in a way that really lent themselves to playing the apes. So we cast a bunch out of the theater scene in Vancouver, and then Terry Notary started to work with them and mold them into their ape characters." Of Konoval, Wyatt says, "It was something about her face. The performance that she gave in the audition had such a stillness and a watchfulness and a wisdom to it that she was an obvious Maurice for me." Her gender wouldn't have been an issue even had she not been buried beneath Weta work because Maurice doesn't speak at all in this film. It so happens that this was a problem that would need to be addressed in the succeeding two films, where the character develops the power of speech, but, with talk of sequels at this point taboo, that possibility wasn't acknowledged. Unlike Serkis and every other ape actor, Konoval did become recognizable from the film because she also takes a small part as an officious human court clerk.

Christopher Gordon was another eyebrow-raising piece of casting. He is actually a stunt performer, but Koba was the sole example of a main ape character whom it was felt didn't need what might be termed a legitimate actor to render his lines. This fact was a holdover from an approach to the film that was gradually sloughed off. Recalls Wyatt, "There was definitely a general belief at the beginning of our production that, [as] the apes were secondary characters to the humans, their stories could easily be performed by stuntmen, stuntwomen. They would be more physical. It was driven by the fact that the big performance that he would be giving would be on the Golden Gate Bridge." The latter is the film's climactic sequence, and as Wyatt notes, "That would require a lot of stunt work."

Gordon was in the right place at the right time: he might not have got the role a few weeks later as the approach to the movie evolved. "Everyone grew in a kind of awareness of the focus of the storytelling," says Wyatt. "There was an ongoing argument that we're making Planet of the Apes here, not Planet of the Humans. . . . We had to essentially go to the studio and really make it clear that in order to get this film to work, we needed actors of the experience and level of . . . the Andy Serkises of this world and Karin Konovals." That said, Koba is arguably the most compelling character in the film. Wyatt says that Gordon "a hundred percent" acquitted himself as well as a legitimate thespian would have. "Many stunt people are terrific actors."

With this film, the word *planet* became even more questionable in the franchise's title than it had been hitherto, reduced to a function that was almost Pavlovian. Leaving aside the vast continuum striven for by the screenwriters that theoretically made the project a prequel to all APJAC Planet of the Apes pictures, what plays out is a localized, circumstance-specific uprising. In fact, this became an issue when preparing to show the extended preamble to that Golden Gate Bridge climax, which involves Caesar and his fellow escapees from an ape sanctuary rustling up a hairy army by freeing simians from a drug laboratory and a zoo. Wyatt recalls a disagreement about this with one of the senior executives at Fox. "There was a desire to cut the scene where they break the apes out of the zoo. To me that was like, 'That makes no sense. If we do that, then the audience is going to be totally bewildered.' We were jumping the shark of reality with that many apes in North America anyway, 'cos there aren't, but we're making a movie, we're not making a documentary. But in terms of the logic of the storytelling, where do all these apes come from?"

The crew responsible for the makeup in Tim Burton's *Planet of the Apes* who are quoted in this book were speaking in 2007. They were clearly aware that they were on the edge of a revolution in their industry.

Mark Alfrey was dubious about physical makeup jobs disappearing: "Digital makeup can work well, but there are actors who want to do all the emoting and directors who want to see it happen on set. So prosthetic makeup isn't going anywhere." Others were not so sure. Jamie Kelman responded in the affirmative to the question of whether CGI was affecting the amount of work offered to him. "And it will continue to. It will change the way everything is done." Like Kelman, Eddie Yang was embracing—if not necessarily passionately—the new technology. "I made the switch a while ago," he said. "Digital is just the next step in the evolution of film."

It was not initially by any means certain, though, that *Rise of the Planet of the Apes* would proffer simians created by CGI. "There was a bit of a perception very, very early on that it was possible that we might use actors in prosthetics," recalls Wyatt. The idea foundered on the fact that apes in this narrative are not the evolved simians of the APJAC films. "Real apes don't actually have the same anatomy as human beings. Their arms are way longer, their torsos are much shorter, all of those things. So there was no way we could actually do a Planet of the Apes in the original mold."

The next option discussed was also ultimately adjudged a dead end. Says Wyatt, "In the first few weeks of my involvement, conversation was very much about the use of live apes. It struck me as wholly and horribly ironic: the idea of telling the story of animal liberation using captured animals that had been trained and forced to perform. But ultimately, that was just put to bed anyway because, practically, eliciting any emotional performance from real apes was never going to happen. And it would have been just prohibitive cost-wise to have got so many apes on camera. But we had to go down the road of doing our diligence, and we went up to one of the last remaining animal sanctuaries in Berkeley College where they had performing apes. . . . It was pretty sad and horrific."

It was only at this point that discussion turned to the creation of digital creatures. "Of course, that had been done and Lord of the Rings had set a certain path and a standard, and *Avatar* of course." Indubitably so, but so had Jar Jar Binks, the much-hated dufus from the Star Wars prequel *The Phantom Menace* (1999), who—as the first-ever completely digital character in a live-action film—had cast a long shadow over the technology. Wyatt doesn't remember having Jar Jar in mind but does say, "We were never certain that it was going to work until we'd actually wrapped the film and we were deep into post and we saw our first fully rendered ape shot which Weta had been working on."

Weta Digital is a division of New Zealand special effects and props company Weta Workshop. As it was cofounded by Peter Jackson, it might be said that its engagement for the new Apes films meant that the New Zealand director had finally, if tangentially, succeeded in stamping his influence on the franchise. Weta is the world leader in performance capture aka motion capture (mocap), the technique by which exotic or otherworldly beings are conjured on film from human performance. "Essentially it's recording movement," explains Christopher Gordon, who has extensive mocap experience even outside of his portrayal of Koba. "You're wearing a reflective suit with reflective balls that are about two or three centimeters round, and they're covering every major joint and facet of your body. When the light shines on you, it reflects back to the computer, and the computer sees the dots only." In postproduction, those dots are used as a grid for the digital superimposition of features and textures. "Put that in the computer and then you can have a body overtop of the motion that your body does. So if you're walking like an ape, it'll look like an ape when you animate overtop, or a martial artist, or whatever you are."

Rise of the Planet of the Apes involved a slight variation on the process, being—Gordon notes—"the first motion capture amongst live action outdoor sets." He explains, "In this case, we did it the other way around, so instead of having reflection—because that wouldn't work in the outdoor space—they had LED diodes that would shine. And then the 'volume' cameras that were all around the entire outdoor set would pick up the shining lights from our suits and effectively give the same end result."

Mocap uses the same "volume" process with faces. Gordon: "There would be a camera like [a] GoPro with a little selfie stick stuck over the helmet pointing back at my face about six to eight inches away and about a hundred little dots all over my face so that you can see every little facial expression, and then that would translate to the facial animation." Is a miniature camera permanently in one's face not distracting? "Well, it can be, but you absorb yourself in the role and then it becomes part of you. Though there's a camera in front of you, there's always a camera right there somewhere filming you."

Although the only time on *Rise* that Gordon and his fellow ape actors ever went into a makeup chair was to have the reference dots painted on their faces, even the cutting-edge digital technology didn't completely preclude an element of old-fashioned practical methods in the transformation to simian. "We had arm extensions that allowed our proportions to be more similar to apes."

There is a comically vast difference between the way motion capture looks when being filmed and the way that it appears in the finished product. In behind-the-scenes footage of such shoots, the body-suited, dot-festooned, mini-camera-bedecked actors look nothing less than ridiculous. How difficult is that to direct? "You get used to it," says Wyatt. "It's a simple step to [tell yourself], 'They will look like apes when all is said and done.' It allows you then just to focus entirely on the performance. It's practically challenging at times. Face cameras would always get in the way of actors trying to get close to each other. Kissing scenes were really hard, or any kind of physical interaction in a close proximity."

It being their task to transform such awkward raw material into a plausible vista, Weta naturally had an on-set presence. "There was always a representative anytime there was any motion capture going on," recalls Gordon. "They worked quite closely together to bridge the digital and real world." "Their team were invisible in the main," says Wyatt. "They allowed for the shoot camera, the cinema camera, to always take front- and center-stage. They didn't slow us down. We had to stick basically to rules in order to minimize additional costs and post [production] and we had to always try and match every shot we did with our performance in the shot, with what we called a clean plate, which was basically we took anything that was going to become digitally rendered out of the shot (i.e., any apes) and then we had the human actors play the scene again." Replaying the scene created problems with eyelines (i.e., the actor looking at something that isn't there). "We didn't have motion control because it was too expensive and time-consuming at the time, so we tried to blend eye match with the camera move. That was a gesture for Weta to always have that as a failsafe in case it became too prohibitive and expensive for them to use the hero shot and have to paint out too much. But to be honest, the human performances were always dropped. They were always less strong."

Although Caesar is shown growing up, only the scenes of him as a newborn baby were not depicted by the very much adult Andy Serkis. Explains Wyatt, "That shot where he's leaving the bathroom, Andy didn't do the entire sequence—he didn't swing on the light fixtures—but he did a lot of the performance all the way up into the attic. We then had to scale him down."

Serkis is currently the top motion-capture performer in the world and enjoys all the rewards that go with that status. However, it doesn't take too much imagination to envisage a time when he might be consumed with self-doubt because of the numbers of people who will always aver that the strength of any of his mocap performances lies in the hands of others. Wyatt is having none of it. "Andy Serkis is the performer. He's the actor behind Caesar. He performs, prepared, blocked, and collaborated before, and on set, and after to create that role and deliver on that role. That's exactly what any actor does. As for how it's then transformed into an ape, and how those subtle intricacies are picked up on and worked on—how when Andy reaches out and grabs a cup of coffee with his human arm the animator turns that into an ape arm that's longer but manages to hold on to what Andy's doing, how he manages to take an ape in the moment that Andy's foot leaves the floor and then keyframe that ape through the air ('cos Andy couldn't do that, we didn't have wirework) and hold on to Andy's performance and the personality of Caesar—that's all in the hands of the animator. It's a total collaboration. But it's a total collaboration when you look at John Hurt in full makeup playing the Elephant Man. One could argue, 'Well, he's so buried beneath the prosthetic, how is he performing?' It's complicated, of course, but I would say that it's plain and obvious that everything's built off of the human performance. That's the whole point of performance capture."

One thing that might enable Serkis to sidestep this postulated crisis of confidence is the fact that his craft is in the process of being formally defined and rewarded. Christopher Gordon recalls *Rise of the Planet of the Apes* being filmed against a backdrop of negotiations and arguments about what rights a motion-capture performer might have in terms of billing and remuneration. Gordon: "He's been somewhat on the front running of that argument 'cos there's an argument [in] the industry that a motion-capture character is not a real actor and all that kind of stuff: you're just a proxy. Andy's been pushing and I think quite rightly so. It doesn't matter if you photograph or digitize overtop, you are still performing and acting. That should be recognized as what it is. The studio's argument [was] that one [actor] could play everything. Well, what the performers were fighting for was if you play a character, that's the character. You're named that character. That's your contract. When you digitize overtop, you theoretically could play every character in the movie, but to only be paid as the one isn't exactly fair. So there's a precedent being fought for during those films."

Some, of course, might argue that the studio's point of view is proven by the conversion of Gordon from a good-looking young man into a scarred old bonobo, and proven even more by Karin Konoval's transformation from attractive woman to molding male orangutan, and proven yet further by the fact that, when a different actor took over from Gordon in sequel *Dawn of the Planet of the Apes*, most people only knew this from the credits. "There's still a soul behind it, though," insists Gordon. "You can see it. It's interesting 'cos I've done a number of films, some of them where you're in full, proper prosthetics. Say there's twenty of us all dressed up. Within ten minutes you know who's who 'cos of how they move and how their personalities come through even though you don't see eyes, you don't see anything. You know who you're dealing with. There's definitely an essence to what is portrayed."

What was being portrayed in *Rise* was not something to which the performers were immediately privy. "I didn't really see any rushes or any cuts or anything like that, how it was coming along, until the final product," says Gordon. His director wasn't much better informed. "Basically the cut was our actors in grey suits with their motion-capture cameras on their heads and dots on their bodies," says Wyatt. "If you heard Caesar or Rocket make an ape sound, it was Andy Serkis basically going 'Oooh ooh ooh, ahh ahh.'" It wasn't until after principal photography had wrapped and "some weeks" after a first edit completed that Wyatt obtained a firm idea of what the apes would look like.

"Joe Letteri, the head of Weta, came to the Fox lot with one single shot and said, 'I have something to show you guys,'" Wyatt recalls. "The studio were terrified. We were all terrified. Like, 'What is this going to be?'" Happily the first evidence of what Weta was intending to do with this project was "just amazing." Wyatt: "It was Caesar behind the bars in the ape sanctuary watching one of the handlers walk past his cage. It really did look like, when you put it up against Andy's performance on screen, the way he did exactly the same thing: his body very still, his eyes just moving left to right. It literally looked like they'd taken Andy's eyes physically out of his skull and put them into a shot and made him into an ape. It was unbelievable. The eyes were a hundred percent digitally created. I think that was the real game-changer. They did many, many other things of course, but they got the eyes right and often with digital creatures that's where everything begins, 'cos it's the windows to the soul. So they managed to pull that off and the rest followed. . . . It was the thing that made everybody just take a breath and realize that we actually had the possibility of making a really strong film."

Not that it should be inferred that Weta's work was ever presented as a fait accompli. "Every day was the cineSyncing to New Zealand," Wyatt recalls. "We would discuss with Dan Lemmon, our supervisor, Clare Williams, our studio supervisor, and we would just go through every shot. We'd discuss the movements, we'd then see the iterations and we'd get the look and lighting back of each of the apes. Then we'd get the final renders. Then we'd discuss the hair movement and the eye movement. . . . I'm directing them, the studio's directing them, I'm directing the studio, the studio's directing me. It's just a massive collaboration." This postproduction collaboration lasted longer than the principal photography. "When you actually break it down, the production itself probably is one-third of the final budget on a film like that. Our post period was like making the film two times."

Asked if he was ever pitched into an identity crisis about how much he can claim responsibility for the outcome of such intricate collaboration, Wyatt laughs. "The story's the story," he says easily. "So how much I feel like I'm an owner of the film—a hundred percent 'cos I was there for nearly two years." Fair enough, but it means he has to take ownership of the bad as well as the good. For instance, a never quite convincing sequence early in *Rise* in which the young Caesar leaves the bathroom in his owner's house and goes up to his attic home in a series of swings and jumps. The acrobatics are breathtaking because they are streamlined and seamless, something assisted by long tracking shots. However, that very perfection creates a sense of unreality: the smooth action seems false because life is intrinsically flawed and fumbling.

Wyatt partly accepts the charge. "I think you've landed on something that is often the issue with digital filmmaking. It's less about his movement, because I do think there's moments where his hands fumble on certain things that he's grabbing. I think it's the perfection of the shot. The shot is basically a bunch of shots all stitched together, because there was no way we could actually get a camera or a technocrane into those small spaces all the way through a house in one go. It creates in your mind's eyes, as you're watching it, a sense of unrealness because you're thinking, 'There's no way a human camera operator could do this.' Once you start to think that, then you start to question what you're seeing."

The grand showcase for the *Rise* digital effects was the apes' mass escape from San Francisco into the natural idyll of the Redwoods by way of the Golden Gate Bridge, with spectacular climbing and ferocious conflict marking the way. How much of it was shot on the real-world bridge? "Er, none of it," Wyatt laughs. "There was a runway in Vancouver that was built for the Roland Emmerich film *Day after Tomorrow*, the end scene where the plane lands. They had left it there. We took it over and we built a portion of the bridge on it, but only up to about six feet high. Everything above that was digital. Weta drove across the Golden Gate Bridge quite a few times, and our effects team, and they 'plated' the bridge and then built it all in post." "We did all the ground stuff: jumping on the cars and all of that aspect was all 'practical,'" says Gordon. "But in general, that was CG. Motion capture was done in a studio where they were swinging around on a jungle-gym thing just to get some reference."

The fact that the mocap work seen in *Dawn of the Planet of the Apes* (2014) and *War for the Planet of the Apes* (2017) was superior to that in *Rise* demonstrates the lightning evolutionary processes endemic to digital technology. In twenty years' time, the world will probably perceive the effects seen in the Chernin trilogy as good for its time but possessing the antiquated patina that now overlays the prosthetics in the original Planet of the Apes quintet. However, at this point in history most cinemagoers would agree that Wyatt and his Weta colleagues created a new paradigm for the Apes franchise that took it into whole new areas of believability.

Most cinemagoers, of course, don't have inside knowledge of special effects. Those who do have a more multifaceted perspective. Tom Burman, makeup veteran of the APJAC films, Tom Burman, adjudges the CGI Apes films "really fantastic," noting that "every aspect is so perfectly done and totally convincing to the eye. The apes look and move like real apes." However, he adds, "For me, they lack the soul and the nuances that a real actor in makeup can bring to the screen. It's like apples and oranges: they both taste good but they are different flavors."

"There's still certain movements and certain things that are very hard to emulate, hence why they have motion capture and not just pure animation," says Gordon. "There's always the difference between what's real and what's generated as a cartoon, and people can see it. People lose connection to it. Sometimes it works great. Sometimes people want to see real live action. So there's a push away from having just Spider-Man flying through the air completely animated to see practical action as part of it because it's more believable."

Gordon has been transformed in his career by both conventional prosthetics (on one job sitting daily in a makeup chair for up to eight hours cumulatively) and CGI. He doesn't view as a sunset industry what is variously known as "practical" and "prosthetic." "I think it's just going to evolve," he reasons. "I don't think it's going to go away. There is going to be a place for prosthetics, and it's just going to get better." However, he then seems to harbor doubt about his own theory. "I suppose at one point it could be completely computer generated. . . . The technology is there to just do away with actual people. . . . There's a lot of enhancement that happens that people don't realize." This enhancement can even be undetectable to industry insiders like Gordon. "It's getting so good now that there's many details that you would never catch, whether it's seagulls flying in the background or it's a different color sunset or it's a building that's not supposed to be there. You'd have to really look and compare."

Burman is stricken by no such doubt. "When I got into the makeup union there were about 350 makeup artists in the union and there were only less than a handful of people who knew how to make prosthetics," he says. "Today there are at least one thousand, eight hundred makeup artists and around six hundred makeup effect artists and ten independent makeup labs just in the Los Angeles area alone, and I don't know how many more there is around the world."

He concludes, "Makeup effects is here to stay."

Making it immediately and graphically clear that the franchise requires us to perceive simians as the victims again, the start of *Rise of the Planet of the Apes* finds terrified chimpanzees being captured in a jungle to be taken for scientific experimentation in the laboratory of biotechnology company Gen-Sys.

That the laboratory is in contemporary America, where all the film's action takes place, marks another departure: this is the first Apes vehicle that's not set even slightly in the future. Another departure is that the animal protagonists are not a physically evolved species intermediate between simians and humans but pure ape: short legs, dopey expressions, dragging knuckles, and all. It takes a little acclimatization: the sympathetic apes in the original series were cute even where they weren't heroic looking.

Despite these differences, one tradition is maintained from the APJAC films: the harking back to previous Apes fare. Sprinkled into the script are at least twenty references to earlier Planet of the Apes projects for the delighted study of a culture that by now fetishized in-jokes, repurposing, and postmodernism and called these kind of things Easter Eggs. A case in point is the previously mentioned character Dodge Landon: his handle is an amalgamation of the names of Taylor's male crewmates in the first movie. Another is the fact that one of the captured apes is dubbed "Bright Eyes," the name initially given to Taylor by Zira in the 1968 film. Here, it is conferred because the chimpanzee becomes the first ape to manifest green flecks in her irises as a result of treatment with ALZ-112, a drug being developed by young scientist Will Rodman (James Franco). ALZ-112 itself is a reference to the 112-minute running time of that first Apes movie.

A casualty of the project's evolution from a human-based film into an apes-dominated enterprise was the importance in the narrative of Rodman. Franco was on an upward trajectory that would shortly see him Oscar nominated for his part in the Danny Boyle flick *127 Hours*, but his excellence was secondary to the makers of *Rise* as they felt their way toward a proper conceptual balance. "It was perceived by many, including the studio, that it was going to be his movie," says Wyatt. "They really wanted to turn James into a movie star. He came on board the movie because he was fascinated by the technology, loved the mythology of Apes, grew up watching them, but had the lack of ego to stand aside and let Andy take center stage. . . . I think actually Franco played really, really well and played the straight man to Andy's Caesar in a way that not many movie stars of his ilk would happily do." Although Rodman's relationship with Caesar provides what Wyatt terms the film's "real core emotion," it is unquestionably Caesar's picture. This is something Wyatt believes is of no little import in the history of cinema. Lassie and King Kong are one thing—as are the evolved apes of the Jacobs quintet—but Wyatt has asserted, "This is the first live-action film that has its main character as a thoughtful, feeling, self-aware animal."

Intended as a cure for Alzheimer's, ALZ-112 is a gene therapy that allows the brain to repair itself. Gen-Sys is desperate to start using it on humans. The necessary approval from the board seems a given when it transpires that the drug is making those simians injected with it preternaturally intelligent. Unfortunately, Bright Eyes runs amok just as

Rodman is giving a demonstration extolling the virtues of the wonder drug. It's a scene that stunningly demonstrates the virtues of CGI, the nonexistent but utterly real-looking chimpanzee bounding and swinging among a group of cowering, white-coated humans. The drug company is run by the dapper, English-accented Steven Jacobs (named after you-know-who, played by David Oyelowo). After Bright Eyes has to be pumped full of bullets in front of the terrified board, Jacobs closes down the drug trial.

Too late, it is discovered that the reason for the chimp's aggression was the fact that, pregnant when captured, she was worried that her newborn would be hurt. By now, all the other apes in the experiment have been put down. Rodman's colleague Franklin can't bring himself to do it to the new arrival, but nor can he take the baby home because he is worried that his brother—who works for the company's security division—will rat him out. He asks Rodman to act as caretaker. (Cue the now obligatory pedant-pleasing clearing-up of specific anthropoid suborder: "I can't take care of a monkey!" / "He's not a monkey—he's an ape!") When Rodman duly takes the baby back to his house, we discover that the Alzheimer's issue has a particular resonance for him because his resident father (John Lithgow) suffers from the condition.

Three years later the adopted ape is an established fixture at the Rodmans'. Will originally intended to keep the baby for a couple of days until his colleague was able to find it a sanctuary. He then noticed that not only have the benefits of ALZ-112 been passed from mother to son but that Caesar is exhibiting intelligence levels far in excess of a human child of the same age. He has kept the ape as the only way he is now able to study the effects of his synthesis. The new member of the household is christened by Rodman's father, who happens to be reading

Shakespeare's *Julius Caesar*. The obverse of the stunning effects in the board meeting is the fact that the limitations of 2011 CGI are evident in the way that Caesar's features sometimes resemble a toy brought to life rather than the face of a young ape.

Rodman sneaks home some ALZ-112 to inject his deteriorating father with it. His dad not only quickly shows signs of improvement, but cognitive abilities superior to those he'd possessed before his condition struck. Also showing signs of improvement is Rodman's love life. When Caesar gets injured by Rodman's obnoxious next-door neighbor Douglas Hunsiker (David Hewlett) after venturing into the man's backyard, Rodman takes Caesar to primatologist Dr. Caroline Aranha (Freida Pinto). She notices Caesar—taught sign language by his owner—suggest to Rodman that he ask her to dinner. The realism of the signing communication method is somewhat undermined by scenes in which Caesar seems to understand English long before he is shown to have developed any ability in this area. (The fact that such artistic license is not necessary was memorably established as far back as 1986 by *Children of a Lesser God*, the film in which William Hurt played the lover of a deaf woman and simultaneously spoke words as he signed them.) When Aranha advises Rodman that Caesar needs space, the three of them begin making day trips to the Redwoods.

Five years later Caesar is much bigger. He is also melancholy, beginning to question his origins and where he fits into the world. Meanwhile, when antibodies find a way to fight ALZ-112, Rodman's father's Alzheimer's returns with a vengeance. It culminates one day in him getting into Hunsiker's car on the misapprehension that it's his own and smashing into other vehicles. When the neighbor starts prodding an old man who has never shown Caesar anything but kindness, the chimp rushes out and attacks Hunsiker, resulting in Animal Control taking Caesar away to the San Bruno Primate Shelter.

At this point a hitherto nuanced movie descends into cartoonish cliché, with Konoval's officious judicial clerk taking it upon herself to tell Rodman—lodging an appeal against the seizure—that he is lucky that Caesar wasn't put down. The shelter's orderly, Dodge Landon (Tom Felton), is shown as viciously contemptuous of his charges (even to the extent of—horror of horrors—calling them "stupid monkeys"). The latter character—the grunge-chic-dressed son of the shelter's manager—is the franchise's traditional human character with an unaccountable but plot-convenient hatred of apes.

Caesar is initially bullied by other apes, particularly chimpanzee Rocket, who tears his shirt off him. (After which point, clothed apes will almost never be seen in the trilogy again.) When Caesar cultivates the friendship of his fellow shelter residents, it becomes clear that this film picks up the baton from the Tim Burton picture in one respect at least: there is no particular demarcation of intelligence or temperament between chimpanzees, gorillas, and orangutans. Nor indeed bonobos, represented for the first time in the franchise. One of the apes Caesar befriends is Maurice (named in tribute to Maurice Evans). The Maurice character is visually delightful, especially the magnificent flanges that give him a face like a dinner plate. The orangutan can sign—a legacy of his days as a circus performer—and his fingers warn Caesar, "Careful—humans no like smart ape."

At work, Rodman is given permission to start testing ALZ-113, a revised, vaporous version of his creation. Rodman begins his experiments on Koba. The latter is another CGI triumph, even if his scars, snaggle teeth, and milky eye represent the lazy old cinema shorthand of ugly-for-evil. Rodman's father declines treatment with the new variant and shortly thereafter dies of natural causes. Determined that he won't lose the other part of his "family," Rodman bribes John Landon (Brian Cox), the manager of the primate shelter, into letting him have Caesar back. However, after looking around at his newfound ape friends, Caesar refuses to leave them and gently closes the door of his cage on his would-be rescuer. The chimp's attempt to rally the apes into some sort of uprising, though, is an uphill struggle because, as the orangutan signs to him, "Apes stupid." Caesar's solution is to sneak out at night and steal some ALZ-113 from the refrigerator of his former owner, then release canisters of it into the shelter's air.

It turns out that the drug does something to humans that it doesn't do to apes (i.e., it kills them). Franklin, accidentally exposed to the gas, develops symptoms of severe illness. He tries to alert Rodman. He doesn't find him at his house, but ends up projecting blood onto Hunsiker, who comes bumptiously out to investigate.

Catching Caesar in the primate shelter's recreation area when he's not supposed to be there, Dodge produces a shock baton. As Caesar grabs his wrist, Dodge snarls, "Take your stinking paw off me, you damn dirty ape!" The back reference is the preamble to another one of sorts when Caesar then speaks for the very first time. In the style of Aldo, the word he enunciates is, "No!" "That's a jumping of the shark because vocal cords take millennia to develop," admits Wyatt. When Dodge again resorts to the shock baton, Caesar responds with a water hose, frying him alive.

Caesar sets free every ape in the sanctuary and takes them to liberate the apes at the Gen-Sys labs. Once having done that, they free the simian inhabitants of the local zoo. That accomplished, Caesar leads his army through the hilly, tram-traversed streets of San Francisco toward the safe and natural habitat of the Redwoods. Police cars, helicopters, and horses are mustered to stop them crossing the Golden Gate Bridge. In the confrontation that ensues, the forces of law and order are no match for beasts who have the same brainpower as them but can also swing on the girders beneath the bridge, climb to its fog-wreathed upper reaches, and—courtesy of far superior upper-body strength—overturn coaches and leap onto passing helicopters. They can also apparently charge on horses, although Caesar's gallop toward the enemy may be another Easter Egg, a contrived way of recapturing the astronauts' shock in the first movie at seeing a gorilla on horseback. When Jacobs's helicopter is brought to the ground, Koba takes great pleasure in pushing him off the bridge to his death.

Rodman tracks Caesar to the Redwoods and asks him to come home. "Caesar is home," responds the ape. This is an amended finale. The director recalls the originally shot ending thusly: "Brian Cox's character pursued them into the forest after discovering his son dead, lined up a shot, and Will got the bullet and then died in Caesar's arms. Then Brian's character got eviscerated by the apes." The development was jettisoned as "clearly way too depressing." Explains Wyatt, "It was just not really in keeping with the arc of the story, which is obviously the separation of [Rodman and Caesar] and the idea that the son needed to spread his wings and become his own individual. That didn't require one of them to die."

As if it's not enough that Rodman's next-door neighbor is an obnoxious jerk responsible for Caesar's incarceration, during the closing credits the screenwriters make him the unwitting destroyer of human society. It turns out that Hunsiker is an airline pilot. Having unknowingly picked up the ALZ-113 disease from the now dead Franklin, he gets into his cabin and proceeds to spread it around the world. "That was something that we came up with in post," recalls Wyatt. "We did some additional shooting with him." As well as providing the franchise's usual dovetailing of the apocalyptical reason for mankind's descent and the apes' rise, this sequence also serves to set up a sequel.

It has to be said that, on its own merits, *Rise of the Planet of the Apes* doesn't particularly deserve one. It has its good points. Wyatt's direction is very impressive, full of unexpected switches of angles, sweeping tracking shots, and center-of-action perspectives. Moreover, due to the moving scenes between Rodman and his father, and to a lesser extent the romance between Rodman and Aranha, the film has a substantial emotional core lacking in all previous Apes fare except *Escape*. However, the picture simply fails to justify its premise. Despite the cartoonish human villainy, it conveys no sense that any ape has a reason to engage in an uprising. The maltreatment Caesar suffers under John Landon's auspices amounts merely to being confined to a small, functional cell most of the day, being obliged to eat less refined food than that with which he is familiar, being forced to endure the company of other simians, and having to endure Dodge's (unauthorized) spite. (Dodge's death, supposedly a Bond-movie-style poetic comeuppance like Oddjob's demise in *Goldfinger*, is a completely disproportionate punishment for his "crimes.") It would have made far more sense if Caesar's rebellion had been prompted not by his reduced circumstances but the treatment of the apes at the Gen-Sys labs. However, even those apes have never been subjected to much worse than what Caesar himself does by exposing his supposed friends, without their permission, to Rodman's drug.

Nonetheless, the 110-minute movie was both entertaining and successful. Released on August 5, 2011, it garnered good reviews and an Oscar nomination for Best Visual Effects. It did good box office, too, finishing fourteenth in the year-end worldwide cinemagoing table. Its thoughtfulness also meant that it had a tailwind of goodwill behind it that the last Apes movie hadn't. The upshot was that *Rise* was not destined to be a Tim Burton–style false start.

The birthmark visible on Caesar's chest in *Dawn of the Planet of the Apes* has been postulated as originating as a means to prevent "passing-off." Manufacturers of unauthorized product—in the vein, say, of those Azrak-Hamray generic "Action Apeman" figures—would, the theory goes, be stymied by the crucial missing identifier. Wyatt denies this, saying that the reason was dictated by the fact that this was the first Apes movie where the simians were routinely unclothed. "It was simply put there in the hope that he would be distinguishable to our audience," he says. "Once you start to see these apes move quickly and interacting with each other, how would a human audience be able to tell Caesar apart from Rocket without us caricaturing their faces to the point that they wouldn't feel real?" He adds of the birthmark, "To be honest with you, it didn't really show up in a lot of the shots 'cos he was moving too quickly or his hair was in the way." As for the theory that it had something to do with merchandise, he says, "If it did, then someone would have inserted that into the conversation using a very different tactic, so I think it's highly unlikely." Another reason the rumor is unconvincing is that the merchandise industry was by now very different to what it had constituted in the days of Apemania.

CHAPTER 14

By the time the Planet of the Apes franchise was revived in 2001 after that quarter-century gap, the people who had bought the 1970s Apes merchandise had kids of their own. However, children weren't like they were in their day. Fox launched the Tim Burton Apes movie at the New York Toy Fair, with the film's star Mark Wahlberg attending, but, just as studios had begun to take seriously the importance of merchandising, the wind was beginning to change. Children were certainly prepared to go to cinemas to take in the film, but there was declining appetite among them for ancillary product—yes even wastebaskets. By now, toys were things that they were as often as not given away free, whether on the front of comic books or with meals in fast-food restaurants, even if the latter was admittedly frequently as a tie-in promotion with a motion picture. By the time of the Chernin Apes trilogy, the wind had changed completely. "There really wasn't much merchandise with that," notes Christopher Sausville, offering only, "NECA put out a set of figures." The third word of the name the National Entertainment Collectibles Association is significant. Planet of the Apes merchandise is no longer stuff with which children play wargames or toss into the air. "They were more geared towards collectors, 'cos I think that Fox's assumption is that's who would be buying them," says Rich Handley. "They would be keeping them 'on card' and displaying them on walls. They were extremely detailed. It wasn't like the stuff that Mego did." "NECA's . . . huge here in the States now and they make all the figures for everything and it's all targeted towards adults," agrees Sausville. What about the kids? "Everything's video games," Sausville shrugs. "Everybody's on their phones." Birthmarks or no, adult purchasers were hardly likely to be taken in by sloppy passings-off the way they had been when they were children in the 1970s.

In the aftermath of Burton's picture, Planet of the Apes novels had once more disappeared from the publishing schedules. This, however, wasn't actually the intention. Although Andrew E. C. Gaska's book *Conspiracy of the Planet of the Apes* appeared at the same time as *Rise of the Planet of the Apes*, its appearance had been substantially delayed by the fact that publisher Archaia Entertainment changed ownership. (*Rise* didn't get a novelization, which must have led some consumers to assume that Gaska's novel was the book of that film.)

The fact that this "illustrated novel" featured artwork by the likes of Jim Steranko, Joe Jusko, and Patricio Carbajal indicates its origins as a comic book project. Adapted from a story by Gaska, Rich Handley, Christian Berntsen, and Erik Matthews, the narrative takes place during the events of the original 1968 *Planet of the Apes* film. It focuses on Taylor's crewmate Landon and posits the idea that, during the sections of the film where he is not seen, he comes under the control of the Forbidden Zone mutants. The story also gives a backstory to Dr. Milo, the chimp who later got Taylor's sunken ship working. In order not to contradict the movie canon, the plot does rather hinge on characters unnaturally failing to relate their experiences to others (Dr. Galen doesn't tell Zira that Landon had come into his laboratory, and Milo neglects to inform Cornelius that he too had encountered the astronaut). However, there's no denying that the project is suffused with deep love for and knowledge of all areas of the franchise. Gaska works in Mungwort (although here spelled with two *t*'s), the named-only-in-print character from the animated TV series, and even Jan Adams, an old flame of Burke's mentioned in Apes live-action TV series episode "The Deception."

Seven years later, a sequel to *Conspiracy of the Planet of the Apes* was issued by Titan Books, UK science fiction and licensed-property prose specialists. *Death of the Planet of the Apes* purports to show what happened to Taylor in the large section of the *Beneath* film in which he isn't around. Meanwhile, Milo is still beavering away at space flight. As before, Gaska cares enough to try to address the film series' continuity errors. Running to more than 450 pages, it's more substantial than the previous book, which some might classify as a novella. Such projects can, of course, be dismissed as irrelevant, not least because they are "non-canon" (i.e., no moviemaker is going to be held to their continuity, no matter how painstakingly worked out). However, overwhelmingly positive reviews demonstrate that they served their purpose in pleasing the hard-core fans.

Apes comics also made a comeback. Boom! Studios may not for some have hit the heights that Metallic Rose did, but the Los Angeles company is now easily the most commercially successful Planet of the Apes comic book publisher. Having begun issuing Apes comics in 2011, they have at the time of writing put out ninety-four issues, almost twice as much as Malibu and almost three times as many as Marvel.

As well as two monthly titles each lasting more than a year, Boom! have issued nine miniseries. Their catalogue has explored an unusually large array of the motion picture sector of the franchise. They haven't done any Apes-iteration crossovers. (This may be because Fox wants to keep the strands separate. MR's proposal to feature in *Revolution* both the APJAC Caesar and Thade from Tim Burton's film was nixed by the studio.) However, their various titles have explored Apes universes established by both Jacobs and Chernin. They have also found areas to explore that no other publisher has, such as in their 2018 *Planet of the Apes: Visionaries*. A hardcover graphic novel scripted by Dana Gould and illustrated by Chad Lewis and David Wilson, it adapted one of Rod Serling's scripts for the first Planet of the Apes movie.

Boom! has also enthusiastically embraced the concept of the intellectual-property crossover. On some occasions, this has engendered a real-life company crossover, with them prepared to collaborate with rival comics companies (IDW, DC, Dark Horse) who hold the relevant copyright.

After the previously mentioned Tarzan crossover miniseries with Dark Horse, in 2014–2015 Boom! issued in alliance with IDW the five-parter *Star Trek / Planet of the Apes: The Primate Directive*. Writers Scott and David Tipton and artist Rachael Stott posit a scenario wherein the *Enterprise* from the original series *Star Trek* visits Earth in the time frame between the first and second APJAC Apes films, encountering Cornelius and Zira as they do. *Planet of the Apes: Green Lantern* (2017) saw writers Justin Jordan and Robbie Thompson and illustrator Barnaby Bagenda put Cornelius into the DC Comics world, where he puts on his finger the ring of the protectors of the galaxy from the planet Oa, thus conferring on himself superhero powers. The 2017–2018 six-part *Kong on the Planet of the Apes* (writer Ryan Ferrier, artist Carlos Magno) created a story set in the time frame around the original *Planet of the Apes* movie wherein the Apes characters venture to Skull Island to investigate the source of a mysterious giant ape carcass. Kong—in classic style—takes a shine to a comely female no bigger than his fist, in this case Zira.

The idea of such ventures is automatically intriguing (if sometimes also laughable), and the writers usually find inspired (if sometimes contrived) ways for Planet of the Apes characters to encounter people from other franchises. For Handley, though, crossover is where the Boom! line falls down because, as a matter of course, severe continuity, logic, and sometimes aesthetic issues arise. "There is some stuff Boom! has done that I think is outstanding," Handley says, singling out for praise the work of Boom! scripters Corinna Bechko, Daryl Gregory, and Gabriel Hardman. "The one that I genuinely liked was Star Trek / Planet of the Apes. It worked surprisingly well. . . . Tarzan was surprisingly not bad. Tarzan and Kong on the Planet of the Apes, I give them those two in that, if you have to do a crossover, doing a crossover with a story that has apes in it makes more sense." However, he adds, "Things like Green Lantern / Planet of the Apes crossovers don't make sense, for either franchise. I think crossovers in general tend to dilute both franchises." He not only feels that the idea of connected universes "takes away the uniqueness of Planet of the Apes" but also questions the notion of compatibility. "If the Star Trek crew were visiting Cornelius and Zira between *Planet* and [*Beneath*], that means that when we went into [*Beneath*], they shouldn't be surprised that Brent exists—they just met the entire starship crew. Once the crossover is done, unless every character has their mind wiped, how are the characters not then aware of another entire universe?"

The type of people writing such material grew up in an era when crossovers between the intellectual properties of rival companies were rare, hence the hullabaloo in 1976 surrounding DC Comics' Superman battling, then befriending, Marvel Comics' Spider-Man. Beyond that historic publication and a scant few like it, devotees could only fantasize about such punch-ups-cum-team-ups. Yet Handley thinks that the proliferation of crossovers is not so much down to them being the pet projects of people who finally have the power to execute the frustrated fantasies they had as children but instead the baser impetus of mammon. "If you're going to do Star Trek / Planet of the Apes, you just doubled your audience." For those who think that the crossover craze won't descend into something like *Planet of the Apes Meets Every Which Way but Loose*, it should be remembered that the comics medium has already witnessed the bisecting of the universes of freckly innocent Archie and pitiless vigilante the Punisher.

A more pressing issue, though, is the fact that comics may be a sunset industry. The interactive digital publication *Planet of the Apes Sketchbook* produced by Dark Horse was perhaps the first attempt to address this threat. Additionally, the Boom! Apes one-off *Before the Dawn* started life as a webcomic, while their *Rise of the Planet of the Apes* prequel was serialized in six parts on the internet for a period. Madefire is the only publisher so far to have issued a digital-only comic. Their five Planet of the Apes "Motion Books"—which take place in the new continuity—were uploaded to the DeviantArt website in 2016. However, although they came complete with sound files, kinetics-wise they hardly lived up to their billing, resembling a cross between a comic book page being turned by an unseen hand and a slowly moving pan. None of these publications can any longer be experienced in their original form, having been taken down, with the copies preserved as PDFs by fans only inexactly approximating the experience. Such dependence on third-party upkeep makes propositions like motion books innately ephemeral. Moreover, the fact that this was a free download produced by Fox—they were official tie-ins to *War for the Planet of the Apes*—renders this particular example little more than a grandiose type of advertising, ultimately no different in purpose to the various videos Fox placed on YouTube to spread the word about the three Chernin films. It certainly didn't prove the existence of a market for e-comics.

The brutal reality is that none of these innovations may be enough to placate a generation that every day plays on its computer screens things that, though they may be very akin to comic books, are far more satisfying because they are interactive. Video games also keep this cohort occupied for a far longer period than it takes to passively consume a comic book story spanning only twenty-two paper pages.

"The comics industry is kind of imploding," laments Handley. "I think we're going to see the death of 'floppies' eventually. They'll try to keep it going with trade paperbacks, but how long can they keep it going? . . . If there's not a next generation buying into it, then the whole market will collapse in twenty, thirty years from now."

A depressing thought for anyone weaned on comics, but even if the whole industry does go under, many of the creatives behind the medium's Planet of the Apes publications can take pride in the fact that they did something that was in no way inevitable: generate from a licensed property comics that were interesting and high class in their own right.

15

APE SANDWICH

With pleasing box office results coming in for *Rise*, 20th Century Fox gave the green light for that follow-up that no one had been allowed to talk about during production.

"I did want to make the sequel very much," Wyatt recalls of what would be the first successor Ape movie since 1973. "I worked on a script with Scott Burns. We were really happy with the script, and the studio was very happy." Interestingly, Wyatt recalls that one of the things his preparatory work addressed was whether the franchise should return to the iconic imagery of dressed apes. "We started to think about them using clothing in the same way that humans did, to stay warm or things like that."

That idea and every other one besides unexpectedly became someone else's responsibility when in 2012 it was announced that Wyatt had left the project. Wyatt's explanation seems couched in the carefully vague terms of a still-active Hollywood director for whom candor can be career impairing. "It was at a time when Tom [Rothman] left Fox," he says. "I can't really remember all of what went down back then, but I was just exhausted. I was tired and wanted a break. Making these films is seven days a week. And I wanted to get better as a filmmaker, 'cos sometimes when you're making a film of that size, filmmaking itself takes a second place to delegation, navigation, politics, all of that. I just wanted to make a smaller film and then come back to the sequel. And ultimately, they wanted to turn it in a different direction. Part of me was very sad, but I also knew that I made that choice for all the right reasons." Of Peter Chernin—the only person to be listed as a primary producer on all three films—Wyatt says, "He thinks I made the wrong decision for sure, but there was no animosity ever. Our relationship is pretty good. I'm still in touch with him." He summarizes, "It was the first film for Chernin Entertainment and it was a massive success and I think whatever happened after that, we set out to achieve something and we succeeded."

~

Dawn of the Planet of the Apes—a title that, in conjunction with the previous film, seems as oddly transposed as do those of *Conquest* and *Battle*—was instead directed by Matt Reeves. Reeves, who had a half dozen films to his name including *The Pallbearer* (1996) and *Cloverfield* (2008), stayed the trilogy's course. The credits inform us that the script is based on characters "created" by Jaffa & Silver. Mark Bomback polished the script of the latter team.

The film opens with a montage of news footage, which cumulatively explains the pandemic dubbed the "Simian Flu" and the civil war and decline of human civilization it sparked. The Hunsiker-caused catastrophe that has struck humanity is of little interest to the escaped apes. They are living in the Redwoods in a society that is no less organized for it being alfresco. (As a human later notes, "They don't need power, lights, heat. Nothing. That's their advantage.") The society styles itself a "family," the head of which continues to be Caesar. The main method by which they style themselves anything is sign language, in which all are now proficient. This time, few shortcuts are taken with this communication method, subtitles explaining the exchanges. There seems no logical reason why the other apes wouldn't have mastered language like Caesar did in *Rise*, as they took an improved version of the drug with which he was infused at birth. However, Koba is the only other ape seen talking to any significant extent. The latter is now played by Toby Kebbell, yet another English actor.

Although the action takes place "ten winters" after the events in *Rise*, even Caesar and Koba can only manage halting, conjunction-less speech. Ape children, however, are learning to write, one of several echoes of *Battle for the Planet of the Apes*. Maurice acts as teacher, and one of the things he imparts is the familiar sacred ape edict, here rendered as "Ape not kill ape." Caesar's more domesticated hinterland is circumnavigated, including the delicate fact that in reality he might be disgusted by the lack of interest of his fellow apes in using toilets: the previous movie had demonstrated he was potty trained.

Weta's apes are now more consistently real looking. Fur is textured and rippling, faces are pockmarked with character, and expressions are as fluid and animated as any human's. An early example of this improvement comes when chimpanzees are shown swinging en masse through the branches of the Redwoods in a far more believable way than boy-Caesar's cavorting in *Rise*. (When it comes to gorillas, as in the last movie, the production sidesteps the issue of the fact that they are a species that do not have much in the way of arboreal ability.) Among the few gaps in believability are Caesar's never-quite-lifelike baby son (whom actors additionally don't manage to look at square-on). The impact of the effects is assisted by the superb direction of Reeves, which is—perhaps paradoxically—very naturalistic. Astonishingly this was his first experience with motion capture.

The Redwoods are not necessarily the idyll that might have been imagined from the previous outing. Not only is it seen almost exclusively in drizzle, but it's shown to hold its own dangers, including grizzly bears, one of which attacks Blue Eyes, Caesar's older son, when the apes are hunting elk. (Unless it's a coincidence, the name Blue Eyes is an Easter Egg relating to the animated Apes TV series, being the name that production's Zira gives to one of the astronauts.) That Blue Eyes is teenaged (in ape years: they live to around a half century) hardly seems to account for his extreme prickliness. Blue Eyes picks up some chest scarring from the attack, another handy means of identification for viewers in the sea of furry bodies. The female apes are differentiated by the likes of hair ornaments, such as those of Caesar's wife Cornelia, a chimp seen briefly at the primate shelter in the last film.

In the first meeting of human and ape for two years, Blue Eyes and Ash (son of Rocket) come upon a man strolling in the forest. Spooked, the human shoots and wounds Ash. Hearing the gunshots, the apes descend on the small group of humans he has come with. The humans' leader Malcolm (Jason Clarke) apprehends the fact that these are no ordinary apes and apologizes, stressing that they mean no harm. Caesar screams at them, "Go!"

On Caesar's instructions, Koba follows the strangers. The humans return to a San Francisco colony made up of people who had transpired to be genetically immune to ALZ-113. By now, moviemakers are able to represent ruination via far more impressive methods then child-like matte paintings and atmosphereless interior sets. San Francisco is vividly shown as a postindustrial wasteland losing ground to moss, vines, and Father Time.

Koba wants to go to war on the humans, but Caesar says no (literally), before signing, "If we go to war, we could lose all we've built." Instead, Caesar leads a delegation of apes. The novelty of the first glimpse of a gorilla in saddle in the original *Planet of the Apes* movie can never be replicated, but the sight in this scene of Caesar, Koba, and Maurice on horseback surrounded by multitudes of apes on hindleg and knuckle is quite arresting. The leader of the human colony is Dreyfus, played by Gary Oldman. Such is the realism of the Chernin trilogy that it seems quite obvious why the British actor resists any temptation to go with the tradition of Apes characters with inexplicable English accents.

The humans, focused on their own problems, have never become conversant with the fact that the apes they remember rampaging across the Golden Gate Bridge have cognitive parity with them. Moreover, Dreyfus has instructed that the reconnaissance party do not mention to the colony the extraordinary sight they had witnessed in the forest. The humans are therefore shocked when Caesar verbally addresses them. "Apes do not want war, but will fight if we must," he announces, before telling the humans to stick to their own turf and not to reenter ape territory.

The humans no more want war than the simians. However, Caesar's decree is problematic. The party of humans had been in the forest because they were investigating the possibility of reactivating a nearby dam so as to generate enough power to keep the lights on in the colony. Having confirmed that the dam is operable, they need to go back to get it working. Malcolm wants to reason with the apes. The more belligerent Dreyfus says he'll give him three days, after which he will go up into the woods and take with him the one form of strength humans have in abundance courtesy of the Fort Point armory just below the Golden Gate Bridge.

The party Malcolm takes includes Carver (Kirk Acevedo). As he is the one who shot Ash, he might seem an odd inclusion, but he is the only one among them who knows how to operate the dam. He also fulfils the franchise's timeworn role of a human with a convenient hatred of apes, in his case stemming from bitterness about the Simian Flu wiping out vast swathes of the human race. The party also includes Alexander (Kodi Smit-McPhee), Malcolm's teenage son from a previous marriage. He is passively resentful of his father's new partner Ellie (Keri Russell), the kind of intricate subplot that didn't really exist in science fiction movies in the days of the original quintet. Also marking the picture out as one from a more sophisticated era is the impressive lack of chiseled features or heroism among the humans: these are ordinary-looking folk, while Malcolm is shown as terrified when he ventures into the apes' stronghold (past, incidentally, eerie scarecrows). Caesar allows the humans passage as long as they surrender their guns. He admits to a disgruntled Koba that he is taking a risk but says that the humans seem desperate enough that, if they are denied what they want, they will attack them to secure it. Koba is not mollified, especially when Carver turns out to have a hidden gun. Koba's suspicions are aroused further when he takes some apes along the top of the rusting, moss-covered Golden Gate Bridge (stunning CGI work and awe-inspiring direction) and notices humans testing the weapons at Fort Point for use in the event of Malcolm's overture failing.

In the aftermath of giving birth to Caesar's new son, Cornelia is seriously ill. Caesar reluctantly allows Ellie—a trained nurse—to give her antibiotics. His realization that not all human science is bad makes Caesar disinclined to turn the other cheek when Koba—furious at what he has just seen from atop the bridge—accuses him of loving humans more than either apes or his own children. A fistfight erupts in which the two apes battle as you would expect them to, pinning down their opponent and bringing both fists down simultaneously in a rotating method. (Serling wrote something similarly naturalistic in his script.) Caesar attempts to throttle Koba, before remembering the apes' sacred edict. Koba makes a perfunctory apology but, significantly, doesn't tell Caesar about the gun cache he observed. Koba proceeds to make friends with Blue Eyes. The reason for the chip on the latter's hairy shoulder now becomes clear: the scriptwriters needed a reason for him to be a receptive audience for Koba's disingenuous claims that Caesar doesn't understand the dangers that humans pose.

At the dam, the humans react with joy as light suddenly floods a nearby gasoline station and the strains of the Band's "The Weight" drift across the air. Meanwhile, Koba and friends have liberated guns from the armory after killing the two men guarding it. Koba shoots Caesar with a purloined weapon and sets fire to the apes' home, laying the blame at the feet of humans. Celebrations in the newly lit-up San Francisco come to an end as a vengeful ape army bearing torches and machine guns descends on it, a sight Reeves makes suitably terrifying. The ensuing battle is magnificently staged, the night peppered with gunfire and explosions and the clash intriguingly poised as humans deploy rocket launchers and apes exploit their ability to swing on telephone wires. The rich detail is almost impossible to take in, the viewer not knowing whether to focus on foreground or background. When the apes wince and shrink at explosions and gunfire, it's almost as though we're watching a documentary.

Malcolm and Ellie come upon Caesar, left for dead by Koba, and scoop him up. Seeing that the colony is on fire, they realize they can't go back to San Francisco. Caesar, meanwhile, has recognized his old home on one of the streets they are driving down: the house belonging to Rodman. We infer that the latter became a casualty of the drug he invented because, like all of the human cast of the previous film, he is nowhere to be seen. Caesar indicates that they should hold out there. Ellie needs to operate on him but has nothing to do it with. Convinced that Caesar is the only one who can stop this war, Malcolm elects to go back to the colony to fetch a surgical kit. The fact that apes tried to kill him and humans are saving him—as well as nostalgia induced by memories of Rodman—rather alters Caesar's conception of family.

Koba's army presses on, swarming on all fours over the ornate steps of City Hall. However, Koba is finding that some of his soldiers are more in thrall to the pacifist sensibilities of Caesar than his warmongering. In a scene that is genuinely shocking in its brutality, Koba drags Ash step-by-step up to a balcony and then throws him off as punishment for refusing to kill a helpless human. He then locks up Maurice and Rocket for being too loyal to Caesar. Other doubters are intimidated into obedience.

Malcolm, meanwhile, is searching the human colony for medical supplies. Reeves excels in a scene wherein Malcolm is trapped inside a building just as apes invade, the human alternately pressing himself into corners and hastily switching paths as the simians rampage down corridors in a hail of hooting and machine-gun fire. Malcolm encounters Blue Eyes and is able to alert him to the fact of what really happened to his father. Blue Eyes consequently leads a rebellion against Koba's crew and frees the imprisoned humans and apes. Caesar gets off his sick bed to go and confront Koba.

As apes swarm up a steel tower on top of the human holdout, Dreyfus gets ready to blow it up. Malcolm desperately tries to hold him off at gunpoint in order to give Caesar time to regain leadership of the apes. When Caesar struggles his way to the top of the tower to confront Koba, there follows a grand version of the arboreal fight between Caesar and Ursus in *Battle for the Planet of the Apes*. CGI enables the scenario to be drawn far more richly and dynamically than that brief treetop *contretemps*, the two apes tumbling down latticing, careening across planking, and undulating on chain-link. In a truly immersive experience, the viewers feel they are tumbling and whirling with the participants. When Koba is left hanging for grim life to the end of a girder, he holds out his arm to Caesar and reminds him, "Ape not kill ape." "You are not ape," responds Caesar and lets him plunge to his death.

Dawn of the Planet of the Apes is a considerable step up from *Rise*, being a classy, convincing, and nuanced narrative as well as a breathtaking spectacle. Such is the depth of quality of the CGI that we almost take for granted the utterly fanciful sights it proffers. We also find ourselves forgetting that it's predicated on a clumsy preceding film in which there was never any profound impetus for apes to wage war. *Dawn* possesses no major faults, with even the perennial one for which the Apes fan has learned to make allowances not present. Whereas scriptwriters previously ignored the issue of whether there were any other civilizations or countries because to do otherwise would open up too many questions, here the reactivation of the dam is explicitly stated as being partly about getting a radio transmitter working so as to open communications with some of the other enclaves of mankind that must be dotted around the planet. In the closing minutes, Malcolm warns Caesar that Dreyfus has made contact over the newly working radio and that the military—alerted to the ape attack—is on its way. Not only are war and a climactic third movie inevitable, so is an opening out of the usually parochial Apes canvas.

The complaints, then, have to be minor. One is the contrived symbol of allegiance based on the distinctive window that Caesar spent much of his childhood gazing through in *Rise*: it would mean nothing to those apes who have never seen Rodman's house. Another is that the film is pretty much lacking in humor. And of course there is the inapposite title. There again, the truly appropriate title—*Well-Crafted Bridging Movie in a Planet of the Apes Trilogy*—would have been too nakedly honest, even if audiences became cognizant of the fact that pictures could be excellent holding actions as far back as 1980's *The Empire Strikes Back*.

Dawn of the Planet of the Apes—which runs to 130 minutes—was released on June 26, 2014. Joe Letteri, Dan Lemmon, Daniel Barrett, and Erik Winquist lost out on a Best Visual Effects Oscar to the talents behind the dull space-travel flick *Interstellar*. Outrageously, Reeves wasn't even nominated for Best Director. The public were more impressed than were the Academy of Motion Picture Arts and Sciences.

Also impressed was Rupert Wyatt. The *Rise* director didn't get to use the rapidly developing motion-capture techniques to which Reeves had access. "Jealousy's possibly the wrong word," says Wyatt. "It was a bittersweet experience."

~

When it comes to the issue of the first Chernin Apes film not having been granted a novelization, Rich Handley offers, "I don't think that they were banking on how popular these new movies were going to be. They were probably [cautious] because a decade earlier Burton's film had bombed." It's difficult to assess whether Andrew Gaska's *Conspiracy of the Planet of the Apes* convinced Fox or publishers of the viability of Apes tomes: the inordinate time it took for Gaska's sequel to appear hardly suggests stratospheric sales. However, when *Dawn of the Planet of the Apes* came out, it was accompanied by no fewer than two tie-in books. Perhaps this was down to something in the air. That very year, the validity of novelizations seemed to have been reconfirmed when Greg Cox's *Godzilla* adaptation shifted enough units to make the *New York Times* bestseller lists.

The *Dawn* "official movie novelization," written by Alex Irvine, is slickly done if, as ever, clearly based on an earlier script containing scenes and plotlines later jettisoned. It goes into considerable detail about the precise nature of the task Malcolm faces in getting the dam going and provides an epilogue not seen in the film wherein the military arrives to confront defiant apes. The other tie-in—published like the novelization by Titan—was prequel novel *Dawn of the Planet of the Apes: Firestorm* by Greg Keyes.

An acclaimed SF writer in his own right, Keyes is also a prolific author of adaptations and tie-ins, including books related to *Babylon 5*, *Star Wars*, *Interstellar*, *Independence Day*, and *Pacific Rim*. *Firestorm* is set between *Rise* and *Dawn* and is essentially the story of the Simian Flu, telling of its consequences from the points of view of both humans and apes, including Caesar. It also provides the backstory of Koba. As with all "before the events" stories—from the Star Wars prequel films on down—it can assume a grand sense of redundancy. However, it's adroitly written and the subject matter (the decimation of human civilization) intrinsically interesting.

Things were looking good in Planet of the Apes land. The outstanding question was, Could the quality of the new iteration be maintained, or would the trilogy sputter out in a damp-squib finale *à la The Godfather Part III* or *Return of the Jedi*?

16

A FULL CIRCLE, SQUARED

On *War for the Planet of the Apes*, the concluding part of the Chernin trilogy, Amanda Silver and Rick Jaffa acted as producers but for the first time in the new series weren't the writers (although, of course, we are reminded in the credits that they "created" the characters). The screenplay is by the team of Mark Bomback & Matt Reeves, the latter also returning to the chair that he filled so majestically in *Dawn*, becoming the first director to helm successive Apes movies since J. Lee Thompson back in '73.

The story jumps on rather disjointedly from the last episode via a lengthy and slightly arty written precis (capitalizations reproduced faithfully):

> Fifteen years ago, a scientific experiment gone wrong gave RISE to a species of intelligent apes and destroyed most of humanity with a virus that became known as Simian Flu.
>
> With the DAWN of a new ape civilization led by Caesar, the surviving humans struggled to coexist. But fighting finally broke out when a rebel ape, Koba, led a vengeful attack against humans.

CHAPTER 16

The humans sent a distress call to a military base in the North, where all that remained of the U.S. Army was gathered. A ruthless Special Forces Colonel and his hardened battalion were dispatched to exterminate the apes. Evading capture for the last two years, Caesar is now rumored to be marshalling the fight from a hidden command base in the woods, as the WAR rages on.

Despite the contrivances to come, it's certainly plausible that humans would consider the apes to be a threat after the Golden Gate Bridge incident and the clash in San Francisco. The army battalion—which, in another franchise back-reference, styles itself "Alpha-Omega"—is assisted by former followers of Koba who are fearful of what Caesar will do to them. The humans are hardly grateful for the turncoats' assistance, daubing their fur with the derogatory designation "donkey."

The opening scene finds an ape camp under attack by Alpha-Omega rescued by a simian cavalry. Reeves quickly conveys that his masterly direction is not just about a 360-degree immersive technique, but now takes in atmospheric slow motion and drifting aerial shots. This is the final major section of the film that will be seen exclusively from the humans' perspective. The first Chernin Apes production with simians in every scene, *War* is depicted primarily from the point of view of Caesar.

At the ape family's hideout behind a waterfall, Caesar is informed of events. He is now speaking fluent American-accented English. In a sign of his now somewhat more serious mien, he speaks that English in a low growl through clenched teeth. Most of the apes, however, still communicate via sign language.

There is happier news when Blue Eyes and Rocket return from reconnaissance work and reveal that they have found a safe location for apes: because it's beyond a desert, it's believed the resource-strapped post-pandemic humans will not venture there.

Caesar shows mercy to the captured elements of the human attack squad and sends them home with a message of live-and-let-live. Even so, a retaliatory human raid is mounted on the hideout. After killing Cornelia and Blue Eyes in the mistaken belief that one of them is Caesar, the soldier's leader gives the radio signal, "King Kong is dead," an illustration of the fact that these soldiers are cartoon villains devoid of the ambiguity about conflict with apes that we saw in the humans in the last movie (none of whom reappear here). The raiding party is forced to retreat, but not before Caesar catches sight of the leader. Placing his younger son (who we now discover is named Cornelius) into the care of Blue Eyes's widow Lake, Caesar instructs the apes to seek the promised land without him. He wishes to exact revenge on both the human soldier and Winter, a traitorous ape who had clearly led the humans to their hiding place. He feels that by taking out the human, he will become the enemy's main target, giving his tribe the opportunity to slip away.

A trio of other apes insist on accompanying Caesar. It so happens that this gives rise to a group of protagonists composed of a variety of different species and hence handily distinguishable individuals: chimpanzee (Caesar), bonobo (Rocket), orangutan (Maurice), and gorilla (Luca). However, the effects are now progressing so rapidly that soon the viewer may not require such contrivances. The CGI is so detailed that it includes specks of debris attached to ape coats, gently dilating nostrils, and Caesar's facial fur being newly flecked with mid-life gray.

The ape eyes are also extremely lifelike, particularly the gentle orangutan orbs and startled bonobo peepers. If, despite this verisimilitude, the apes do sometimes look artificial, this is nothing more than an example of the curious fact that occasionally animals resemble models of themselves (see sharks).

Discovering a remote shack, the group is forced to kill a human army deserter, only to then find that he cares for a young daughter. The little girl is unable to speak, an affliction that the ape party will soon encounter in other humans. Fearing for the child's safety, Maurice insists that they take her with them. Maurice dubs the girl "Nova" after coming upon a hood ornament for a 1960s brand of Chevrolet Chevy II. This is all very well, but she must have had a name before—or perhaps she forgot it as quickly as she appears to have her slain father?

Sneaking into an Alpha-Omega camp, the group finds Winter. They obtain as much information as they can from him before strangling him to death. The writers missed a trick in not making this striking-looking albino gorilla one of the heroes, particularly as it would have been in line with the necessity to ensure viewers can tell furry creatures apart (not to mention the impetus to feature characters who can be turned into covetable collectibles). Although it's left ambiguous about whether Winter was placed in a chokehold only because the four were trying to prevent him raising the alarm, Caesar is haunted by a dream in which Koba admonishes him, "Ape not kill ape."

The group follows the Alpha-Omega men to their home base, negotiating freezing cold as they do: after the drizzle of *Dawn*, this is a snow movie. In the process, they come upon Bad Ape (his given name, played by Steve Zahn). The humor that was completely absent in the last movie is present here in the form of this stunted, jug-eared, bumbling, cowardly, kindly chimpanzee, a former resident of a zoo. He is the only adult ape character in the modern series to voluntarily wear clothes, implicitly because of his depleted coat, but of course really because it looks funny. We first see him in a parka, and when he gives that—in an act of typical compassion—to the shivering girl, he switches to a sleeveless puffa jacket and bobble hat. Although Bad Ape is engaging rather than irritating like his spiritual antecedent Jar Jar Binks, the origin story he relates is, disappointingly, a return to the sloppy science of both the original quintet and Boulle's novel, with him being posited as having learned his halting speech by simply listening to humans. The scriptwriters' motivation for this seems to be nothing more than the fact that, if he had been exposed to ALZ-113, he would be intelligent and they therefore wouldn't have been able to depict him as a lovable fool. Moreover, we are asked to believe that humans have behaved toward him in a consistently cruel manner (hence his name) when the law of averages dictates that he would have been shown kindness far more often than malice. (How many bad-asses are there working in zoos, after all?)

The Alpha-Omega HQ on the Californian border is a massive abandoned military base once used as a quarantine camp for people dying of Simian Flu. Bad Ape knows its location and leads the group there, if reluctantly. Caesar becomes even more vengeful when Luca gets killed by guards outside and he finds the path lined by apes spread-eagled on X-shaped crosses (the first time the echo of the scarecrows in the 1968 film has been reinvented in the same continuity). When Caesar is taken prisoner and transported inside, he finds the ape family, who were captured on their way to the safe haven. Half-starved, they have been put to work building a wall outside the building.

Caesar is introduced to the leader. Colonel McCullough is a shaven-headed, muscle-toned career soldier, played by Woody Harrelson. The Colonel has gone rogue because of his belief that his superiors are failing to take seriously the fact that the Simian Flu is now worsening. The mute humans whom Caesar's group encountered previously are examples of its effects. A medic has theorized to the Colonel that the ape virus, still resident in its human survivors, has mutated and may wipe out the race for good this time, not by killing them but by robbing them of speech and higher thinking, thus turning them into beasts. It's similar to Pierre Boulle's ideas about man devolving but is far more scientifically plausible. Not quite so plausible is the Colonel disdaining his superiors' talk of developing a vaccine and lunging instead for what he terms a "holy war," at which point we are reminded yet again of the franchise's dependence on humans with an irrational hatred of simians or vice versa. "All of human history has led to this moment," the Colonel insists. "If we lose, we will be the last of our kind. It will be a planet of apes, and we will become your cattle." So absolute is his conviction that, he reveals, he shot dead his own son when he succumbed to the muteness. Nova's father, it turns out, deserted the Colonel's camp precisely because he refused to follow his example and dispatch his own similarly afflicted offspring. Although his army superiors share the Colonel's fear of the apes, they are sending soldiers to deal with his unauthorized behavior, hence the wall.

"What have I done?" Caesar says aloud when he sees the demoralized state of the enslaved apes. This attempt to demonstrate the deleterious effects of being consumed by hatred doesn't quite come off, not least because of the conceit implicit in him assuming that the family would never have been captured if he'd remained to lead them.

Outside the base, things are getting silly, whether it be Bad Ape looking at the proceedings inside through the wrong end of binoculars or Nova strolling into the heavily guarded grounds unseen. Once inside, Nova gives Caesar—thrown in a cage—much needed food and water, all somehow unobserved by the guards.

The previously discretely veiled issue of ape toiletry habits is at least tangentially addressed when a guard finds himself being pelted with feces, just like visitors to zoos containing less mentally evolved simians. In this case, it's a ruse, designed to lure in the guard so that his keys can be seized from him. Caesar takes things from there, organizing a surreptitious escape, which is not noticed until the soldiers have far bigger things to worry about as helicopter missiles begin raining down on them.

Once again, this is an Apes movie with an inappropriate title, as the promised war never materializes. The film is more a combination of *The Great Escape* (wartime prison break), *The Bridge on the River Kwai* (forced wartime labor), and *The Ten Commandments* (trek to a promised land). There is a set-piece battle, although it's not much larger in scale than that seen in the last film. It's also not essentially the expected combat between man and ape but rather one between two human factions: Alpha-Omega versus the legitimate army. It does, however, give Reeves the chance to strut his stuff, him once again pulsatingly capturing carnage and chaos, this time with the photogenic bonus of snowbanks and spiraling choppers.

Nova responds to Maurice's praise for her bravery by delightedly signing, "Me ape?" Going in the opposite direction to such harmony, Caesar resigns himself to Koba-like hatred and stays behind to kill the Colonel. However, he finds that the military man has himself been struck by the muteness he dreaded. Allowing the Colonel to shoot himself, therefore, is an act of compassion.

Making his escape, Caesar is felled by a soldier's arrow. Unexpectedly, his life is saved by Red, a donkey gorilla who tormented him during his incarceration. This enables Caesar to throw a grenade at a fuel tank, which sets off a chain reaction that enables Reeves to treat us to yet another splendid destruction-fest. More is to come. The chain reaction turns out to include an avalanche. As tumbling ice consumes the base and rogue and liberating soldiers alike, Caesar scurries away on all fours.

The snow, literally and symbolically, gives way to sunny uplands as Caesar successfully leads his ape tribe to their new home. Although he lives long enough to secure this sanctuary, the wound he picked up from the soldier's arrow finally claims him. In an echo of the finale of the last series, a tear is seen to trickle down Caesar's face. The ending seems inappropriately optimistic—the apes have no way of knowing that more humans will never pursue them here. However, it provides a reasonably efficient sense of conclusion to what is a very good film, if not a great one like *Dawn*.

Released on July 10, 2017, the 140-minute *War for the Planet of the Apes* was a smash, something by now pretty much expected. The cycle that afflicted the original Apes quintet—reduced budgets, leading to lower box office takings, leading to even further reduced budgets—was not replicated with this series. *Rise* had a budget of $93 million and did $481.8 million in cinemas. *Dawn* was provided $170 million and rewarded that largess with takings of $710.6 million. *War* had a slightly reduced budget of $150 million, but it was still higher than the trilogy's opening film. Additionally, its profits of $490.7 million beat the opener's takings. At this point, it is permitted to make the species-erroneous joke that Fox in the Chernin era had finally realized that if you pay peanuts, you get monkeys. That said, it should be admitted that Peter Chernin had an advantage that Arthur P. Jacobs did not: whereas 1970s audiences expected an installment to be cranked out every year, modern cinemagoers are prepared to accept three-yearly sequel cycles, which affords the luxury of time and care.

The series had not just concluded but had provided, like *Battle for the Planet of the Apes*, a series full circle. With the vast continuity, in fact, a double full circle. Or a loop. Or a full circle squared. Whatever it was, it was pleasingly symmetrical. It begins in *Rise* when a background newscast speaks of the disappearance of a deep-space flight, implicitly that crewed by Taylor, Dodge, Landon, and Stewart. It concludes in *War* with the human species losing their vocal faculties, one of them being a young girl named Nova, whom Taylor will meet down the line when she is an adult. All of which renders the 1968 *Planet of the Apes* what George Lucas might call "Episode IV." The first epic of filmed science fiction had once again proceeded in the grand and ambitious way that had made the world love it from the get-go.

As time marches on, what was once so impressive becomes less so. Just as John Chambers's makeup now seems less stunning than it did in 1968, so the vaunted Planet of the Apes continuity and social commentary have not weathered well.

In the latter case, this is down to it being a victim of its own success. The Chernin trilogy demonstrated that the franchise had reached a curious place. Subtext was certainly present in the new films. Animal rights and the uprising of the oppressed runs like a thread through the trio. In *War for the Planet of the Apes* specifically, we are shown soldiers in search of Caesar's encampment wearing helmets festooned with slogans like "MONKEY KILLER" and "BEDTIME FOR BONZO." This is a clear allegory to Vietnam, the first American conflict where the practice was tolerated by top brass of daubing battle dress with slogans that demeaned the enemy. Meanwhile, black-slavery analogies become explicit again when the apes are set to work on what amounts to a chain gang and are whipped for clumsy behavior. (Sometimes, though, a cigar is just a cigar. Critics assumed that the wall being built by the Colonel was a dig at Donald Trump's proposed barrier on the US border with Mexico, ditto the line, "His wall is madness." Matt Reeves insists it was pure coincidence.)

Yet the social commentary in the second series of Apes movies was profoundly less noteworthy than that in the APJAC films. Subtext was now unremarkable because lots of people did it. We can be charitable—probably justifiably—and say that this is a measure of the triumph of the original Planet of the Apes films, which proved that consistently serious discourse and outlandish entertainment were in no way incompatible, thereby setting the ground for much imitation, which in turn rendered it unexceptional.

It is societal change and technological development that have rather called into question another part of the franchise's reputation. When in 1971 *Cinefantastique* magazine enthused about "the first epic of filmed science fiction," the series was only on its third movie. Frederick S. Clarke, the contributor in question, must have been delighted at the way the subsequent two movies developed further the series' story arc and even made it circle back on itself. Incredibly important as that continuity was in terms of both Planet of the Apes' internal aesthetics and the wider development of cinema, however, we have now reached a stage where Rich Handley feels obligated to say, "If you examine it, it's not there."

"The whole thing has become a very logical development in the form of a circle," Paul Dehn told the media when he was preparing the fifth movie. "I have a complete chronology of the time circle mapped out and, when I start a new script, I check every supposition I make against the chart to see if it is correct to use it." The carefully designed continuity of Dehn—assisted by Rod Serling, Michael Wilson, John & Joyce Hooper Corrington, et al.—was certainly painstaking and groundbreaking, but society was not yet equipped to see it was highly flawed or, to use Handley's term, "bonkers."

The cats-and-dogs origin story in *Escape* is itself totally inconsistent with the previous films, where simians barely grasp the fact that humanity was once the dominant species, and the few who are cognizant of it know that the odd course of evolution is down to a man-made catastrophe. Meanwhile, the apes that human society so misuses in *Conquest of the Planet of the Apes* would logically be simians as we know them today rather than the broadly upright creatures with human mannerisms into which they had evolved in the time frame of the previous Apes movies. However, the only visible physical difference between these slave apes and the likes of Cornelius and Zira is that they can't speak.

Having authored two books on the franchise and edited three more, Handley is staggered by the number of inconsistencies he has had cause to confront. "It goes back to *Beneath*," he says. "*Beneath* is said to take place in 3955, which is twenty-three years earlier than the first film, so things don't line up at all. In the first movie, ape culture is twelve hundred years old. They don't believe there's anything before twelve hundred years because that's how old the Sacred Scrolls are. Yet in the future films we find out that the apes know about the plague of cats and dogs two thousand years earlier. Nobody knows humans can talk, and yet Caesar says that everybody celebrates the holiday on which Aldo said 'No' to his human overlords. It's funny because all the sequels are written by the same person, and yet it's almost like he didn't watch them."

While Handley acknowledges, "It's very easy for writers to screw something up," he also states that some of the plot holes are simply a matter of exigency. "Where things go awry with that original quintet is the need to keep Caesar in the story, because obviously the desire would have been strong to keep Roddy McDowall involved. But the problem is, just from the dialogue in *Escape*, it seems like the ape revolution was supposed to be several hundred years after *Escape*. There's no way to do that unless Caesar lives for centuries. So they sped everything up in the next movie and made it within Caesar's lifetime."

Handley admits that he can't locate such internal discrepancies in the Chernin trilogy. "The three new movies hold up remarkably well as one story," he says. "I've seen each movie several times and I've never really seen anything from one movie to the next that made me say, 'Wait a minute, that doesn't make sense.' I think they've done a remarkable job. . . . The spin-off materials—the novels and the comics—do a great job of filling stuff in too. There's more of an attempt to remain cohesive than there was back then."

The reason for the first Apes series' inconsistencies is that Dehn, for all his meticulous stitching together of a coherent arc, knew he could paint in broad brushstrokes and didn't need to worry about fine detail. As Handley points out, "They figured that it had been a year since you've seen the [previous] movie." The modern conscientiousness to which

Handley refers, distinct from the APJAC quintet's failed or pretend continuity, is the result of a new mentality brought about by superior consumption technology, particularly the instant playback mechanisms of video cassette, DVD, and streaming. Handley: "If a casual fan is watching the five movies spaced apart and is not really paying attention, the 3978/3955 discrepancy might go right past them. If you watch them back to back you go, 'How is this movie twenty-three years before the other one?'" The Jaffa/Silver generation has a wholly different mentality. They are cognizant of the fact that, since the 1980s, films have been steadily demystified by ready accessibility and that the public has therefore a far less fragmentary knowledge of their contents. Moreover, the current filmmakers themselves benefit from that new accessibility. Handley: "They're working as professionals in an era where they can just pull up the Blu-ray and watch a scene six times to make sure they understand it. And when they were younger, they were probably the fanboy types who were noticing these things themselves and they don't want to be caught in the same way. Their perspective is different than say Wilson's or Paul Dehn's because they have grown up seeing what happens when you make mistakes and the entire internet breaks over it. But also they have resources that Paul Dehn simply didn't have." Those resources also include web-assisted instant retrieval of statistics and at-a-glance comparisons. In Dehn's day, it was a matter of leafing through paper files, looking up facts in books, and other laborious processes that engendered a disinclination to double-check. Tom Burman's view on the issue of the generally unremarked-on fact that the ostensibly alien planet on which Charlton Heston's character lands happens to speak English ("When they are a big success, who cares?") may have been prevalent in film circles in his day, but that attitude is increasingly rare.

Yet the Chernin trilogy does have its continuity faults. If it were indeed an "origin story" for the original quintet, it would make all Planet of the Apes films a vast continuum unprecedented in motion picture history (albeit with a necessary wiping from that history of the inconveniently intervening and incompatible Tim Burton film). Says Rupert Wyatt, "I can only really speak for *Rise*, less for *Dawn* and *War*, but to be able to place [it] in the timeline of the original film was important to us." For all his respect for the internal continuity of the Chernin trilogy, Handley points out that it simply does not slot together as intended with the Jacobs quintet. For him, the task was doomed from the get-go, and not just because of the irreconcilable facts already resident within the APJAC series. "It starts in 2011," he says of the Chernin films. "The Apes would have already been in charge. There's also the fact that Taylor left in 1973, but the astronaut mission in *Rise* is leaving in 2011. . . . You have talking apes in 1973 and then there are no talking apes in 2011. You have an ape revolution in 1991 but the apes are not in control in 2011." One might say that those are petty objections insofar as Jaffa & Silver can't do anything about real-world passing time, but Handley also points to irreconcilables that didn't need to exist: "ANSA instead of NASA. . . . A totally different reason for talking apes to exist now: it's a cure for Alzheimer's. . . . There was a revolution involving both Caesars and the second one [is] unaware of the first one. . . . I just don't see how the current films could really in any way be seen to be part of the same universe." As for the plague in the Chernin trilogy that renders humans mute and the fact that one of those voiceless humans is a young girl given the sobriquet "Nova" by Maurice, Handley says, "But see, that right there would knock me right out of calling it the same story. The only reason Nova's Nova two thousand years from now is Taylor nicknames her that. I am fascinated by the idea that they might have had the intention of making it a loop, but I would say it failed."

Perhaps Handley isn't giving enough credence to the immutable law known by anybody with even a passing knowledge of time-travel stories: that one tiny action by people who have no right to be in a particular point in history can change the future. Surely, by going back in time in *Escape*, Cornelius and Zira have altered what transpired in the first two films, thus explaining away pretty much all inconsistencies? This suggestion that the future has been altered is present in the bookends of *Battle*, where the mortal, long-dead Caesar has taken the deity place in Ape culture that the Lawgiver once had, and the Lawgiver role is now that of a living teacher, and furthermore a rather liberal one. Corrina Bechko, in the Planet of the Apes comic books she has written with Gabriel Hardman, has certainly adopted this stance. "The original movies have time travel in them," she says. "We figured if the time travel happened, it could have reset into a different universe. Maybe that happened a bunch of times. So perhaps all of the time lines of Planet of the Apes are correct. They're just in slightly different universes affected differently by the time travel." This explanation was, of course, handed to her and her ilk on a plate when in *Escape* Dr. Otto Hasslein explained to a TV presenter (and at such length it was as though Paul Dehn was trying to make his own excuses for discrepancies) his multiple-road theory of time. At its conclusion, Hasslein summarizes, "Time is like a freeway with an infinite number of lanes, all leading from the past into the future. However, not into the same future. A driver in Lane A may crash while a driver in Lane B survives. It follows that a driver by changing lanes can change his future." "It's such a free pass," laughs Bechko.

There again, Handley can hardly be blamed for declining to embrace a magic wand that waves away all inconveniences and, in the process, renders all his own continuity efforts redundant. He has taken the trouble to write an entire book attempting to place everything seen in Planet of the Apes media—not just the films and TV series but also spin-off prose, comics, and video games—on a consistent time line. Moreover, the acceptance of this theory would break the golden rule of art: a writer has to state facts rather than an audience infer them—convenient but unintended effects don't count. If Dehn had meant that speech to be a *deus ex machina*, he should have written the expository dialogue that would make it "real." Additionally, as mentioned previously in this text, Dehn himself thought that the escape to the past of Cornelius, Zira, and Milo would not have changed the future.

The indifference of the general public to such discrepancies is a given: if Jo/e Public has been entertained, and their children distracted, for two hours, they simply laugh at the idea that they should brood over elements that don't add up. However, this unconcern in the end even applies to someone like Handley. He has an attitude that is not uncommon among Apes fans and illustrates the great dichotomy at the heart of the whole Planet of the Apes franchise. Despite the two Apes film series having always tilted for an overarching consistency and connectedness, their failure in this ambition has never really mattered to the very parts of their audience who respect and adore the franchise precisely for its efforts in this regard. "You gotta roll your eyes, throw up your hands and say, 'I still love the movies,'" Handley states. "I love all of them, warts and all."

~

Greg Cox (of *New York Times* bestseller *Godzilla* fame) handled the 2017 novelization of *War for the Planet of the Apes*. He is also the author of the novels of *Man of Steel* and *The Dark Knight Rises* as well as several Star Trek books. The *War* book is as thoughtful and well crafted as might be imagined from his résumé.

Meanwhile, Greg Keyes was once again given the job of the film's bridging novel. He has less scope in *War for the Planet of the Apes: Revelations* than he did in his previous effort. A pandemic wiping out much of humanity is a wide-ranging subject with a lot of dramatic possibilities. Here, he is confined to smaller drama: depicting Caesar and his army getting ready for the attack of the human military, the genesis of Koba's plotting, the tragic story of the Colonel and his son, and Blue Eyes's search for a new homeland for his brethren. Somehow, he manages to produce a readable yarn from what is essentially an exercise in plugging holes.

Also in 2017 came the collection *Tales from the Forbidden Zone*. The contents of these short stories all take place in what is now termed "Planet of the Apes classic continuity" (i.e., the original movie quintet, the live-action TV show, and the animated TV show). "That was Titan's license," explains Rich Handley, who coedited with Jim Beard.

While some stories in *Tales from the Forbidden Zone* seek to address and correct internal contradictions in Apes screen fare, some can only be justified by Dr. Hasslein's multiple time-lanes theory, such as the stories set on Earth a few years on from it being destroyed at the end of *Beneath*. Nonetheless, the use of accomplished and respected writers (including Gaska) ensured a volume that is highly regarded.

Almost as if to make up for the lack of a novelization of *Rise of the Planet of the Apes*, in 2018 Greg Keyes proffered *Caesar's Story*. Set in the universe of the Chernin trilogy, this Hachette publication uses the lateral storytelling method of a journal written by Maurice for Caesar's son, Cornelius, so as to give him an idea of who his father was. It includes in its chronology not just the three films but the two tie-in novels and related comics. Heavily illustrated, its font alternates between old typewriter lettering and mock hand printing.

The function of novelizations may now, in most cases, be obsolete but—with the Apes film franchise now once again a lucrative industry—Planet of the Apes prose remains a viable proposition. In 2017–2018, Titan even rescued the classic-era Planet of the Apes novelizations from their status of long-discarded, yellowing paperbacks by putting them back into print in omnibuses, including the books of the live-action and animated TV series.

Planet of the Apes fiction has ranged from poor to functional to excellent, but it's a library that these days absolutely dwarfs Pierre Boulle's original slim tome.

When the Apes movie property was resurrected by Chernin Entertainment, video game manufacturers did not seem that interested in capitalizing on it. At least it can be said that the game released to coincide with the third film made up for the lack of previous product.

Planet of the Apes: Last Frontier (2017) was developed by the Imaginati Studios and published by FoxNext, The Imaginarium, and Creative England. It was released on the PlayStation 4 and (eventually) Xbox One and Microsoft Windows platforms. The story line is set between the second and third Chernin films, and gameplay can be either one player or multiplayer. It is a decision-making narrative, with players having no direct control over the cast of fourteen humans and apes, but by choosing the reactions and dialogue of characters, the player can bring about three possible overall outcomes: victory for apes, victory for humans, or peace between humans and apes. Boasting movie-style opening credits, photorealistic footage (for which Andy Serkis and others provided stop-motion performance), and a remarkably high number of "cutscenes" (non-gameplay sequences), not to mention lasting two to three hours (depending, of course, on skill level), it sometimes resembles less a game than a fourth Chernin Apes movie. Mixed reviews demonstrate that some were left unsatisfied by the lack of action (gamers love to shoot), but there's no denying that it's a beautiful-looking proposition—and an example of a whole new dimension in entertainment.

Another new dimension is the virtual reality game, an example of which is *Crisis on the Planet of the Apes*, released the following year for the PSVR, Oculus Touch, and HTC Vive Gameplay. Developed by Imaginati and published by FoxNext VR Studio, its story line's time frame is five years after the outbreak of the Simian Flu. A first-person shooter, the narrative is seen through the eyes of an ape who, along with a band of other simians, escapes his human captors and tries to find his way home, blasting opponents away as he does. The graphics are impressive, if relentlessly gloomy. It's also a profoundly less passive experience than *Last Frontier* for more reasons than not being restricted to decision making: it involves the player—once he has donned the required headset—physically marching, ducking, and gesticulating to make his character do the same. (For the less fit, it's perhaps a small mercy it only lasts around an hour.) However proactive the gameplay, though, it's also rather repetitive, involving shooting human after human with little feeling of progress.

Lack of progress is not an issue with leisure technology. One day not too far hence video games may seem as laughable as the Planet of the Apes Chad Valley Picture Show Sliderama Projector. In the years and decades to come, there will be new innovations in, and new ways of disseminating, Apes-related product to either the delight or disgust of the franchise's fans.

17

THE FUTURE

Planet of the Apes changed the world—and entertained millions in the process—but where to now?

Many people don't like sequels on a point of principle. Those people (such as, perhaps, *Mad* magazine writers) will not be pleased to hear that more Apes movies are in the pipeline. The Chernin trilogy brought Caesar's story to a conclusive end by having him complete the Moses-like leading of his brethren to the promised land, followed almost immediately by his death. Of course, being deceased has not always meant the end in the Apes franchise, but perhaps modern audiences are a bit more skeptical than the 1971 cinemagoers who barely batted an eyelid about the glib way that APJAC found a way around the previous movie's destruction of every living thing on planet Earth. However, the one thing Hollywood can bank on in today's uncertain world is the market for follow-ups to successful films. Moreover, when what is now called "21st Century Fox" became in 2019 yet another media outlet swept into the voracious maw of the Disney Corporation, a new impetus for fresh Apes product was created. Disney didn't become vastly successful by sitting on its fat assets. It is planning a film (or films) that will make the phrase "modern Planet of the Apes trilogy" redundant.

Mid-2020 saw the announcement that Wes Ball—famed for the Maze Runner series—would be the director of the fourth post-Burton Apes movie. The script will be written by Josh Friedman, scripter of Spielberg's *War of the Worlds* (2005) and Brian De Palma's *Black Dahlia* (2006). Speaking to Chris St Lawrence of the website Discussing Film, Ball said, "Those last three movies are one of the great trilogies we have in modern movie history. . . . They honored the original movies they sprang from . . . but they grounded it in a modern sensibility. . . . So what do you do to follow that up, right? At the same time, I wasn't interested in doing a part four either. . . . We have a take. We have a way of staying in the universe that was created before us, but we're also opening ourselves up in being able to do some really cool new stuff." Any new Apes film seems destined by default to make a mess of the symmetry/loop striven for by Rick Jaffa and Amanda Silver, but, as we have seen, some of the franchise's fans will tell you that that symmetry is a mirage anyway. For the record, Jaffa & Silver are set to serve as the next film's producers.

For Rich Handley, there should be a lot more cool new Apes stuff: "I don't know that Fox has ever fully had faith in the franchise," he says. "I mean, right now we're at a time when it seems like every four days a new Star Trek series is being announced, and a new Marvel spin-off, and DC shows up the wazoo. Yet, despite the fact that those three Planet of the Apes movies are popular, where's the Planet of the Apes TV show? Why aren't Planet of the Apes comic books being announced? Planet of the Apes seems like a really obvious thing for them to be building on and yet they're not.

"I think that that attitude is not new. In the research that I did on the books that I did, it seemed like the people I spoke to would relate a reticence on Fox's part to greenlight things. In the early 2000s, a friend of mine had a publishing company. He went to Fox and he said, 'I'd like to buy the rights to do Planet of the Apes comics now that no one's doing them.' And what he was told was, 'Oh no, they're no longer available. Dark Horse has them.' He said, 'Well, no, that doesn't make any sense because Dark Horse gave up the rights and Mr. Comics has done a comic series since then.' And the person said, 'No, no, no, Mr. Comics never did Planet of the Apes. Dark Horse still owns the rights.' Now keep in mind that the previous year Mr. Comics had released *Revolution on the Planet of the Apes*. 'Oh, well, it's just not available.' That was the end result.

"I think the fact that everything from Apes other than the Boom! comics has been short lived, the fact that the movies were cancelled when they were still really popular, the fact that there was that twenty-five-year dead zone, the fact that the person my friend spoke to didn't even know another company had come and gone since Dark Horse—I think all of this underlies what the problem is, which is that it was probably at the studio's end.

"Titan has done several very good books. Yet Titan is not pumping out Planet of the Apes books. Why? You'd think they'd be riding on this. Did they just run into a brick wall with Fox? Planet of the Apes seems to keep starting projects and then not finishing them. I don't know why that is.

"They keep bringing back Alien and Predator, and when they do there are spin-off comics and spin-off novels and so forth. But when they bring back Planet of the Apes. . . . Yeah, there have been comics but there haven't been any in a while. Boom! really started cutting down on how many titles were coming out and they were largely crossovers with other universes instead of original stories.

"I don't know what the thought process right now is at Fox. I've been waiting for a TV show to be announced and none has. It seems to me that's a no-brainer. These three movies are really, really well regarded. So why would you not do a TV show set in that continuity?"

Handley feels a TV series would be the perfect opportunity to address the recurring issue with the Planet of the Apes franchise—namely, the grand but inapposite use of the word *planet.* He feels that the sight of Hunsiker spreading the virus around the globe in *Rise of the Planet of the Apes* would make a perfect jumping-off point. "All we're seeing in the movies is one little ape village and a human society that's degenerated nearby, but there's so much more, especially given that graphic with it spreading everywhere. An anthology-based TV show could explore everything. That's where the comics came in so brilliantly with the old films. Marvel and Malibu had tons of stuff that showed corners of the Planet of the Apes that you never would have seen in the movies."

Handley is prepared to admit that the Apes franchise is a much more complicated proposition for audiences than, say, Spider-Man. "As much as I love Planet of the Apes, at no point can I say that I relate to Caesar. I certainly can't relate to Zaius. I can't relate to Dr. Hasslein. I certainly wouldn't want to relate to Taylor, 'cos Taylor's a dick. It's easier to relate to characters who are standard heroes."

Despite Handley's opinion about negligence and inactivity, the Chernin trilogy has shown that Planet of the Apes is still a billion-dollar industry. There will be not just further films but also surely a flurry of new Apes product in other media such as prose, comics, and merchandise, even if that ancillary product—due to a changing world—is these days much smaller than its 1970s peak. There will also be more Apes-associated examples of newer media such as video games.

Pierre Boulle had no idea what he started. More than a half century after the publication of *La planète des singes*, the Planet of the Apes franchise continues, grows, and evolves. It would seem that humanity will be tussling with its simian cousin for our entertainment for many years to come.

Acknowledgments

I wish to express my grateful thanks to Corinna Bechko, Tom Burman, Christopher Gordon, Rich Handley, Linda Harrison, Doug Moench, Don Murray, Christopher Sausville, Austin Stoker, and Rupert Wyatt for granting interviews for this book. In addition to these interviews, I drew upon interviews I had conducted previously with Ron Harper, Rob Kirby, James Naughton, and Roy Thomas, some of which material is hitherto unpublished. I am also privileged to be publishing for the first time selections from interviews conducted by Dean Preston with makeup staff who worked on Tim Burton's 2001 *Planet of the Apes*. I wish to extend my grateful thanks to Dean for granting the relevant permission to use quotes from the following individuals: Mark Alfrey, Cristina Ceret, Jamie Kelman, Kazuhiro Tsuji, and Eddie Yang. I would additionally like to thank Mark Arnold, Hunter Goatley, Edward Gross, and Dean Preston for answering queries and providing introductions.

Bibliography

Becker, Lucille Frackman. *Pierre Boulle*. Woodbridge, CT: Twayne, 1996.

Berenato, Joseph F., and Rich Handley, eds. *Bright Eyes, Ape City: Examining the Planet of the Apes Mythos*. Edwardsville, IL: Sequart, 2017.

Bond, Jeff, and Joe Fordham. *Planet of the Apes: The Evolution of the Legend*. London: Titan, 2014.

Cinefantastique (Summer 1972). Multiple articles.

Conlin, William, dir. *Making Apes: The Artists Who Changed Film*. Cleveland, OH: Gravitas Ventures, 2019. DVD.

Dunne, John Gregory. *The Studio*. New York: Vintage, 1998.

Egan, Sean. *Tarzan: The Biography*. London: Askill, 2017.

"Five Questions with Ape-a-Holics Anonymous." *Toys from the Attic*, catalog 3, September 1995.

Handley, Rich, comp. "The Complete Planet of the Apes Comics Index." Last updated January 22, 2021. http://hassleinbooks.com/pdfs/POTAComics.pdf.

Heston, Charlton. *The Actor's Life: Journals 1956–1976*. New York: E. P. Dutton, 1978.

Pendreigh, Brian. *The Legend of the Planet of the Apes, or How Hollywood Turned Darwin Upside Down*. New York: Macmillan, 2001.

Planet of the Apes (Curtis Magazines/Marvel Comics; August 1974–February 1977). Multiple articles.

Russo, Joe, Larry Landsman, and Edward Gross. *Planet of the Apes Revisited: The Behind-the-Scenes Story of the Classic Science Fiction Saga*. New York: Griffin, 2001.

Salisbury, Mark, ed. *Burton on Burton*. Rev. ed. London: Faber and Faber, 2006.

Sausville, Christopher. *Planet of the Apes Collectibles: An Unauthorized Guide with Trivia & Values*. Atglen, PA: Schiffer, 1997.

Woods, Paul A. *The Planet of the Apes Chronicles*. London: Plexus, 2001.

WEBSITES

Hunter's Planet of the Apes. https://pota.goatley.com/.

Planet of the Apes: The Sacred Scrolls. https://planetoftheapes.fandom.com.

Planet of the Apes: The Television Series. http://potatv.kassidyrae.com/articles.html.

Roddy McDowall Reader's Nook. http://www.xmoppet.org/nfReader.html.

Index

About the Author

Sean Egan has contributed to, among others, *Billboard, Book Collector, Classic Rock, Reader's Digest, Record Collector, Tennis World, Total Film, Uncut,* and RollingStone.com. He has written or edited several books, including works on the Beatles, the Rolling Stones, the Clash, Manchester United, *Coronation Street,* Tarzan, William Goldman, and James Bond. His critically acclaimed novel *Sick of Being Me* was published in 2003, while his 2008 collection of short stories *Don't Mess with the Best* carried cover endorsements from Booker Prize winners Stanley Middleton and David Storey. His 2002 book *Jimi Hendrix and the Making of "Are You Experienced"* was nominated for an Award for Excellence in Historical Recorded Sound Research.

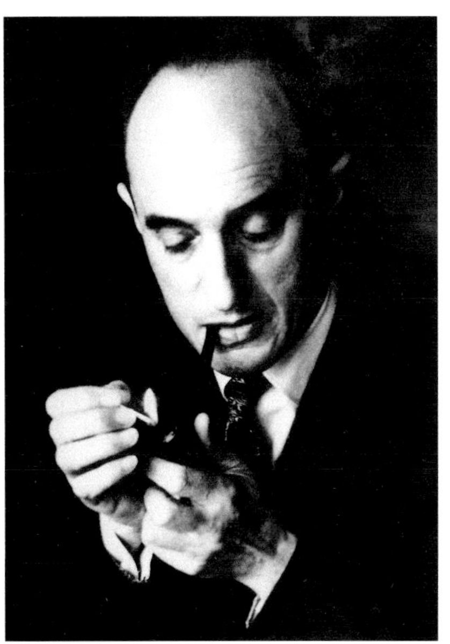

Pierre Boulle. The French author and intellectual was the most improbable progenitor of a science-fiction franchise. PHOTOFEST

The lodestar novel. The mistranslation in the UK version's title has been a running joke, referred to multiple times in the franchise. AUTHOR'S COLLECTION

Arthur P. Jacobs, the film producer who persisted in his dream of adapting Boulle's novel to the screen in the face of multiple obstacles. UNITED ARTISTS/PHOTOFEST

Rod Serling. The man who is a legend in screen SF via *The Twilight Zone* had a long association with the Planet of the Apes franchise. PHOTOFEST

Screenwriter Michael Wilson reworked Rod Serling's screenplay for the 1968 *Planet of the Apes* movie. The combination of the two men's work created a classic. PHOTOFEST

John Chambers (left) predicted to his make-up department colleague Tom Burman (in white behind him) that he would win an Academy Award for his revolutionary prosthetics work on *Planet of the Apes*. He was right. COURTESY OF THE MARK TALBOT-BUTLER ESTATE / ©MARK TALBOT-BUTLER

Tom Burman recommended John Chambers for the *Planet of the Apes* gig. He was rewarded with a job on the makeup team. IMAGESPACE/ALAMY LIVE NEWS

Linda Harrison takes direction from Franklin J. Schaffner. The actress was the silent leading lady in the first two Apes films. TWENTIETH CENTURY FOX FILM CORPORATION/ PHOTOFEST

The moment before the reveal: *Planet of the Apes* (1968). It is the preamble to what is now possibly the most celebrated movie ending of all time. 20TH CENTURY-FOX/PHOTOFEST

A combination of a physical structure and a matte painting conjured this stunning vista. 20TH CENTURY FOX/PHOTOFEST

Roddy McDowall. No single actor is as much associated with the Apes live-action franchise as this gentle-voiced Englishman who played chimpanzees Cornelius, Caesar, and Galen. PHOTOFEST

Paul Dehn. The English-born screenwriter, journalist, and poet had a writing role on four of the original quintet of Apes films.
EVENING STANDARD / STRINGER /GETTY IMAGES

The characters Zira, Cornelius, and Zaius in *Beneath the Planet of the Apes* (1970). The modern era of sequels—follow-ups that were more than simply cheap and exploitative—starts here.
20TH CENTURY FOX/PHOTOFEST

Escape from the Planet of the Apes (1971). Having travelled back in time to 1970s America, Zira and Cornelius find humanity hostile to the prospect of a simian-dominated future.
TWENTIETH CENTURY FOX FILM CORPORATION/PHOTOFEST

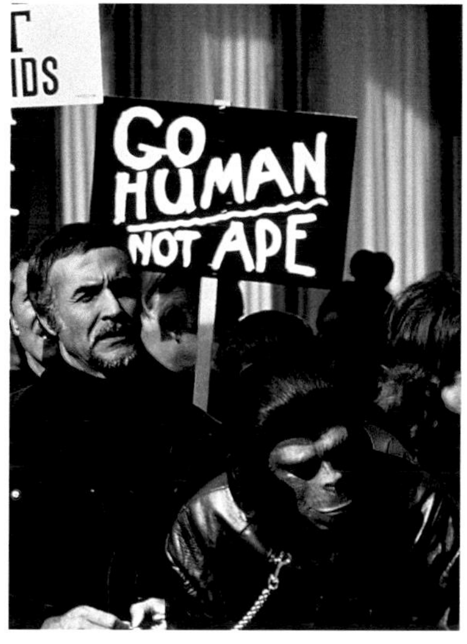

In *Conquest of the Planet of the Apes* (1972), Roddy McDowall played Caesar, son of Cornelius and Zira, who would lead a bloody uprising against a human race that had enslaved apes.
20TH CENTURY FOX / PHOTOFEST

In *Battle for the Planet of the Apes* (1973) the concluding film of the original quintet, man and simian labor under an uneasy and unequal alliance until tragic events cause the two sides to reach an understanding. TWENTIETH CENTURY FOX FILM CORPORATION/PHOTOFEST

The poster used to advertise Seventies *Planet of the Apes* film marathons. The public obeyed the instruction and "Apemania" followed. AUTHOR'S COLLECTION

Comic books have proven to be a surprisingly rich and inspired section of the *Planet of the Apes* universe. Marvel's Doug Moench was the first comics writer to demonstrate the franchise's potential in the medium. COURTESY DOUG MOENCH

Apemania was cemented by the tsunami of *Planet of the Apes* merchandise that swept over the world in the second half of the 1970s. COURTESY CHRISTOPHER SAUSVILLE

A scene from for the 1974 *Planet of the Apes* TV series. In the wake of Apemania, the show was a surprising flop. CBS/PHOTOFEST

Return to the Planet of the Apes (1975) was a low-quality Saturday morning animated series that seemed to auger the end for the franchise. AUTHOR'S COLLECTION

Director Tim Burton and actor Mark Wahlberg on the set of the 2001 version of *Planet of the Apes.* The film was a commercial success but a flop with both critics and long-term fans of the franchise. 20TH CENTURY-FOX/ PHOTOFEST

The only thing about Burton's film that pleased everyone was the stunning makeup by Rick Baker, seen on the right. AF ARCHIVE / ALAMY

Rick Jaffa and Amanda Silver. The married screenwriting team reimagined the Planet of the Apes franchise for the 21st century. STEVEN FERDMAN/EVERETT COLLECTION/ALAMY LIVE NEWS

Rupert Wyatt was a surprising choice to direct *Rise of the Planet of the Apes* (2011) but the little-known Englishman paved the way for a successful new movie series. COURTESY RUPERT WYATT

Andy Serkis as Caesar in *Rise of the Planet of the Apes*. The days of prosthetics were over: the English actor was made into a chimpanzee by Computer Generated Imagery/motion capture. TWENTIETH CENTURY FOX FILM CORP

Andy Serkis on the set of *Dawn of the Planet of the Apes* (2014), directed by Matt Reeves. 20TH CENTURY-FOX/PHOTOFEST

Dawn of the Planet of the Apes (2014), the second in the new Apes trilogy, was a film as dramatic as its poster art suggested. TWENTIETH CENTURY FOX FILM CORPORATION/ PHOTOFEST

In *War for the Planet of the Apes* (2017), a grim Caesar sought to lead his brethren to a land where apes would finally be free from human aggression. TWENTIETH CENTURY FOX FILM CORPORATION/ PHOTOFEST